A history of the
University of Manchester
1951–73

MANCHESTER
UNIVERSITY PRESS

A history of the University of Manchester 1951–73

Brian Pullan with Michele Abendstern

Manchester University Press

Manchester and New York

distributed exclusively in the USA and Canada by St. Martin's Press

Published by Manchester University Press
Oxford Road, Manchester M13 9NR, UK
and Room 400, 175 Fifth Avenue, New York, NY 10010, USA
http://www.manchesteruniversitypress.co.uk

Distributed exclusively in the USA by
St. Martin's Press, Inc., 175 Fifth Avenue, New York,
NY 10010, USA

Distributed exclusively in Canada by
UBC Press, University of British Columbia, 2029 West Mall,
Vancouver, BC, Canada V6T 1Z2

British Library Cataloguing-in-Publication Data
A catalogue record for this book is available from the British Library

Library of Congress Cataloging-in-Publication Data applied for

ISBN 0 7190 5670 5 hardback

First published 2000

07 06 05 04 03 02 01 00   10 9 8 7 6 5 4 3 2 1

Typeset in Sabon with Stone Sans
by Northern Phototypesetting Co Ltd, Bolton
Printed in Great Britain
by Biddles Ltd, Guildford and King's Lynn

Contents

Illustrations

Illustrations can be found between pp. 148 and 149. All illustrations, except where listed otherwise, are copyright of the University of Manchester.

1 Sir John Stopford, afterwards Lord Stopford of Fallowfield, Vice-Chancellor 1934–56.
2 Sir William Mansfield Cooper, Vice-Chancellor 1956–70, as represented by the student publication *Insitter*.
3 Sir Arthur Armitage, Vice-Chancellor 1970–80.
4 The visit of Queen Elizabeth during the centenary celebrations, 1951.
5 The Pharmacy Department, 1958.
6 Mr Patrick Gordon Walker (Secretary of State for Education), Professor George Wedell (Professor of Adult Education) and the leader of a student demonstration on 1st March 1968, when Mr Gordon Walker's extra-mural lecture was disrupted (*Manchester Guardian*, 2nd March 1968). Copyright *Guardian*.
7 'My dear Arthur', spoof letter from a student's father at the time of occupation of the University buildings in February–March 1970.
8 The Great Charter, 1967 (*Staff Comment*, November 1967). Discussion of the University's new Charter and Statutes continued for the greater part of ten years, from 1963 to 1973.
9 '… students with young children must make their own arrangements' (*Staff Comment*, June 1968). The question of a Day Nursery was a controversial subject for many years in the 1960s and 1970s.
10 'Low productivity, Dr Smith' (*Staff Comment*, February 1969). The proposals of the Prices and Incomes Board to reward good teaching by additional salary payments were highly unpopular in the University.

11 'He's never been the same since he got elected to Senate' (*Communication*, November 1973). Elected members were first admitted to Senate in October 1963.
12 Buildings of the new Science Centre to the east of Oxford Road.
13 Manchester Refectory Building – phase 2.
14 One of the last traditional Halls of Residence: Woolton Hall (opened 1959).
15 A new style of student residence: the Owens Park Tower (opened 1964). Copyright Janet Pullan.
16 The Stopford Building.
17 The Moberly Tower.
18 Self-catered, loan-financed accommodation: the Oak House Flats.
19 The Waterhouse Buildings, with the old Dental Hospital (afterwards the Department of Metallurgy) in the foreground. Copyright Janet Pullan.
20 The Mathematics Tower and the Precinct Centre ramp. Copyright Janet Pullan.
21 The Computer Building. Copyright Janet Pullan.

Preface

In 1998 the University of Manchester was preparing to celebrate the one hundred and fiftieth anniversary of Owens College, the institution founded in 1851 out of which the University had grown. As part of the celebrations the University decided to commission an account of its recent history by way of a sequel to H.B. Charlton's centenary publication, *Portrait of a University, 1851–1951*. It was also anxious to establish a sound archive which would preserve, both on tapes and in transcripts made from those tapes, the reminiscences and opinions of people who had been associated in many different capacities with the University in the second half of the twentieth century. Brian Pullan, who had been a member of the History Department for twenty-five years, was asked to take on the job, and Michele Abendstern, an experienced oral historian and a former social worker with a doctorate from the University of Essex, joined him as Research Associate in October 1998. In the time available it proved feasible to prepare a volume covering the period from 1951 to 1973. This spans the period between two centenaries – that of Owens College itself, and that of the occupation, by the enlarged and extended Owens College, of Alfred Waterhouse's buildings on Oxford Road. The book deals with a period of dramatic change, which involved a rapid and unprecedented expansion in the population and the physical capacity of the University. These developments transformed it into a very different kind of institution from the small, intimate pre-war establishment portrayed by Charlton. Described here are the University's attempts to adapt itself to a world in which an organisation founded largely upon personal relationships had to give way to one governed by much more formal procedures, in which rules were much more clearly spelt out, union activity was more intense, and teaching competed with research: a world in which students and junior staff were becoming far less deferential and more determined that their voices should be heard before decisions were made. The book ends in the year in which a new Charter and Statutes became law; in which the University was encountering the first intimations of severe financial stringency, imposed by the government after the the great expansion of the 1960s; in which student protest began to take new directions, both through rent strikes and through attacks on the University's investment policy. Should this book be favourably received, a second volume will continue the story to the end of the twentieth century.

This is an official history only in the sense that the University commissioned it. In no way does it reflect an official point of view, and it seeks to deal frankly and honestly with the University's mistakes and its occasional failures as well as with its achievements. It draws on the minutes of the University Senate and Council, on official reports and statistics, on publications such as the University Calendars, and on the highly informative *Communication*, a magazine first issued by the newly appointed Communications Officer of the early 1970s. But it also uses material drawn from student publications (especially the *News Bulletin* of the 1950s and the *Manchester Independent* of the 1960s and early 1970s), from student manifestoes and pamphlets isued during the time of troubles between 1968 and 1970, and from the journal *Staff Comment*, which was often highly critical of the University establishment. Oral evidence has been taken from people with long memories and good reason to have been in the know about the most important events and developments of the period. But in choosing whom to interview we have not concentrated solely upon the University's leaders, upon senior academics, administrators, lay officers, and experienced members of influential committees. We have also tried to record and present the viewpoints of students, of members of the University's 'support staff', of academics who were then in junior positions, and of neighbours of the University. Needless to say, this is not an oral history of the University, and it is not based on interviews with a random sample of the University's members. Rather, it is one which uses oral evidence to capture anecdotes, ideas, impressions and personal insights which would be unlikely to leave any mark on official records or even upon newspapers and magazines.

We have attempted to write a social and political history of the University, of the framework within which research and scholarship were pursued, rather than of the research and scholarship themselves. The sheer range and variety of the University's intellectual undertakings would be too vast to allow us to write a coherent and comprehensive account of them all, even if the time to do so were available and even if we possessed the necessary intellectual versatility and technical knowledge. It may be that this book, by its very incompleteness, will encourage individual faculties and departments to write their own histories, as a few of them have already done, and that other scholars will pursue in greater depth subjects on which we have barely touched in our effort to provide a general view of what occurred.

Readers will soon realise that the book is mainly concerned with Owens and not with the Tech. In other words, it deals only incidentally with the University's famous partner in Sackville Street, with the institution which, in our period, was first called the Municipal College of Technology, then the Manchester College of Science and Technology, and finally the University of Manchester Institute of Science and Technology (UMIST). Like all faculties of the University, UMIST calls for a full, recent history of its own, which will discuss in detail the great changes of the later twentieth century. Needless to say, it was always far more than just the University's Faculty of Technology, since it was also a separate institution, with its own Principal, Council and students' Union.

A list of some of the people who were formally interviewed by Michele Abendstern – those whose remarks and reminiscences relate to the years 1951–73 – appears in the form of a brief Who's Who at the end of this book. We are most grateful for their willingness to give of their time and delve into their memories, and we hope to have the opportunity of drawing on other interviews in a later volume. Our heartfelt thanks are also due to the following people and organisations who have helped us in various ways with the preparation of this book: to David Richardson, Jeffrey Denton and Ken Kitchen for their encouraging comments on a late draft of the book; to Will Eades and the staff of the Development and Alumni Relations Office of the University for general support and assistance; to Estates and Services for finding us spacious rooms in which to store materials and from which to conduct operations, first over the Senate Committee Room and then in the region of the Department of Pharmacy; to Peter Nockles, the University archivist, for guidance to materials held in the University Library; to the Vice-Chancellor's office for enabling us to consult Senate and Council minutes not available elsewhere; to Alan Ferns and the staff of the International and Public Relations Office for back numbers of *Staff Comment* and *Communication*; to Richard Davies for material on the Athletics Union and other matters; to George Brooke for materials on the Faculty of Theology, Hilary Kahn for materials on Computer Science, and Tony Trinci for materials on Biological Sciences; to Steve Chick, for compiling the graphs in the Statistical Appendix; to Tracy Carrington and Marian Haberhauer for transcribing the tapes of the interviews; to Peter McNiven of the John Rylands University Library and Andrew Schofield of the North West Sound Archive for arranging to store the transcripts and tapes in their respective institutions; to Helen Pearson for the verses which appear in the Epilogue; to Jeffrey Denton, John Griffith, Christopher Kenyon, Ken Kitchen, Vincent Knowles, Barbara Lees and Joan Walsh for lending us materials from their own collections of papers on the University's history; to Sir George Kenyon for allowing us to see the typescripts of unpublished writings concerning his own connection with the University; to Sheila Hammond for putting us in touch with several of her contemporaries at the University in the 1950s; to Michael Tant for sharing with us his interview with Anthony Arblaster, and to Anthony Arblaster for allowing him to do so; to Derek Whitehead, Joan and Jim Wood and many others for anecdotes; to Colin Divall, Colin Lees and Alex Robertson for offprints of their articles; to Alan Tallentire for a photograph of members of the Pharmacy Department, 1957–58; and to Vanessa Graham, Alison Whittle, Rachel Armstrong and the staff of Manchester University Press for their efforts in seeing this book through to publication.

B.P., M.A.

Abbreviations

AUT	Association of University Teachers
CAFD	Council for Academic Freedom and Democracy
CVCP	Committee of Vice-Chancellors and Principals
DSIR	Department of Scientific and Industrial Research
IBM	International Business Machines
JCUD	Joint Committee for University Development
ICI	Imperial Chemical Industries
LSE	London School of Economics and Political Science
UGC	University Grants Committee
UMIST	University of Manchester Institute of Science and Technology
WEA	Workers' Educational Association
YMCA	Young Men's Christian Association

1

At the centenary of Owens College

In 1951 the University of Manchester marked the centenary of the college established by the will of John Owens, a bachelor merchant, in a house in Quay Street, near the border between Manchester and Salford. From this small, unpretentious establishment, originally intended for local boys of at least fourteen, the University itself had sprung. The celebrations culminated, though they did not end, in a royal visit on 31st May by Queen Elizabeth, George VI's affable and popular consort, and were noted in a radio broadcast featuring a commentary delivered by a leading royal watcher, Richard Dimbleby. By nature austere and thrifty, impatient of fuss, the University had in the past been slow even to accept the traditional notion of a Founder's Day at which honorary degrees were bestowed on distinguished people personifying the values of the scholarly community. But the ceremony was skilfully contrived in such a way as to combine the military formalities of a royal occasion with the slightly whimsical rhetoric of an academic speech day, to commemorate the University's complicated history, to honour the female minority in an institution dominated by men, to remind spectators of the importance both of the city of Manchester and of the Commonwealth.

Her Majesty inspected a guard of honour recruited from the University Training Corps. Lord Woolton, who as Chancellor was the University's own constitutional monarch, conferred upon her a Doctorate of Laws, the degree generally awarded to persons prominent in public life and administration. Her fellow graduands included the Vice-Chancellors, not only of Manchester itself, but also of Liverpool and Leeds, which had once (under a royal charter granted in 1880) been joined with Owens College to form the Victoria University, a federal institution straddling the Pennines. In the public orator's words, they were the 'academic Siamese triplets' divided by King Edward VII when he granted the new charter of 1903 and incorporated Owens College with the Victoria University of Manchester, first

Liverpool and then Leeds going their separate ways and incidentally allowing the newly independent University of Manchester to establish the Faculty of Theology which they had persistently opposed.

Another doctorate was conferred on Mildred Pope, a specialist in Anglo-Norman studies who had after forty years of teaching in Oxford become in 1934 the first woman to hold, albeit for only a few years before retirement, a professorial chair in Manchester. The current charter provided that 'All the degrees and courses of study of the University shall be open to women ... and women shall be eligible for any office in the University and for membership of any of its Constituent Bodies.' In the early 1950s about 20 per cent of the University's students were women, but women were very thinly represented, in Manchester as elsewhere, in the higher academic posts and administrative offices. Indeed, in 1951 the philosopher Dorothy Emmet was the only woman professor in office, and no other was to be appointed until Violet Cane became Professor of Mathematical Statistics in 1972. The only woman in 1951 to hold a leading administrative office was Phyllis Crump of the French Department, who had served as Tutor to Women Students since 1925. Professor Pope was honoured, as were most honorary graduands, because she was a rare bird and not because she was typical of anything. But a women's residence, Ashburne Hall in Fallowfield, which was certainly the largest and perhaps the most gracious of University hostels, was given the honour of playing host to the Queen in the afternoon. There she met a selection of students from all the halls, took tea in the Morley Library, and planted a maple tree sent as a gift to the city of Manchester by the Department of Lands and Forests in Ontario.

At the Arts Library the Queen had received a presentation copy of *Portrait of a University, 1851–1951*, by H.B. Charlton, a Shakespeare scholar and a lover of Browning, the senior professor in the University Senate after the Vice-Chancellor himself. Charlton had held his chair since 1921. He was an inspirational teacher whose mannerisms in the lecture room were at once disconcerting and entertaining, for he was given to harrumphing in public and to traipsing back and forth as he talked so that his audience watched him with the fascinated attention of spectators at a Wimbledon match (in private he was kindly, unintimidating, and well liked by his students). Disclaiming any intention of writing an exhaustive history of the University, Charlton chose rather to provide a sharply focused account, like the foundation myth of a Renaissance Italian city celebrating the wisdom of its ancestors, of the ideals of the founders and of the achievements of subsequent generations of 'shaping spirits' who had striven to 'unfold' them and to translate them into reality. As Charlton, following in the steps of earlier historians such as Thompson and Fiddes, reminded readers, the founders and shapers had created a 'University of the Busy', practical, hard-headed and innovative, a bourgeois-entrepre-neurial institution which provided a simpler and cheaper alternative to the more gentlemanly and supposedly more leisurely universities of Oxford and Cambridge. Manchester's was a centralised University founded upon departments subject to a Senate rather than autono-mous colleges; a University shaped by the personalities and vision of the enlightened professors who were given almost absolute power over those departments; a University which, though not irreligious, imposed no religious tests upon academics or students, insisted on no compulsory chapel, and gave no preference to the Church of England or any other denomination; a University rooted in the city and the region, which, in the recruitment of its students, was neither cos-mopolitan nor metropolitan in scope, though it was very much aware, intellectually, of developments in continental Europe. For inspiration, it had looked to the Scottish universities and after 1870 towards Ger-many, in such a way as to attract the favourable attention of liberal German families of manufacturers, engineers and businessmen who had migrated to Manchester – among them the Simons and the Renolds who were still prominent among the University's councillors, governors and benefactors in the mid-twentieth century.

As Frank Kermode (a professor of English Literature from 1958 to 1965, in a very different mould from Charlton) was to write in his autobiography, *Not Entitled*, 'The university had a kind of grim friendliness and a justified assurance of its own value, at a time when the metropolitan claims of Manchester were weakening but still pretty strong ... The mood of the place was always to oppose the south, and the university had, or professed, no inferiority feelings about the ancient universities.'

If the University professed a single, overriding educational objec-tive, it was to discover and communicate the general principles, sci-entific and philosophical, behind the practicalities of life. Its charter stipulated that 'Degrees representing proficiency in technical subjects shall not be conferred without proper security for testing the scientific or general knowledge underlying technical attainments'. But it had not attained distinction solely in science, engineering, economics and other subjects of practical use in the creation of wealth and employ-ment. The University had been equally famous for its Arts Faculty, although Tout, the founding father of Manchester's distinctive history school, had sought to emphasise the methodical, scientific character of the research in which it engaged, and which it required, in a small way, even of its undergraduates. Charlton's commemorative volume reprinted an essay by the Manchester philosopher Samuel Alexander, whose bust by Epstein was the icon of the Arts Faculty's foyer. University education, wrote Alexander, should be founded on a 'systematic and deliberate effort to understand by principles, to discover the reason of facts'. Charlton himself, as he told a student journalist, strongly believed that the purpose of university lectures was to communicate ideas, not facts. The ideal was clear enough, even though in practice the facts might threaten to clutter the foreground and obscure the middle distance. Before the end of the 1950s some students would be complaining in print that dry information alone was being flung at them, as though in response to the dictates of some latter-day Gradgrind, fresh from the pages of *Hard Times*.

As the Queen's speech implied, the centenary being celebrated was not that of Manchester alone, but of all civic universities, for it could well claim to be the pioneer, the senior and archetypal 'red brick' university of the North and Midlands. 'The hundred years of your history', pronounced the Queen politely, 'prove that it is not a disadvantage but an advantage, that you stand in the centre of a great commercial city in the midst of a great industrial region.' Manchester University in 1951 was as much black stone as red brick; was it actually built of coal, as a legendary foreigner wondered? Smokeless zones were still some years away, and Waterhouse's soot-encrusted buildings on Oxford Road were not to be sandblasted until 1971, when the red shades of their steeply pitched roofs were at last to be rediscovered, and admirers reminded that Victorian architects loved colour as well as form. But the city had more to give to it than the dense fogs, industrial illth and bronchitic sub-climate that depressed most newcomers. Even though the University was relying increasingly for financial support upon grants from the Treasury, it still leaned heavily on the good will and generosity of local businessmen prepared to regard it as one of the worthiest city amenities, happy to profit by employing its graduates, and willing to serve on its Council.

The University also set out to give something to the city and the region. Since the late nineteenth century extension lecturers had striven to bring 'the University to the people when the people cannot come to the University'; the University had contributed generously to the Workers' Educational Association, and a fully-fledged Department of Extra-Mural Studies had been founded in 1920. By the 1950s the middle-class clientele of the Department was becoming proportionately larger, and the tastes of clients had begun to turn away from the natural and social sciences towards things of the spirit – towards music even more than literature. Thanks to the generosity of Sir Leonard Behrens, a member of Council, the University now possessed, in Holly Royde in West Didsbury, a 'short-term residential college for adult education', a gracious house where once 'Grieg's wife found hospitality and Joachim played his violin'. It could now play host to University concerts and choral weekends. Extra-mural tutors taught in person and organised others into teaching outside the walls; indeed, a survey conducted in the mid-1960s was to show 'that no less than 90 of the 100 or so departments of the University were engaged in some form of extra-mural activity'.

The Vice-Chancellor had acquired a car and a chauffeur, not because of the dignity of his University office, but on account of his other duties as Chairman of the North Western Regional Hospital Board. His Rolls Royce sported the numberplate ONE 1. This harmless brag appeared to symbolise, not the Vice-Chancellor's supremacy over his colleagues, but the University's capacity for unity and innovation. There were no league tables designed, as in the 1980s and 1990s, to quantify the relative standing of the country's universities in research, but Manchester's claims to intellectual distinction and innovation, at least in certain areas, appeared to be very strong. As Anthony Sampson would write some years later in his widely read volume *Anatomy of Britain*, 'the outward appearance of universities is no clue to their scholarship: Manchester, one of the bleakest, has produced three Nobel Prize winners in a row and for twenty years contained the most distinguished British historian, Sir Lewis Namier, while several pleasant places are classed as "Academic Siberia"'.

When, in 1953, the third Manchester winner of the Nobel Prize for Physics, the Langworthy Professor, Patrick Blackett, departed for Imperial College London, and Namier retired to direct a great collaborative history of Parliament, there may have been a certain sense that the glory was departing. But Blackett's successor, Samuel Devons, brought with him much expensive equipment from Imperial College and was soon elected to the Royal Society. The Arts Faculty was still the home of Eugène Vinaver, editor of the works of Sir Thomas Malory, a refugee from the Russian Revolution who was constructing one of the finest departments of French Studies in the country. 'Manchester firsts' were eagerly looked for and recorded: the recent invention in 1948 of the world's first electronically stored programme computer; the role of Manchester's Hebraists in interpreting, deciphering, editing, purchasing and popularising the Dead Sea scrolls, together with that of the Technical College's Professor of Mechanical Engineering in successfully opening the oxidised Copper Scroll discovered in Cave Three at Qumran; the presentation, under Professor Jack Diamond's direction in 1954–55, of the first full-time course in nuclear engineering to be given anywhere in Europe; the period, which began in the session of 1956–57, when Sir Harry Platt (a no-nonsense orthopaedic surgeon) was President of the Royal College of Surgeons and Professor Robert Platt (a renal specialist, much concerned with the evil effects of smoking) of the Royal College of Physicians. As the Vice-Chancellor's report pardonably boasted, 'No other Medical Faculty outside London has ever before provided the Presidents of the two premier Medical Colleges in this Country.'

Critics, however, spotted some 'Manchester lasts' to set against these triumphs: the lifeless architecture of its dull new buildings, which seemed to belong to the 1920s and 1930s rather than to the middle of the century; the slowness of the University to provide residential accommodation on an adequate scale; the churlishness of the Men's Union, which ensured that Manchester retained the last segregated Women's Union in the country. In the opinion of Stopford, the Vice-Chancellor, who was no friend to complacency, Manchester was a great university in the making, rather than a great university *tout court*.

In the 1950s, indeed until 1973, the University was governed by the charter of 1903. This document seemed to echo the mixed constitution of a republic in Renaissance Italy or the Holy Roman Empire, for it aimed at combining the virtues of government by the One, the Few and the Many. It sought to establish collaboration between academic authorities, chosen from within the community of scholars, and so-called 'lay' or 'honorary' officers and advisers, recruited from the civic community outside it. Functioning on the principle of 'much to the great, little to the humble', it allowed little weight to university teachers below the rank of professor, to the great body of readers, senior lecturers, lecturers, assistant lecturers, demonstrators and research assistants who formed the bulk of the University's academic forces. Their job was to carry out teaching and research, not to legislate, administer or help to rule.

Supreme authority lay in theory with the Court of Governors which, with its 120–130 members, consisting of some academics and a large body of lay persons who served *ex officio* or were nominated by various important bodies, formed the element of the Many. Court's function, like that of the Great Council of Renaissance Venice, consisted mainly of endorsing decisions already taken elsewhere, of hearing reports and speeches from the active University officers at meetings normally held twice a year, and of providing a pool from which members of the University Council could be selected. The career of most lay officers began with their recruitment to Court, usually at the suggestion of friends, golfing partners or business acquaintances who had spotted their suitability for an exclusive club which would eventually, when they were fully-fledged members of it, make exorbitant demands on their time and patience. Elections, as distinct from nominations, from Court to Council were rare, but they could happen: the election in 1960 which brought George Kenyon into the Council was, he believes, the first since 1913.

Council was the 'Executive Body of the University', an element of the Few (it had some twenty-eight members in the early 1950s) composed according to complicated rules of the Chancellor (in theory) and the Vice-Chancellor (in practice), and of various members of the Court, both lay and academic. Not all the academics were professors; some were elected representatives of the Boards of the Faculties, which plumbed the academic scale as far as lecturers. Council was charged with managing the University's finances, property and investments, and its business was 'To provide the buildings premises furniture and apparatus and other means needed for carrying on the work of the University' – to control, and where possible enhance and improve, the environment and other resources which enabled research and teaching to be carried out.

If the Council provided the hard protective shell, the Senate constituted the soft vital organ of the University. It exercised sovereignty over the function for which the University was designed, for it was to 'have control and general regulation of the instruction and education within the University'. In the early 1950s there were almost eighty members of the Senate and nearly all of them were professors. The three others entitled to be present were not tribunes of the people but University grandees, in the form of Dr Moses Tyson, the University Librarian and Special Lecturer in Palaeography; of Sir James Myers, the Director of the School of Education; and of Dr Vivian Bowden, fresh from Ferranti's, the newly appointed Principal of the Manchester Municipal College of Technology.

Subordinated to the Senate were the nine faculties of Arts, Science, Law, Medicine, Music, Economic and Social Studies, Theology,

Technology, and Education. These were clusters of teachers and researchers which varied greatly in size, from the huge Faculty of Science to the tiny Faculty of Music. The larger faculties consisted of loose and sometimes uneasy alliances of departments in cognate disciplines, whereas the small ones, such as Music and Law, were not divided into departments. Arts was particularly sprawling and miscellaneous, boundaries were sometimes arbitrarily drawn, and there was some duplication, especially between Science and Technology. The boards which ruled faculties, each presided over by a Dean, generally included all permanent and full-time members of the academic staff, not only professors, but also readers, senior lecturers and lecturers. They did not usually embrace the large academic plebs of insecure probationers, in other words assistant lecturers and demonstrators, who were on trial for periods of three or four years and struggling to make their mark – though there could be exceptions to the rule, and Peter Bromley, arriving from Oxford as an assistant lecturer in 1947, found himself at once on the board of the Faculty of Law.

All members of Faculties, taken together, formed a large body, seldom active or visible, known as the General Board of the Faculties. In no way did this resemble the august committee of the same name which ruled the academic affairs of the University of Cambridge. Rather, Manchester's General Board was a consultative general assembly, which had had no duties until 1917, when it was made responsible for the Ph.D. degree. This new-fangled doctorate had then been the only degree which the whole University had in common, for there were many variations in the titles of bachelors' and masters' degrees, according to the faculty concerned (Bachelor of Arts, of Science, of Medicine, of Commerce, and so forth). In practice, general issues affecting the entire University were most likely to be openly debated in a semi-official body called Staff Forum, which was usually rather sparsely attended, no matter how fascinating the topics it discussed. Since most senior members of the University ate together at lunch-time under the same rafters, even more discussion probably took place in Staff House.

Though not officially recognised in the charter of 1903, departments were the building blocks of the system. They generally revolved around professors, and where there were several professors in a department they were all presumed to be equal, at least in a formal sense. No professor could be legally superior to another professor, although there were some directorships (for example, of the Physical Laboratories) which conferred on those who held them a large measure of administrative power. Seldom was the title of Head of Department used, its nearest equivalent being simply the professor or professors of the subject, who were presumed by virtue of their scholarly distinction also to possess minimal managerial skills. Professors were at liberty to call staff meetings and consult with them if they would, but were under no constitutional obligation to do so, and not bound to regard expressions of opinion by such meetings as tying their hands.

According to the charter the University was 'free from liability to admit or remain in association with any College other than the Owens College', but it was also empowered to 'affiliate other institutions' and 'to enter into any agreement with any other institution for the incorporation of that institution in the University'. Two faculties, those of Technology and of Education, brought into the University's ambit certain other establishments which had once been wholly independent and to a large extent remained autonomous.

The Faculty of Technology consisted of those members of the Municipal College of Technology who taught courses which the University recognised as being of degree standard. The College had been established towards the close of the nineteenth century by the Manchester City Council, and in the near future it was to undergo more than one change of title and status. In 1955, in response to national demand for technologists and engineers, it would acquire its own royal charter, become entitled to its own grants from the Treasury by means of the University Grants Committee, cease to be financed from the local rates, and assume the new name of 'The Manchester College of Science and Technology'. Courses not of degree standard would be transferred to other colleges in the city. During the 1950s and early 1960s its Principal also held the office of Dean of the Faculty of Technology in the University, though the offices were to be separated when Bowden was invited to join the government as part of Harold Wilson's first administration.

As a freshers' guide to student jargon explained, the University as a whole should be referred to as Coll, and Coll was divided into two parts, known as Owens and the Tech. Realistically, the Victoria University Act of 1904 had provided that, though Owens College 'shall cease to exist as a separate corporation and shall be merged in the University', 'the buildings in Manchester which have been erected by and which immediately before the passing of this Act belonged to the College may continue to be known and designated by the name and style of "the Owens College"'. Owens was the collective name for those whose lives revolved around the Waterhouse buildings on Oxford Road, Tech for those who frequented Sackville Street and the site of the factory, now vanished, which had once manufactured Joseph Whitworth's guns.

Concerned with the training of teachers and with research into the history, theory and techniques of education, the measurement of intelligence and other such matters, the Faculty of Education included not only several departments of education in general and in particular, but also a recent creation of the later 1940s. This was the School of Education, by means of which a number of teachers' training colleges in the region were affiliated to the University, which assumed some responsibility for examining their courses. The heads of those colleges and some of their deputies became lecturers in the School of Education. R.A.C. Oliver, the Professor of Education at the time, advocated the principle that the Department of Education should train graduate teachers and the colleges teach for the Teachers' Certificate. When the School had been imminent, the Vice-Chancellor's report for the session of 1947-48 had proclaimed it 'a meeting place in the fullest sense for the Ministry, the local authorities, training colleges, the teaching profession and the University'. Oliver had urged in a letter to the Vice-Chancellor in 1948 that 'We have never been an "ivory castle"; on the contrary, we have felt ourselves to be part of our regional community ... for the first time all those directly interested in education ... will be brought into direct contact and co-operation to survey and tackle the common problems, with their joint resources and with the full support of the University in seeing that the whole job is done at the only standard a University can set before itself, the highest.'

In the University's elaborate constitution the Vice-Chancellor was the element of the One. Like the Doge of Venice he owed much of his authority and power to his ability to draw together the two main spheres of government, those controlled by the Senate and the Council. The top people who counted for most in the development of the University formed an inner cabinet which included three lay officers, the Chairman of Council, the University Treasurer, and, at times of expansion, the Chairman of the Building Committee too. Privy to most secrets and of crucial importance to the conduct of business were the Registrar, who headed the academic civil service, and the Bursar, the steward and manager of the university's money and property. No attempt was made to unify their two fiefs into a single domain. Much depended on a happy relationship between the Vice-Chancellor and the Chairman of Council and their ability to collaborate in such a way as to provide the resources for the most important intellectual under-takings.

To most people then in high authority it seemed undesirable that academics should be required to be businessmen or administrators on a large scale, to raise funds, manage budgets or wade through heavy paperwork other than examinations scripts. They should devote themselves to the things they did best, leaving the world of action and affairs to other, more worldly beings, like a medieval religious com-munity entrusting the defence of their monastery and its estates to lay protectors. It was easy to believe that academics would never be good at making collective decisions, however quick they were to resent any failure to consult them at interminable length. Their passion for debate, their suspicion of other people's initiatives and their tendency to conduct business meetings as though they were seminars, were daunting to some businessmen – who were, after all, devoting much time and energy to solving the university's problems and were entitled to believe that time was money. As one distinguished industrialist was to write, after thirty-three years serving the University between 1955 and 1988, 'the lay members, entirely independent as they are with great experience of affairs, stand between the outside world and the universities and what they represent. Those lay members who get to understand and sympathise with the academics introduce a decision-making process into what is an unwieldy mass of people of high intel-ligence with special knowledge and abilities but mostly with an innocent and naïve understanding of the outside world.'

Many civic universities had been invaded by graduates of the uni-versities of Oxford, Cambridge and London, which produced far more potential academics and administrators than they could ever employ themselves, and exported a large proportion of them to other places. But Manchester in mid-century was governed to a surprising extent by senior administrators who had grown up within the Uni-versity and devoted most of their working lives to the institution. They were not careerists perching for a few years in the University or aliens in exile from another academy and determined to impose its ways on Manchester. There was perhaps a risk that inexperience of other institutions might make them a shade parochial, a touch com-placent, but they enjoyed the enormous advantage of having grown gradually into the job and of having seen the University from below as well as from above.

Sir John Sebastian Bach Stopford, the Vice-Chancellor in 1951, had already held office for seventeen years with outstanding success. He was the kind of Vice-Chancellor who, as he liked to put it, used an oil can rather than a stick. Born in 1888, he was the son of a Wigan colliery manager. His intellectual standing, both as teacher and as scholar, was of the highest. Stopford was a 'surgeon's anatomist' whose interests lay chiefly in neurology, well known for his book on *Sensation and the Sensory Pathway*, published in 1930, and for work on 'the supply of blood to the brain, on the loss and recovery of sensation in the peripheral nerves arising from nerve injuries in the war of 1914–18, and on the structure and functioning of the autonomic nervous system' (to quote from the account of him in the *Dictionary of National Biography*). Famous for plain language and personal simplicity, easily mistaken for the gardener by a young electrician sent to carry out repairs at the Vice-Chancellor's official residence, popular with the officers of the students' Unions, addicted to watching football even when played by small boys in the street, Stopford liked to describe himself as a reluctant administrator who had three times refused the office which he now held. 'I was never intended by nature to be an administrator and I don't think I'm much better at it now.' So he told an interviewer from *News Bulletin*, the Unions' paper, and the remark may have seemed like a piece of outrageous self-deprecation, since his services were much in demand from bodies outside the university and he was greatly concerned with the reorganisation of local hospitals in his capacity of Chairman of the Regional Hospital Board.

When Stopford retired in 1956, tributes went far beyond the ordinary politeness to be expected on such occasions. One of them, probably written by his successor, emphasised his extraordinary ability to sympathise with people of all disciplines, ranks and persuasions within the University, and if any note of criticism was sounded it was very delicately qualified. 'His capacity, medical scientist though he was, to absorb the major sense of the Arts men's variously and imperfectly formulated values was almost miraculous ... Occasionally, perhaps, there may have seemed to creep into his later manner a note which to one who did not know him might have sounded somewhat arbitrary, and even, maybe, dogmatic. But a Vice-Chancellor must be definitive, and whatever the form of speech the point of view it expressed sprang always from his deep religious sense and its immediate moral implication, that is, to do to the full the task you are appointed to do.' Pat Case, who as Pat O'Gara was President of the Women's Union in 1953–54, remembers him as 'somebody who enjoyed the company of students. He felt it was his job to walk around and chat like a sort of extremely good headmaster.' At the retirement dinner given him on 19th June 1956 by the students' Unions, senior students of Halls and chairmen of societies, he received, together with a television set, a tiny green plant for his rock garden. The Latin name of the plant was 'Semper Vivum', 'Everlasting', and the student reporter who covered the event was deeply touched to see the plant clutched tightly in the Vice-Chancellor's hand for the rest of the evening: 'he would not let go even to put on his coat'.

William Mansfield Cooper, who succeeded Stopford, was another old Manchester hand. His career had been less conventional. He moved between the position of Registrar and a chair of Industrial and Commercial Law; the two offices were not thought to fall within two separate and mutually impenetrable spheres. Now approaching fifty, Mansfield Cooper had left school at the age of fourteen and worked in a hat factory for a year. Afterwards he had spent thirteen years with a firm of accountants, attending WEA classes in the evenings. After winning a scholarship to Ruskin College Oxford, he had matriculated at Manchester at the age of thirty-one, and had proceeded to take a first and second degree in Law, and to be called to the bar of Gray's Inn. From his appointment as assistant lecturer in 1938 he had risen rapidly, serving as an officer in the University Training Corps during the war years, and humbly taking instruction in map-reading from a student of Geography and Anthropology who helped him to improve his technique. Becoming assistant to the Vice-Chancellor, he was charged with drafting documents for Stopford. At the end of the war, as a former mature student himself, he was well equipped to deal diplomatically with the large numbers of ex-service students flooding into the university. He was appointed Registrar in 1945, and succeeded to his law chair a few years later after initiating his successor, Vincent Knowles. When Stopford's health gave serious cause for concern and he was sent with his wife on holiday to Australia by the University Council in the winter of 1953–54, Mansfield Cooper was the natural choice for the position of Acting Vice-Chancellor. His experience of University affairs would soon qualify him to be the permanent holder of the office. Sir Raymond Streat, the Chairman of the Cotton Board and the University Treasurer, was pleasantly surprised at the professoriate's ability to show so much enthusiasm for anyone. ' ... the way in which the entire professorial body, normally so apt to argue and differ, being such individualists, showed virtual unanimity in preferring Cooper over many distinguished outsiders, was a matter to marvel at. I think he will do great service.'

A profile of Mansfield Cooper in the students' arts magazine, *The Serpent*, for autumn 1953 proved to be not merely deferential but fulsome, calling him 'A man of infinite charm, an urbane and witty speaker who is always popular at Union functions', and testifying to his lasting popularity with Union officers. It was to be the paradox and tragedy of Mansfield Cooper's career that changes in students' attitudes and opinions in the late 1960s were to expose him to distressing abuse which he could only interpret as personal attacks. To John Carswell, sometime Secretary of the University Grants Committee, Mansfield Cooper was among the great Vice-Chancellors of the mid-twentieth century, and one who successfully presided over an important phase of sustained expansion. Sir George Kenyon, a lay officer closer to him, praised his achievements generously, but detected in him 'a certain waspishness and an aloofness which could be forbidding ... He was a bit of an NCO' Some of that aloofness sprang from a self-imposed ban on making particular friends among the academics of the University. In the words of Margaret Young, who became Adviser to Women Students in the mid-1950s, 'To say that I made friends with him would be incorrect because he was absolutely scrupulous and he mustn't be friendly with anyone, particularly a woman, but he did like me, I know that, I got on very well with him and I got to know his wife.' The Coopers were not naturally convivial and Professor Flowers, who arrived from Harwell in 1958 to take a chair in Physics, was critical of their failure to entertain at The Firs. Outside academic circles, however, Mansfield Cooper could be relaxed, informal, unassuming. Arnold May, the foreman binder of the University Library, was astonished, indeed 'over the moon', to discover that the 'little chap' who had often sat on a bench in the sun to pass the time of day with him as he ate his sandwiches at lunch-time was in fact the Vice-Chancellor.

Mansfield Cooper's trenchant replies to unjustified criticism sometimes earned him respect, as witness, for example, his reminder to the great Professor Blackett that 'more academic projects have been killed by academic colleagues than ever have been destroyed by University bureaucrats'. Blackett, having thought it over, decided that Cooper was right. But Cooper lacked Stopford's straightforwardness and could seem quirky and obscure: as Sir George Kenyon has complained, 'he certainly had a good line in triple negatives; I often wondered whether I had missed one'.

As Registrar Mansfield Cooper was followed by Vincent Knowles, likewise a Manchester graduate and also a man of some academic

standing. As a student in the 1930s he had bicycled to the University
from his home in Northenden and had eventually taken a First in
Classics, followed by an M.A. in Greek. He had been appointed a
part-time lecturer by Semple, the Professor of Latin, and had served
as a tutor in the Lancashire Independent College, an institution in
Whalley Range chiefly designed to prepare students for the Congre-
gational ministry. Knowles was to retain his lectureship in Greek and
Latin throughout almost thirty years as Registrar, it being with him an
article of faith that although administrators existed to save academics'
time they must have some claim to be their intellectual equals. No gulf
between the two species should be allowed to develop. After appointment he was duly paraded before the good-hearted but forbidding
Lord Simon of Wythenshawe, the Chairman of Council, who thought
him very young for the appointment and said so (Knowles was still in
his thirties and far from portly). 'Age will modify that, my lord.' 'Oh,
cheeky as well ... we'll make it a three-year appointment.' Stopford
also assured Knowles of his autonomy: no individual, not even the
Vice-Chancellor, could give him instructions, since his responsibility
was directly to Senate, Council and Court, the legislative bodies
which he served.

On Knowles's appointment, the administrative, as distinct from
clerical, staff was tiny. The Calendar for 1951–52 listed an assistant
registrar, a secretary for examinations, a chief assistant, three administrative assistants, an officer for men students in lodgings, and a personal assistant. It was the new Registrar's policy to appoint young
administrators whose qualifications resembled his own, beginning
with the amiable George Ashworth, a former pupil of Bury Grammar
School who had gone to Corpus Christi College Cambridge and taken
high honours in the Classical Tripos. They were reasonably well paid
and their salaries were, or came to be, closely related to those on the
academic scales. Their duties at first were not hugely demanding and
Knowles's arrangements were sometimes sneered at by colleagues in
other universities: did one need functionaries of such high calibre to
call and service committees, pay out state studentship cheques, edit
the University Calendar and prospectuses and compile statistics? But
they began (to use Vincent Knowles's verb) to 'infiltrate' both the faculties and some very large departments such as Physics, offering their
services as secretaries and relieving academics of the need to perform
some heavy administrative chores. Perhaps, like the citizen secretaries
of early modern Venice, they contributed continuity and a knowledge
of proprieties and precedents to a republican system which at certain

levels depended on the rotation of office. Deans in most faculties came and went after a year or two in post, but faculty secretaries served for longer stretches. In the course of time sixteen of Knowles's protégés were to become registrars in other universities. They had the initiative and intelligence to deal with jobs that became increasingly demanding, as universities were increasingly called upon to account for the public funds which they spent and as academic planning became an increasingly complicated task.

Subject to the Registrar was a staff of women Clerical Assistants, 'Vincent Knowles's girls', who worked in the General Office on the first floor of the Main Building under the supervision of the efficient Mrs Wright. They dealt with a variety of administrative matters, including examinations, awards, statistics and appointments. Some of these concerns swelled to such dimensions over the next few years that they had to be organised into separate departments on separate premises – especially awards, which dispensed grant cheques and chased up students who failed to attend or disappeared altogether from the scene. Mr Knowles was a popular and approachable boss who, in the absence of an effective trade union and a personnel department, could be relied upon to attend to the problems of his staff. There was a certain social distance, however, between administrators and clerical staff. Whereas administrators would associate with academics as equals and take their meals in Staff House, the clerical assistants foregathered in a small common room on the upper corridor of the Main Building.

In some parts of the University support for the academic staff lay in the hands, not of the Registrar's colleagues, but of secretaries who were also highly efficient and versatile administrators, even if their administrative contribution was not formally recognised. This was true of the School of Medicine, which was always conscious of being, as the direct descendant of an independent Medical School, older than Owens College and of standing midway between the University and the National Health Service. Here great responsibility rested with the Dean's secretary, later called his personal assistant, Rita Davies, who had succeeded to the office in 1942 and was to hold it until 1965, when she became Public Relations Officer to the Blackpool and Fylde Hospital Management Committee and was, in her new role, instrumental in arranging placements for Manchester medical students, to enable them to do their 'clinical clerking' in the Blackpool region. When the first Registrar's man, Gerard McKenna, was appointed to the Medical Faculty in the 1970s, it was as though he were an ambassador from a foreign power (so says Gay Rhodes, a later personal assistant to the Dean). In the course of a long career Ellen Carling, who became secretary to the Professor of Astronomy in the mid-1950s, organised members of the department into travelling to observatories abroad (particularly the Pic du Midi in the Pyrenees); went out there herself to set up the observing schedules; organised conferences and other functions at venues from Manchester itself to the northern Peloponnese; edited conference proceedings; and acted as editorial assistant to two journals, *Astrophysics and Space Science* and *The Moon* (later entitled *Earth, Moon and Planets*), which were edited by Professor Kopal and put out by a Dutch publisher, Reidel.

In the 1950s the administrative assistants of the Registrar's Department were no more than gifted amateurs compared with the highly professional accountants, building officers and engineers of the Bursar's domain. Their chieftain, master in his own house but responsible to the University Council, was R.A. (Richard Alan) Rainford, a formidable and effective officer of commanding presence and physical as well as moral stature. Rainford had joined the Bursar's staff in 1929 and become Bursar himself in 1950. Businessmen on the University Council were relieved to find in him a kindred spirit. 'He was a nice man to deal with, funnily enough, but he could also be very strict', in the words of Harry Cameron, who became an apprentice electrician soon after the war and rose through the hierarchy to become Electrical Engineer. The Bursar's Department in the early 1950s comprised a finance officer, a chief administrative officer, a buildings officer, a cashier, a personal assistant, two assistant buildings officers and a book-keeper. Recruits to the administrative staff might well find that their tasks included the ordering of coal on a large scale and the conduct of altercations with finicky professors who wished to be supplied with a particular brand of dustless chalk.

With its ever-expanding demands for technicians, electricians, maintenance staff, catering staff and porters, the University was a large-scale employer of local skill and labour (partly through contract work) and a purchaser of local goods and services which exerted considerable influence on the economy of Manchester. Some of its staff had served for many years in a variety of jobs – Walter McCulloch, for example, had started at the age of fourteen in 1935 as a 'two-year lab boy' in the Perkin and Schunck laboratories of the Chemistry Department, had then become a porter in the University Library, and after the war had become involved with the huge, slow photocopying machine acquired by a Librarian with progressive ideas. There were hierarchies among the support staff, ranging for example from Junior Technician to Chief Superintendent, just as there were among academics. The University's educational function extended not only to the education of students but also to the training of apprentices, to whom its attitude was often more strict and paternal. Having noticed the young Harry Cameron smoking a cigarette in a departmental mess room, the Chief Electrical Engineer said that he intended to inform his father of the fact. 'When I started you as a young boy I said to your parents that I would look after you and maintain an interest in you and make sure everything's all right.'

Unlike Knowles, Rainford could give the impression of being impatient with academics, even contemptuous of them; having heating bills on his mind, he was famous for remarking that Arts men entered University premises during the Christmas vacation only for the purpose of escaping from their wives. He stood no nonsense from professors and when a haughty dignitary of the Science Faculty requested a service, saying 'Perhaps one of your minions could do this', he received in return a letter signed 'R.A. Rainford (Minion)'. But it was he who, immediately after the war, had greeted Bernard Lovell in a chilly and indifferent common room. He had directed him to the man in charge of the botanical gardens and thereby helped him to find at Jodrell Bank in Cheshire a site on which to instal the army surplus radar equipment which Lovell had parked in the University quadrangle for want of a better place. Somewhat implausibly, the redoubtable Rainford confessed to being scared to death by one woman. This was Olwen Williams, secretary to Harry McLeod, the University's first Staff Officer. Appointed to have 'wider responsibility for the welfare of the non-salaried staff', the unfortunate Mr McLeod was regarded with suspicion by most of the old-established administrators and by some of the wage-earners themselves. Miss Williams was his staunch defender.

The least conspicuous member of the caucus at the heart of power was the University Librarian, Moses Tyson, a painfully shy bachelor who shunned the company of women. Described by his successor as 'one of the great unsung figures of the University', he was said to have planned its future while firewatching during the war with Mansfield Cooper. Tyson's staff were generally scholars like himself rather than professionally qualified librarians. They regarded him as a 'generous father figure behind the scenes' who often bought books for the Library out of his own pocket, and also gave them all Christmas presents, making a nice distinction, a guinea for graduates and a pound for others. When once they reciprocated and bought him a cigarette lighter to feed his habit, he was covered in confusion. 'Never, never, do this again!' He was an innovator who established in the Library both a photographic section and a bindery. Above all he was a book collector, more interested in adding to the stock than in expanding the numbers of his staff, and was very much alive to new opportunities for collecting in, for example, the history of science. But he also spotted the potential of microfilm, and purchased for the Library a complete set of microfilms of books published before 1700, in order to fill gaps in the Library's collection and provide an excellent resource for scholars. It was a way of extending the holdings without having to provide more space in which to house them. But, since he had the ear of successive Vice-Chancellors, he also pleaded effectively the case for extending the Library buildings. He prevailed upon Senate and Council to strengthen central control in such a way that the Science, Medical and Main Arts Libraries (though housed in different places) all clearly became part of the University Library and the departmental libraries were treated as subsidiaries thereof.

In Tyson's day the Library had at least two special characteristics. It allowed, to an astonishing degree, open access to its collections – even incunables, books published before 1500, were kept on open shelves, and readers did not have to order them at a counter, so low was the sense of any need for security. Furthermore, a kind of do-it-yourself librarianship was made possible by a system of cataloguing by subject which had been developed since the late nineteenth century; there was no question, as there might well have been, of putting the books on the shelves in chronological order, just as they came in.

The day-to-day running of the University was in the hands of an oligarchy, but it had the undoubted merit of being visible, accessible and predictable in its habits. Members of the inner ring had the power to 'be definitive', to give crisp answers in a short time to most of the questions put to them; there was little need to refer minor matters, involving small sums of money, to committees and to wait on their decisions. Wherever possible business was transacted by word of mouth and the writing of letters was discouraged. One able administrator who felt compelled to put his lengthy thoughts on paper was suspected of holding shares in a log firm and liable to be summoned to Knowles's office to see his communications torn up. The Registrar, the Bursar and the Librarian would generally repair to Staff House between half-past ten and eleven o'clock of a morning, do the *Times* crossword jointly with one of them acting as scribe, and make themselves available for discussion with anyone from any part of the University who cared to approach them. The great men of the University were also on display at lunch-time, for the oak-panelled dining room of Staff House contained a high table on a daïs, where the senior administrators and the professors sat; the high table waitresses went to the front of the queue to ensure that their charges were promptly served, in advance of the lesser beings below the salt. Only professors of exceptionally liberal outlook, such as Vinaver, would defy convention by choosing to eat with their junior colleagues and friends.

At the summit of the University, even above the high table of Staff House, Lord Woolton, who had been Chancellor since 1944, and Lord Simon, Chairman of Council since 1941, were philanthropic capitalists of differing political allegiances and contrasting personalities, inclined to dislike each other. Woolton's election by Convocation, the body of graduates of the University, broke with the established tradition of choosing landed aristocrats who had been educated in some more fashionable place. Woolton, formerly Frederick Marquis, was an alumnus of Manchester, and could boast of having been one of three undergraduates in his year privileged to listen to the notoriously demanding lectures in which the philosopher Samuel Alexander thought aloud and invited his tiny audience to join him as fellow students. As a young man early in the century he had subscribed to the Fabian Society and derived from his time as Warden of the Liverpool University Settlement a lifelong interest in eliminating poverty. But he was now no socialist, and as a highly successful retailer he had come to see the solution to social problems in reducing the cost of living and increasing employment, in bringing down the prices of goods while maintaining their quality. Better labour conditions should be pursued, in his opinion, not only out of humanity, but because they would bring in more profit. As Minister of Food during much of the war, the nation's genial and avuncular schoolmaster appealing for the avoidance of waste, he had used his exceptional powers to help stamp out the diseases that arose from malnutrition. He had been chairman of Lewis's, the department store chain, and had served on the University Councils of Liverpool and Manchester. Woolton seemed well attuned to the University's philosophy; he claimed in his memoirs that his had been the first retailing firm to adopt a policy of recruiting graduates, 'people who had had a basic training in straight and analytical thinking and had built their technical experience on this foundation', and of training them for management after acquiring considerable experience behind the counter. At first an independent who never stood for Parliament but entered Churchill's government by means of the House of Lords, he had at last joined the Conservative party, recoiling from the prospect of nationalised industries, in the post-war days of 'Cheer Churchill. Vote Labour.' Whilst serving as Manchester's Chancellor in the 1950s he was Lord President of the Council, Chancellor of the Duchy of Lancaster, and Chairman of the Conservative Party.

The role of Manchester's Chancellor was somewhat mysterious and ill-defined. Apart from his ceremonial duties and his obligation to preside over the Court of Governors, the Chancellor was vaguely supposed to exercise influence on the university's behalf in the exalted circles to which he belonged and generally to enhance its standing in the world. Woolton, however, also held strong opinions on practical matters to do with the University, and particularly on the importance of making it at least partially residential. He was prepared to lend his personal prestige and his knowledge of fund-raising techniques to an appeal for halls of residence which he launched in partnership with Stopford in 1954–55; he was involved as a politician in the decision to grant a new status to the College of Technology. His talent for writing appreciative notes was long to be gratefully remembered, as witness one sent to the Registrar after a Founder's Day close to the Coronation in 1953:

> My dear Knowles,
> Perfection as usual. I'll tell Norfolk where to come for advice.
> P.S. What a bloody steak.

Whereas both Stopford (known as Jock) and Woolton (known as Fred) were renowned for their common touch and their fondness for homely language, Lord Simon was a more intimidating figure. Born in Didsbury in 1879, he was the son of Henry Gustav Simon, a liberal German inspired to emigrate from Prussia to the north of England. While still an undergraduate reading for a degree in engineering at Cambridge, Ernest Simon had inherited responsibility for the two firms of Henry Simon Ltd, which originally made machinery for flour mills, and Simon Carves Ltd, which began by exploiting a French patent for a by-product coke oven. He had much experience of ordering others about, and little of being ordered about himself. As his biographer, Mary Stocks, has written, 'It is possible that this early assumption of leadership, plus the enjoyment of comparative wealth, isolated him from the day-to-day experiences of common men and intensified a natural shyness which made him appear both impersonal and insensitive. He was in fact a dedicated and altruistic humanitarian with a sensitive and self-searching social conscience ... he thought statistically rather than personally ...' Stopford said of him, 'the vigour, tireless energy and "youth" of my Chairman leave me breathless and a trifle exhausted'. Ever eager to collect information, even to constitute himself a one-man Royal Commission on university affairs, he had the disconcerting habit of making notes on every serious conversation in the presence of the person with whom he was holding it. He had been a member of the University Council since the First World War, and his wife Shena, herself a member of the Council from 1920 to 1966, shared his interests and sometimes joined him in pursuing a cause, as on the occasion when they visited Jodrell Bank together and immediately began to bombard the Bursar with demands that he provide more acres for the development of radio astronomy. Lady Simon, indeed, was responsible for one of the few questions ever asked in Court around this time: 'The Treasurer sounds very optimistic. I cannot see how he can be optimistic, and could he tell me why?'

Ernest Simon was best known as a social reformer rather than a successful industrialist (he was that as well). Four tangible memorials to him in the University were to bear witness to his passionate belief in the power of education to make the world a better place. The Simon Fellowships, established in 1944, were designed to promote research of practical value in the social sciences. Broomcroft, his house in Didsbury, was left to the University and intended in part to provide a place of residence for Simon Fellows. The towering, cliff-like Simon Engineering Laboratories, eight storeys crowned by a green excrescence on the roof, the largest building in the new Science Centre, were named after him in the early 1960s. The Simon Fund, which financed modest entertainments, was designed for 'the furtherance of social contact between members of the University within the University'.

Simon had joined the Labour Party in 1946. His overriding concerns in his later years were over-population, nuclear disarmament, and higher education. He was dedicated to the cause, not of Manchester alone, but of all universities, and had founded in 1946 a journal, *Universities Quarterly*, devoted to discussing their affairs. He was perturbed by the country's failure to provide sufficient numbers of graduates in general, and of qualified engineers in particular – though his interest was never in technology alone, but in good citizenship and understanding of the world. His eloquence in the House of Lords in May 1960, a few months before he died, was to lead directly to the appointment of a committee under Lord Robbins to investigate the state of higher education in the country.

In the early 1950s the University of Manchester was a strongly hierarchical institution, but it was governed by trusted people of manifest ability and sustained by a sense of participation in the reconstruction of the post-war world. Austere, utilitarian and overcrowded as it was, its dense population jammed into a cramped and inconvenient site, it retained, perhaps because people were forced to live cheek-by-jowl in unlovely conditions, a sense of unity which was later to be lost. Because the laboratories west of Oxford Road opened into each other and the technicians and maintenance men all knew one another and borrowed each other's tools and equipment, there was a feeling of community, even a kind of family atmosphere, which would disappear in the days when every principal branch of science had its own building, an island entire of itself. The truly intimate world of the Edwardian university which Woolton recalled in his memoirs was gone for ever. But there was, by way of compensation, the knowledge that governments of either complexion believed in universities and were prepared to finance their growth.

Common criticisms of the University were not so much that it was undemocratic as that it offered its students a one-dimensional experience, which concentrated on academic achievement alone and equipped its students poorly for the world, endowing them with no social polish or intellectual breadth. With time it began to appear that the academic staff and their students were becoming isolated from each other. Those very words, 'staff and students', argued the Men's Union in 1951–52, ought to be replaced by the term 'senior and junior members', as though to confirm the participation of everyone in a corporation called the University – as the wording of the charter implied.

There was also a risk that senior members of the University, particularly in periods of rapid growth, might begin to retreat into their own specialisms and lose any sense of the University as a whole. It was true that on one front the University had struck its own blow against over-specialisation. With the Universities of Oxford and Birmingham, Manchester had recently become a sponsor of the new University College of North Staffordshire at Keele Hall in the vicinity of Stoke-on-Trent, and occasionally lent it lecturers. This new institution, advocated and for a time headed by Lord Lindsay, the former Master of Balliol, was designed, with its foundation year and subsequent three-year degree course inspired by Oxford's Philosophy, Politics and Economics, to counter both over-specialisation and departmentalism.

But was Manchester itself free of those ills? Increasingly rare by the late 1950s were academics who, as did Michael Polanyi, crossed intellectual frontiers. Originally trained in medicine and once a professor of Physical Chemistry, he had moved in 1948 to a chair of Social Studies; it was said at his retirement ten years later that he 'had the courage to dare to enter fields of study in which he was not a specialist, and to do research and writing which cut across the conventional boundaries of academic subjects … '. In the same session another eulogist lamented the departure of Ely Devons, the Professor of Applied Economics, saying 'he has been, what is becoming rare in Manchester, a University character and a University politician … '. Dr Helen Rosenau, a refugee from Hitler's Germany and a lecturer in the tiny department of Art History, warned in an interview with a student journalist in 1955 that 'We are losing sight of the fact that we are a university. We must break away from over-specialisation, following in the steps of Tout and Alexander, who certainly knew the dangers of a narrow view of education, and were masters in relating their subjects to wider interests.'

It remained to be seen whether, under the strains of the 1950s and 1960s, the University would be able to retain a sense of common identity – whether, in a world made more impersonal by increasing numbers and physical expansion, it would be able to resist a division into specialisms which knew little of each other, and a division into social orders, consisting of professors, non-professors, students and support staff, who were increasingly set apart.

I
1950s expansion

2

Government, Science and Humanities

Shortly after the Second World War the student population of the University of Manchester more than doubled. This unprecedented expansion created a kind of Malthusian crisis in which the pressure fell, not upon inelastic food supplies, but upon restricted space – upon laboratories, libraries, lecture theatres, accommodation, and everything that they contained. Although the resources available to higher education were increasing, they seemed always to march at least one step behind national needs. Official reports in four successive years noted record entries to the University. Total numbers of students at Owens and in the Faculty of Technology began to level off at just under 6,000 in 1948–50. In the last session before the war, 1938–39, 2,774 students had been registered; numbers had remained much the same since the early 1920s. Hence the post-war expansion represented an entirely new experience for the University administration. To feed the five thousand on campus (sometimes there were six) was no easy task; there were reports of twenty-minute queues for lunch in the Refectory in 1946–47, despite the provision of an additional large dining room. A couple of years later the Men's Union officers noted that 'The Entrance Hall is now definitely a "Union Room", so continually full is it of members unable to find elbow-room anywhere else in the building.'

The immediate task was not only to admit school-leavers proceeding directly from sixth form to university, but also to take in an extraordinary influx of mature students made up of ex-servicemen and women. Most of them were supported by grants for Further Education and Training, bestowed by the Ministry of Education. Some were starting courses from scratch, others resuming in mid-stream studies interrupted by call-up. An unlucky few found that Senate had abolished certain of the more unusual and enterprising courses, such as Geography and Anthropology, in their absence. This meant that they now had to choose between accepting an ordinary degree (granted to those who had taken the Intermediate but not the Final Honours examinations) or embarking on some course which was entirely new to them. Some new courses were devised for the convenience of ex-service people, however; a three-year ordinary degree in Theology was set up for ordinands who could not afford to qualify in the old, leisurely way by spending three years on an Arts degree and at least another two on becoming a Bachelor of Divinity.

As a result the student population fell into two contrasting groups, very different in terms of age, experience and outlook. One consisted of youngish people who had had to grow up quickly and had often held rank, wielded authority and risked their lives in battle; some were married and most were eager to make up for lost time and pursue their careers with urgency and the benefit of good qualifications. The younger students who had missed call-up were in awe of the ex-service men and women and conscious of their own indebtedness to them for the defence of the country. Joyce Boucher, who arrived from Withington Girls' School to read English in 1946 at the age of seventeen and a half, found herself part of a 'frightened little crew'. Only six students in a departmental intake of about a hundred had not served in the forces. She had to reconcile herself to several years as one of the departmental children, too diffident to associate with older colleagues or to join any of the committees which attempted to organise student life.

War veterans were rewarding to teach and often remembered with affection by their tutors. But they were inclined to be impatient of footling regulations, to resent some of the scientists who had enjoyed deferment or exemption from military service, even to despise some of the 'old aunties and wimpish men', innocent of battle experience, who addressed them from the podium of the lecture hall. Old hands such as Professor Charlton rose to the occasion, saying of all students: 'Here they are. Now I will instruct them.' Though outwardly self-confident, the veterans, conscious of having forgotten what they once knew, were liable to be just as disconcerted by his habit of asking sudden questions – 'What is a casement?' – in the course of his lectures. But some of the younger lecturers must surely have been intimidated by the mature and assertive audiences which faced them.

By 1952–53 the cohorts of ex-officers, rankers and ratings had passed through the system and the average age of the student population had fallen dramatically. True, National Service was an obligation for most male students and the period of service with the colours had lengthened, in 1950, at the time of the war in Korea, from eighteen months to two years. However, although a few chose to perform their duties before entering the University, there was a strong temptation to postpone them and perhaps prepare for National Service through the University Training Corps. The University did not, as did many Oxford and Cambridge colleges, insist that students of Arts and Social Sciences should serve in the armed forces before matriculating as undergraduates. Although the student population was now younger and said to be more apathetic by those (such as Union officers) who wanted to organise it, students were scarcely less numerous and soon to proliferate again. In the early 1950s the totals fell back towards 5,000, but they rose again from 5,205 in 1953–54 to 7,215 in 1959–60. Much of this growth occurred in the Faculty of Technology, as though in recognition of the changed status of Bowden's newly chartered Tech from municipal to national institution.

Among academic planners there was much talk of 'bulges' and 'trends' which would have to be absorbed by the whole system of higher education, either by expanding and pouring resources into established universities and university colleges or by creating new ones which would become their rivals. The original bulge was created directly by the presence of the war veterans themselves; the second was formed by their children, and the steep increase in the birth-rate shortly after the war could be expected to impinge on universities towards the middle of the 1960s, when post-war babies would reach the ages of seventeen or eighteen and clamour for admission. To contend with meanwhile were the effects of the trend, of the inclination of more pupils in schools to stay on in sixth forms with a view to taking their A-level examinations and seeking university places. It was widely believed that the population contained a large fraction of highly intelligent young people who were being deprived of the opportunity to obtain degrees by the country's failure to provide a sufficiency of university places. Soon after the war Patrick Blackett, the Langworthy Professor of Physics, himself a dynamic expansionist who had greatly enlarged and improved his department, had investigated the I.Q. of the top half of the students in Manchester and concluded 'that in each age group there were four times as many people outside the university with as high an I.Q. as the top half of the students'.

University authorities in the 1950s inclined to the belief that the University would forfeit all sense of identity and coherence if its numbers exceeded 5,000. However, this estimate was probably not intended to take account of the Faculty of Technology, for the Tech was in many respects a separate though neighbourly institution, with its own Council and Principal, its own students' Union, its own strongly masculine ethos, its own bright prospects of growth. At a meeting held on 2nd March 1956 the University Council recorded its opinion that '4,500 is the maximum number of full-time students which should be contemplated in the University in the foreseeable future, assuming that suitable accommodation and adequate staff are available', but then added a note to the effect that 'an increase from 700 to 1,500 full-time students is envisaged in the Faculty of Technology'.

During the 1940s and 1950s more staff were indeed provided. There was no expectation, as in later decades, that the University would be able to absorb larger numbers of students simply by finding more 'efficient' (i.e. cheaper and quicker, if otherwise inferior) methods of teaching them. As in most boom periods, very large numbers of inexperienced junior staff had been drafted in after the war, but by 1949–50 Stopford was talking of increasing the proportion of professors, readers and senior lecturers in the interests of intellectual well-being. There was a general rule that when senior people, other than professors, vacated their posts these would revert to the level of assistant lectureships. But a professor suddenly bereft of several colleagues could appear before the Standing Committee of Senate and plead that perhaps one of their replacements might be a full lecturer. There was little or no talk of suppressing posts, and at intervals the Council would release packages of money for development to be squabbled over by the faculties. At the end of the session 1956–57 the new Vice-Chancellor, Mansfield Cooper, remarked that 'the staff–student ratio is better today than it has ever been in our history', though he also complained of a 'silent revolution … in the terms of university service', which took the form of burgeoning teaching, examining and administrative responsibilities and threatened to drive research to the wall. Some students, meanwhile, complained that the staff were taking life too easy and did not care to see much of them, certainly not outside working hours; pastoral care and friendly interest, such as they were, were said to take the unlovely form of over-regulating and over-examining the student population.

Growth did not proceed at the same rate in all parts of the University, nor were the benefits evenly spread. By the end of the 1950s the Vice-Chancellor was commenting on the failure of the humanities to keep pace with the rest of the University, though their erosion was still a fairly slow process (the Arts Faculty accounted for 24.85 per cent of total numbers in 1953–54, and for only 22.50 per cent in 1959-60). Their modest performance seemed to reflect a swing from Arts to Science in the school population, so that the expected bulge might never press upon the humanities at all and the balance of the University be disturbed. Was the University stunting its own growth by excessively rigorous methods of selection and by demanding evidence of achievement rather than mere promise at school? But careful admissions procedures, he reflected, brought low rates of 'failure and attrition'. In his judicious style he continued, 'It may be questioned whether there is cause for anxiety in all this; whether in fact a stable University might not have much to commend it; whether we are not in danger of growing too large.' For all these delicately formulated doubts, the Vice-Chancellor went on to recall that the University had accepted additional grants from the University Grants Committee and was thus 'deeply committed to a policy of expansion'.

Universities could not absorb these ever-increasing numbers or provide their students with adequate buildings or up-to-date equipment without relying heavily on grants provided by the Treasury (they came from the Treasury and were not passed through the Ministry of Education). Some critics regretted this heavy dependence on public money and consequently upon the fluctuating opinions of politicians, their views on public spending, and their sense of what, in higher education, might be deemed most useful to the country. But such critics had few or no alternative schemes to propose. Before the war no university had depended upon the Exchequer for more than half its money; St Andrews, receiving 46 per cent of its income in the form of Treasury grant, had relied most heavily on public funds. In 1952–53, when Manchester's general Treasury grants amounted to exactly £1 million, they accounted for 75.7 per cent of the University's total recurrent income, which then added up to £1,321, 231. Student fees, the level of which had not risen since 1926, totalled approximately £160,000, and contributed 12.1 per cent of the whole, whilst endowments, investment income, donations and subscriptions raised something in the region of £90,000 or 6.8 per cent. At the end of the decade, in 1959–60, the proportions were still much the same, with the Treasury grants providing about 80 per cent of the whole, £2 million out of about £2.5 million

Moneys were not assigned to the universities by the Treasury directly, but funnelled through the University Grants Committee. First established in 1919, this body acted as a buffer between the universities and the government and was designed to preserve the autonomy of universities whilst giving them access to public funding. Manchester had provided the first full-time chairman of the UGC, Sir Walter Moberly, who held office from 1934 to 1949 after resigning his vice-chancellorship. As Lord Simon explained in 1958, the UGC then had sixteen full members: ten serving university academics, three industrialists, one Director of Education, a grammar school headmaster, and one retired head of a university college (the only woman on the panel). There was a secretary appointed from the Civil Service, and a staff of about thirty. It was the business of the Committee both to advise the Treasury on the needs of universities in general, and to distribute grants to particular institutions according to the judgments the committee had formed of their requirements and perhaps also of their achievements and competence. The extent of recurrent grants over the next five years would be announced in advance, and over the quinquennium they could be expected to increase modestly but steadily; it was known, by December 1952, that Manchester's grant would rise in steps from £1,054,000 in 1953–54 to £1,238,000 in 1956–57. Additional grants could be made in the course of a quinquennium if it appeared that for some reason the needs of universities had been underestimated, as indeed happened in the late 1950s. This system of quinquennial planning offered a degree of certainty, an opportunity for looking confidently at least into the near future, that would be remembered with nostalgia in the uncertain last decades of the century.

Apart from the recurrent grant, universities would apply repeatedly to the Committee for specific grants to assist with building, with the acquisition of sites, and with the purchase of some scientific equipment. For the most expensive instruments of scientific research, it might well prove necessary to apply to other sources of funding, for example to the Department of Scientific and Industrial Research, or else to the Royal Society, or perhaps to a great philanthropic organisation such as the Nuffield or the Rockefeller Foundation. Although answers were often favourable, cherished plans had sometimes to be postponed. When the University wanted money for a new students' Union building in 1953, the Grants Committee replied that 'as this University had been enabled to start one large building scheme in each of the last three annual programmes, it would not be possible in fairness to other Institutions to grant permission to start a further major project in the fourth successive year'.

Since universities now relied so much on public money, it seemed reasonable to the Public Accounts Committee that they should be caused to account for their spending in greater detail. In the summer of 1954, for example, the Committee were seeking assurances that universities and colleges were observing proper rules of accounting, controlling expenditure strictly, and placing contracts in the most economical ways compatible with efficiency. Within three years the University of Manchester would be mired in deep trouble over its failure to control expenditure on the great radio telescope at Jodrell Bank. It was to attract the unwelcome attention of the Public Accounts Committee, which may have sensed an opportunity to charge academics with being incompetent to manage large sums of money – even though, by the standards normally applied by the Committee, the sum involved was still fairly small.

For all their talk of autonomy, the universities could scarcely be so impolitic or so unpatriotic as to ignore national needs, however these were defined. Soon after the war ended, indeed, their guild of chief executives, the Committee of Vice-Chancellors and Principals, had asked for closer guidance from government in identifying these requirements. For the purposes of higher education national needs were explored by a number of influential reports drawn up by government committees and also by the University Grants Committee themselves. The UGC's brief was extended in 1946 to include 'the preparation and execution of such plans for the development of universities as may from time to time be required in order to ensure that they are fully adequate to national needs'.

In practice such needs were strongly associated with the defence of the country and the promotion of its economic prosperity rather than with the nurturing of good citizens or the encouragement of a critical attitude to authority. The Barlow Committee of 1945–46, on which Blackett of Manchester served as one of six independent members, recommended that the production of science graduates by British universities should be doubled as soon as possible and, at the latest, within ten years. However, it also urged that the expansion of the sciences should not be effected at the expense of the humanities, a principle which Mansfield Cooper was to invoke a decade later. Far from transforming themselves into technological institutes, universities ought to preserve a balance between disciplines. After hearing a lecture by Blackett in the Central Library of Manchester in May 1946, Sir Raymond Streat shook his head at 'the way in which so many people talk about University education in terms of training more and more scientists. This is due to the spectre of the Atomic Bomb as well as to all this modern talk about Scientific Research. It will be a pity if the arts and philosophy get submerged along with the classics.' But government reports were not wholly concerned with the natural or even the social sciences. The Scarborough Committee stressed the Foreign Office's interest in Slavonic and Oriental languages, and the University received a grant which enabled it to build up book collections in Russian, Hebrew, Arabic and Persian, and in the general field of Near Eastern Studies and Semitic languages.

Never had the prestige of British science stood higher. There could be no dispute about the role of scientists, mathematicians and engineers, 'men of the professor type', in winning the war. Several such pundits returned to Manchester or came to it for the first time soon after the war ended. Their work on electronic digital computers and on radio astronomy was to win recognition, sometimes promptly, sometimes belatedly, for its relevance to national interests and was to bring great prestige to Manchester. Some scientists succeeded in exploiting their wartime connections in order to secure expensive surplus equipment that would otherwise have been scrapped or jettisoned; certain of their wartime associates sat on powerful grant-giving bodies or acted as government scientific advisers; they themselves had become accustomed to thinking and planning on a grand scale in the expectation that the means would promptly be found to finance the large installations and provide the loyal and laborious teams that they required. Some of these Manchester entrepreneurs, however, were equally distinguished by their achievements in forms of pure science which could hardly have been dubbed immediately useful to society's needs.

Patrick Blackett, F.C. Williams and Bernard Lovell had served the University in the 1930s, Blackett as a professor and the other two as assistant lecturers. Max Newman, appointed Professor of Pure Mathematics, and Alan Turing, appointed at Newman's instigation Reader in the Theory of Computing in 1948, were new arrivals from Cambridge. Involved with defence policy and the development of radar since 1935, Blackett had been, among much else, Director of Naval Operational Research during the war and a major influence on the techniques employed against U-boats. His forthright opinions on atomic policy, critical of the Americans and considerate of the Russians, excluded him for many years from government favour. But he remained a master tactician in obtaining grants for ambitious projects (including Lovell's) and was, despite his innumerable outside interests and his habit of living on trains, an able Dean of Science and a Pro-Vice-Chancellor capable of understanding, not just the interests of the

Faculty of Science, but those of the University as a whole. Turing, well described in Manchester as 'a kind of scientific Shelley', had long ago begun to dream of machines that would be able to think and learn, indeed, perform most of the functions of the human brain: conceived as a logical system, independent of cells and tissue, the brain could be reproduced in another medium. His paper, 'On computable numbers, with an application to the *Entscheidungsproblem*', had attracted little attention when first published in 1937, but it was cited in support of his election to the Royal Society while he was in Manchester in 1951; Max Newman and Bertrand Russell were his sponsors. In wartime Turing had directed the counter-offensive in Hut Eight at the Government Code and Cipher School at Bletchley Park against the German Enigma, a code made on a machine which could also be broken on a machine, the British Bombe of Turing's contriving. Williams and Lovell had both served at the Telecommunications Research Establishment at Malvern, Lovell working principally on airborne radar, Williams on identification of friend or foe and airborne interception systems.

One urgent task was to solve the main problem associated with the huge electronic calculating machines created during the war, to make it possible to re-set the monsters rapidly in such a way as to enable them to perform an almost infinite variety of tasks. For that purpose it would be necessary to provide them with a large electronic digital store holding hundreds of numbers, including numbers that were codes for instructions. Plans were made and projects undertaken at the National Physical Laboratory in Teddington, where Turing was for a while a Principal Scientific Officer, and where his vision focused on a machine called ACE; at the Department of Electrical Engineering in Manchester; at the Mathematical Laboratory in Cambridge, where the projected device was named EDSAC. In Manchester, it was Newman the pure mathematician who secured a grant of £36,000 from the Royal Society for the development of a computer and used part of the money to attract Turing, the mathematician involved with machines, to Manchester. But it was Williams the engineer, intent on finding ways of using in peacetime the skills developed in connection with radar during the war, who developed the cathode ray tube as the means of storing the information and instructions which the computer would need. It was he and two assistants seconded from Malvern, Tom Kilburn and Geoff Tootill, who succeeded in beating all rivals to the post and in running the first successful programme on 21st June 1948. The Manchester team achieved its aim by simply getting on with the job and not being over-ambitious – perhaps even, as Williams told a scandalised American audience at IBM, by not thinking too hard.

Known as the Baby, the Manchester product was, writes Turing's biographer, Andrew Hodges, the first embodiment, albeit on a very small scale and far more modest than the projected ACE, of a Universal Turing Machine. As Williams himself described the collaboration with the mathematicians, 'We knew nothing about computers, but a lot about circuits. Professor Newman and Mr A.M. Turing in the Mathematics Department knew a lot about computers and substantially nothing about electronics. They took us by the hand and explained how numbers could live in houses with addresses and how if they did they could be kept track of during a calculation.' It had once been thought that Williams would build to Turing's instructions, but, paradoxically, Turing, the conceptual pioneer of the machine as a whole, now had the job of making Williams's machine work.

The national importance of the machine was swiftly recognised; at times government agencies seemed to be impressing this on the University, rather than the other way about. In October 1948 the Ministry of Supply placed an order with Ferranti Ltd, the local electrical engineering firm, 'to construct an electronic calculating machine to the instructions of Professor F.C. Williams', thus establishing records (in Williams's opinion) both for speed of reaction by a civil servant and for brevity of specification. Hence the invention became the first electronic computer to be sold commercially. In a letter of 30th January 1952 the National Research Development Corporation 'sought an assurance that the University appreciated the great national importance attending the use of this machine in the next two or three years while it was the only one of its kind, and the hope was expressed that the cordial collaboration between the University team and Ferranti Limited would continue'. The machine was used, among other things, to perform calculations related to the construction of the British atomic bomb.

If the Baby was the loudly applauded midget of Manchester research, which had brought about the hoped-for collaboration between University science and local industry, the radio telescope at Jodrell Bank, the 'Horticultural Grounds and Physics Out-station', was Manchester's insatiable and embarrassing giant. Under Blackett's umbrella, in the post-war years, astronomy developed in the postgraduate sections of the large, many-professored Physics Department: optical astronomy under Zdeněk Kopal, radar and then radio astronomy under Bernard Lovell. The new astronomy offered the prospect of exploring the universe by the reception, not of light waves, but of radio emissions from outer space received by a gigantic aerial. Radar beams could be directed into the solar system to pick up objects such as meteors which might be invisible to the eye, at least in bad weather. For both these purposes the ideal instrument was a 'fully steerable paraboloid', in other words a huge steel saucer with a pylon-like pointer at its centre, which could focus with the aid of powerful motors and gear-racks salvaged from obsolete battleships upon any part of the sky.

In September 1951 the University Council accepted with gratitude the offer of an 18 in. reflecting telescope from Mr G.T. Smith-Clarke of Coventry, in the belief that it would be most useful to Professor Kopal. About £500 would be required to dismantle and transport this object, and a small building would be erected to house it at Jodrell Bank at a cost of approximately £1,000. The demands of radio astronomy were on a grander scale and introduced the University forcibly to the problems of 'big science'. In 1952 the University received the largest grant in its history for a scientific project. This sprang from two sources: the Department of Scientific and Industrial Research and the Nuffield Foundation, of which Stopford, himself enthusiastic for the project, was then Vice-chairman. Their bounty added up to £335,450: £289,200 for capital costs, £21,250 for staff salaries, £25,000 for running expenses. But it was not enough. Over the next five years the cost of constructing the radio telescope more than doubled. It left the University heavily in debt, since the grant-giving agencies, though willing to produce some further funding, were unable to help beyond a certain point, and could only suggest that the University seek other sources of finance. Industrialists, when appealed to, did not prove unstintedly generous, because they thought that the government ought to pay.

So new was the venture that many of the pitfalls could hardly have been foreseen, and yet it would have been impossible to proceed at all without some kind of estimate, however approximate. Difficulties were caused, for example, by underestimating the tonnage of steel required for the construction and by questions concerning the possible effects of high winds upon the structure. When, in March 1957, the deficit on the telescope had reached £260,000, the Public Accounts Committee began an investigation, as a result of which the consulting engineer for the project, Charles Husband, was wrongly accused of having altered the design without consulting Lovell, and

Lovell was charged with making irresponsible use of public funds. Since Husband's professional reputation had been gravely, perhaps fatally, impugned, he demanded that Lovell, with whom he had in fact been working closely every day for five years, should write a letter to *The Times* refuting the slur on Husband. But Rainford, the Bursar, advised Lovell that he could not and must not do so, because the Committee's report was a privileged document and not therefore open to challenge. Hence there was for a time a serious risk that Lovell would be personally sued for a huge sum of money which he could never have afforded to pay. However, it was not he but Charles Melville, the new Secretary to the Department of Scientific and Industrial Research, who had made the misleading statements to the Public Accounts Committee. He had visited Jodrell Bank only briefly and was therefore poorly informed. Fortunately Melville was brave enough to admit his error handsomely and publicly, and the report was duly corrected, thus clearing Husband's name.

Fortunately, too, the public reputation of Jodrell Bank began spectacularly to improve. Known locally as the fairground, Jodrell Bank had been suspected by Cheshire neighbours of harbouring more than its fair share of communists. At Brereton church a visiting cleric had likened the telescope to a goldfish bowl and its operators to 'open-mouthed goldfish searching gaumlessly for things they have no business to be sticking their noses into, because the Universe is God's province and not man's'. But in 1957, the year of the embarrassing investigation, the telescope was able to prove its own relevance to national defence by successfully tracking the carrier rockets (potential inter-continental ballistic missiles) which had launched the Russian satellites, Sputnik I and Sputnik II, into orbit. Although the military uses of the telescope were incidental to its main purpose, Lovell was astute and pragmatic enough to appreciate their value in enhancing its reputation and attracting finance.

There were many theories as to how the debt should be cleared and the extent to which the government, or one of its agencies, should be obliged to pick up the bill. One of the crasser suggestions, discussed in August 1957 by Sir Raymond Streat, the Treasurer of the University, and Lord Heyworth, the Chairman of Unilever and a member of the University Grants Committee, was a proposal which originated from neither of them. It was to the effect that 'the government might as well pay up for the telescope, since if they forced the University to meet deficiencies or over-expenditure on the telescope the only result would be to reduce the University's income from investments and the

University Grants Committee would have to make good the difference from Treasury funds if the University were to provide the
required contribution to the national programme of University facilities'. Heyworth dismissed the argument as impolitic and untrue, urging that 'In our efforts we must tell the truth and accept whatever
blame or criticism were involved.' Streat departed believing that the
University 'is going to suffer in three ways – (i) financially, (ii) in reputation, and (iii) in having to struggle for a year or two with money-
raising, legal complications and difficult negotiations with the DSIR
and UGC' Luckily, events did not justify his pessimism, because the
University's reputation gained handsomely from Jodrell Bank's easily
appreciated contributions to the Space Age, and the last debts were
eventually paid off by a godfatherly act on the part of Lord Nuffield
himself. The final £50,000 came half from his personal fortune, half
from the Nuffield Foundation. As he wrote to the University in 1960,
'I find it quite humiliating that this great research tool, which has done
so much to raise the prestige of our country throughout the world in
this particular field, should be in such an invidious position.'

In recognition of the generosity of the man and the Foundation, the
University Council resolved to rename the Cheshire outpost – in so far
as it was concerned with heavenly bodies and not with horticulture –
the Nuffield Radio Astronomy Laboratories. Lovell, once taxed with
wasting public money, was knighted in 1961; Husband, once close to
suing him, received an honorary Doctorate of Science in 1964 for
'achievements in structural engineering'. Jodrell Bank was now on the
verge of great discoveries in the physics of the stars; in the early 1960s
Henry Palmer and his group produced a catalogue of about one hundred small objects in the radio sky, well outside our own galaxy, which
proved to be the most powerful objects in the universe and were
termed 'quasars' or 'quasi-stellar objects', thus opening the way to an
extra-galactic astronomy which would range far beyond the Milky
Way.

The great telescope itself became a landmark in the Cheshire coun-
tryside, the focus for a lively community of technicians and support
staff drawn from Congleton, Macclesfield and the neighbouring villages. As the University's most wondrous and most visible piece of
apparatus, it had a powerful attraction for visitors who might not
have connected it with the University at all. It was reported in 1964
that 35,000 visitors had seen the laboratories during open weeks in
July and August, and that the profits to Jodrell Bank were now considerable. Lovell was moved to suggest that permanent facilities for

visitors should be constructed, and the University Council took the hint. In 1972 Lovell and David Valentine, the Professor of Botany, proposed that an arboretum, 'a collection of trees and shrubs unique in the north of England', should be added to the attractions of Jodrell Bank. The trees would, incidentally, help the telescope to function better by suppressing interference. On one occasion the opportunity to see the telescope itself – a privilege seldom granted – disarmed even an official of the Amalgamated Engineering Union who had been sent to investigate complaints about the long working hours imposed upon the technicians. 'Look here, Kent, this industrial relations matter, it's a doddle, isn't it!' cried Lovell to the member of the Bursar's Department who had been responsible for softening the trade unionist up.

It was easy enough to imagine that, despite the Vice-Chancellor's repeated admonitions concerning the need to preserve balance in the University, the future would lie with its spectacular achievements in science and engineering, and these alone would be likely to win public attention. Two cultures would divide the University, a process symbolised by the expansion of science and engineering on the east side of Oxford Road, a thoroughfare notoriously difficult to cross in fog. One culture might ultimately triumph over the other. Frank Kermode describes his own resounding defeat at the hands of Lovell at a University committee before which he was endeavouring to make out a case for an additional assistant, or assistant lecturer, in English. 'I was challenged by a famous astronomer, who wanted another helot to man his telescopes, and when in the course of his impressive oration he passionately asked whether Professor Kermode was really ruthless enough to strengthen his department at the cost of closing down Jodrell Bank, ... I was so amazed by this brilliantly shameless tactic, and so abashed, that I abandoned the competition at once.' Science and humanities professors appeared to think on entirely different financial scales. In those years, or a little later, Flowers of Physics and Gee of Chemistry looked on incredulously as a professor of one of the ancient languages justified to Senate the addition of a few pounds to his budget for the purpose of buying a second-hand mechanical typewriter and saving his department from the necessity of copying out documents by hand. There was a danger that because Arts did not cost very much it might not be valued very highly. However, the University's development was not altogether one-sided, and extended to the fine arts as well as to science and engineering. It had the means and the inclination to rescue neighbouring institutions, both useful and beautiful, from financial quicksands. Among those salvaged was the Whitworth Art Gallery.

This gallery formed part of the generous bequest to the city of Sir Joseph Whitworth, the versatile, indefatigable Victorian engineer who, in his biographer's opinion, was probably the greatest educational philanthropist before Nuffield. Endowed with a fine collection of English water colours and drawings, the gallery depended for support partly on the yield of its investments and partly on a grant from the Corporation, which had been contributing since 1921 to its support. But a decline in the value of the investments and a rise in costs forced the gallery to run at a loss. The Whitworth's director, Margaret Pilkington, a shareholder in Pilkington Tiles Ltd, had served without salary for many years; after her retirement, no other director would be likely to do so. Under its charter of 1889 the gallery could impose no charges on the public who came to see its treasures, and could not recoup any part of its losses by making visitors pay. In September 1954 the governors of the gallery approached the University Council, suggesting that it might be transferred to the University and the directorship fall to the head of the Department of Art History. To ensure its survival as a living institution it must be enabled to make acquisitions and its curator be empowered to go frequently to London ('the only active art centre in this country') and occasionally to continental Europe. The Council agreed in principle to accept the transfer of the gallery, which happened to stand at the southern end of the area reserved for University development, and seemed calculated to complete it gracefully. Before long their decision attracted a generous benefaction, for Margaret and Dorothy Pilkington offered in 1956 to transfer to the University shares to the value of £20,000, to be used to establish a professorial chair in association with the Department of the History of Art – thus enhancing the possibility that a scholar and administrator of high calibre would be attracted to the directorship of the gallery. The transfer was eventually accomplished after prolonged legal proceedings during the session 1957–58, and John White, the first Pilkington Professor of the History of Art, took office on 1st August 1959.

Throughout the 1950s students of science and engineering remained a privileged body within the University. Their potential contribution as scientists to the country's well-being was expressly acknowledged, they had better career prospects, and they enjoyed more opportunities of escaping the tedium and humiliations of National Service. Service obligations cast a long shadow over the University and were regarded with scant enthusiasm by the body of men students in general, many of whom were all too well acquainted with the parades and manoeuvres of school cadet forces. OWENS, suggested a University wit, was an acronym for the Obvious Way of Escaping National Service; a correspondent of *News Bulletin* called National Service an unacceptable euphemism for conscription; a Union debate in 1956 passed overwhelmingly a motion to the effect that 'National Service is a waste of time.' Even those who, as did Peter Taylor, a dental student, chose to get their service out of the way before coming to the University, found themselves still obliged to devote a chunk of their almost non-existent leisure to discharging their obligations to the Territorial Army. This body's claims persisted for several years after service with the colours. They could be met by attending a stipulated number of parades with the University Training Corps, and the Training Corps also provided a relatively gradual introduction to service life: it was possible to take the War Office Selection Board from the University with a view to a National Service commission, and army service with the Corps would enable the recruit to choose, up to a point, which of five arms he would serve with – the Royal Engineers, the Royal Signals, the Infantry, the Intelligence Corps, or the Royal Electrical and Mechanical Engineers.

By the mid-1950s the University Appointments Board was reporting that the desire to avoid National Service was exerting a strong influence on choices of career. As abolition drew nearer it seemed doubly futile to have to postpone careers on account of military service. With conscription's abrupt disappearance, competition for jobs among those leaving the University would become especially intense, and it would be good to be in post before the queues for employment lengthened, as they surely would in 1961. At various times science and technology graduates enjoyed deferment for such time as they were carrying out classified defence work in industry or in government departments, especially, perhaps, in the design and production of aircraft. In 1955–56 indefinite deferment was granted to scientists working for the National Coal Board and two years' deferment for industrial graduate apprenticeships. The University was also entitled to identify and seek deferment for 'a strictly limited number of scientists of outstanding ability and capacity to undertake fundamental research', their names at first being brought before the Standing Committee of Senate that they might be formally approved.

From the mid-1950s there were fewer vacancies in defence work. But well-qualified scientists and mathematicians – i.e. those who bore away first- and second-class degrees – could now obtain deferment by becoming schoolteachers. Reports on the employment of Manchester graduates over the period from 1949 to 1954 suggested that of scientists only 13 per cent of men and 26 per cent of women were teaching in schools (as compared with 63 per cent of male arts graduates and 47 per cent of female arts graduates). Improvements in the recruitment of science teachers could now be expected, as the Appointments Board noted in satisfied tones.

To go in for science and engineering, to communicate their principles and techniques to schoolboys and girls, was in effect a form of National Service, one of many ways in which universities and their graduates could minister to national needs. Ways in which the humanities could contribute to national needs were not so expressly stated, although the Vice-Chancellor continued to declare that 'the intellectual health of any University demands the maintenance of a reasonable balance between disciplines', and the University's tradition of pursuing and communicating knowledge for its own sake was not seriously placed at risk.

By the end of the 1950s, the University, like most others in the country, had become heavily dependent on government funding, though not to the exclusion of all else. It could only become more so, and be made more publicly accountable, as its need for expensive buildings and scientific equipment increased. The number of students it admitted, and the number of places to be made available in particular disciplines – science, engineering, medicine, law were to be strongly influenced by government-inspired assessments of national needs. In the late 1940s the University had made spectacular efforts to accommodate the men and women who had served the country in the armed and auxiliary forces. In the 1960s it would be urged once more to expand in order to give opportunities to those people's children, to whom the country ought to feel a special sense of obligation. The University Grants Committee stood between universities and the government, although sceptics doubted its ability to be anything other than an instrument of government policy. Partly as a consequence of wartime enterprise, however, far from being a time of unrelieved drabness, austerity and conformity, these were years of extraordinary inventiveness and opportunism. Even today, most people connected with the University, asked casually to name the greatest achievements within the place over the last fifty years, will speak of the development of the computer in Williams's laboratory and of radio astronomy in Lovell's domain at Jodrell Bank.

3

Student culture

A large proportion of students in the 1950s spent three years at the University and set out to obtain honours degrees, although these were not as prevalent as they became in the 1970s, 1980s and 1990s. Most honours degrees were in a single subject, although the possibility of taking double honours in, say, two languages over a period of four years did exist, and there were some joint honours courses. Many students sought professional or vocational qualifications and spent anything from one to six years obtaining them (the Department of Pharmacy, for example, ran an intensive one-year course, known as the Chemist and Druggist course, which led to Membership of the Pharmaceutical Society). Professional courses in Medicine, Dentistry and Architecture lasted for five or six years, and courses in the Faculty of Medicine continued throughout the year, unpunctuated by the vacations which other students enjoyed.

In the first year or two of honours courses, students were generally caused to take subsidiary courses in other disciplines believed to be helpful to their studies or simply intended to broaden their outlook. The notion that scholars and gentlefolk could be trusted to keep up their languages and develop their broader cultural interests on their own initiative was somewhat alien to the University's outlook, and it thought mostly in terms of courses of lectures leading to examinations which had to be passed. History Honours students, for example, would be called upon to study a language and 'something ghastly called Political Economy' (as one former student now puts it) in their first year. Students of Social Administration took a wide variety of courses outside their own department. Though admirable in its intentions, the system tended to crowd students' days with lectures, and allowed them little time to develop close relationships with particular tutors, at least until they reached an advanced level and embarked, as some did, on individual projects or began to write short theses in their final years.

Less focused general courses usually led only to pass degrees, and were sometimes called by derogatory titles such as Ord. Arts ('General Arts' or 'General Science' were more proper and dignified). In the Faculty of Economic and Social Studies the B.A. in Economics was an honours degree, whereas the B.A. in Commerce was not. Honours in Combined Studies was a thing of the future, to be introduced in Arts only in 1972. However, the advent of American Studies in the Arts Faculty soon after the war hinted at the possible development of a planned multi-disciplinary honours degree in history, literature and politics, and the example of Leeds University in establishing an honours degree in general studies was much commended in the late 1950s. General studies in Manchester suffered from administrative failure to timetable courses in such a way as to make certain interesting combinations practicable. Broad and incoherent courses were also handicapped by a confusion between their roles, which called on them both to provide a menu for open-minded students who did not wish to specialise, and to act as a receptacle for those who had failed honours courses after the first or second years. The University usually remained willing to give these unfortunates a degree, whilst they themselves were reluctant to withdraw without one, and general courses seemed to provide a convenient solution to the problem.

Newcomers received little advice about choices of course. Pat O'Gara found that all concerned assumed that convent girls such as herself would continue to pursue school subjects such as English, rather than venture on new ones such as Economics or Law, which might well have suited her better. Pastoral care took the form of closely scrutinising academic progress rather than taking cognisance of personal, emotional or psychological problems. The burden of examinations was heavy, since it included 'terminal' examinations. Despite their misleading name, there was nothing final about them, since they were mock examinations often held at the beginning of term in the first and second years, partly to ensure that students did some academic work during vacations. 'It was death by a thousand exams', says a History student of the 1950s, and there were often alarming rumours to the effect that the Part I examinations the previous year had been 'a real slaughter'. The news of examination failure, as a former Economics student recalls, was likely, at least in the Faculty of Economics and Social Sciences, to be communicated 'administratively', with neither sympathy nor reproof for the victim.

By the charter of 1903, 'There shall be one or more Representative Councils of the students of the University (as may from time to time be determined by the Court) who may approach or enter into communication with the Vice-Chancellor on matters affecting the University.' For most purposes the effective representative council consisted of the officers and committee-members of the men's and women's Unions, whose advice and services as intermediaries were valued by Stopford and, generally, by Mansfield Cooper. It was the Union officers' task not only to represent student opinion (in so far as they could divine what it was), but also to run a debating society, to extend invitations to political and other visiting speakers, to organise social events (especially dances) and to administer buildings. Their premises functioned as a combination of club and department store, providing bars, baths, a barber's shop, a part-time hairdresser, television and games rooms, and a shop which sold stationery. The Unions backed a newspaper, *News Bulletin*, founded in 1934. Originally a free newssheet, this had developed into a sophisticated journal produced in a highly professional manner, the style of which veered, according to editorial policy, between that of a broadsheet carrying high-minded leaders in the manner of *The Manchester Guardian* and that of a tabloid betraying an appetite for scandal. In some sense an official journal published by and for Union members, it was none the less free to criticise the Union officers, and sometimes did so with a gusto which verged upon brutality.

Conscious of being different, the medical students had their own representative council and their own paper, *The Manchester University Medical School Gazette*. It seemed that the arrangement could be traced back to 1901. The Unions might represent all other faculties, but they could not – explained an article written in 1954 – deal effectively 'with medical, especially clinical, matters', and the medical council existed to act as a 'go-between for University and Infirmary authorities and medics ... '. Nevertheless, medical students also supplied a large number of Union Presidents. Since campaigning for Union office was unheard-of until 1956 and frowned upon by many when electioneering was first practised by a bold Commerce student named Michael Scott, much depended on having been around for a long time and made oneself known to the minority of students who were actively interested in Union affairs. Medical students were well placed to do this: Terry Davies, elected in 1957, was the third medical student in four years to become President, and the succession ended only with Netar Mallick (later Sir Netar Mallick, Professor of Renal Medicine) in 1958. Sylvia Manton, a medical student, was the first serious woman candidate for the presidency of the joint University of

Manchester Union in that year, when she finished the race as Vice-President. As *News Bulletin* observed ponderously, 'Maybe a medical course with its preparation for considerable professional responsibility is conducive to the development of the ability to lead.'

Shortly after the centenary, in the session of 1951–52, 4,595 students were registered at Owens, of whom 3,438 were men and 1,157 women. The Faculty of Technology included 670 men and a mere 15 women students; women taking courses in, say, Industrial Management could be sure of attracting in the corridors of Sackville Street the attention accorded to an exotic species. More than 40 per cent of all women at Owens had joined the Arts Faculty, which contained 506 women to 879 men. Women teachers in training occupied 40 per cent of places in the Faculty of Education, which had enrolled 124 women to 173 men. Elsewhere, the distribution of women students was very patchy. In some years virtually all students of Social Administration were female, but for many years to come women would be wholly absent from the ranks of the engineers, and there were even fewer women in Theology (whose students were mostly in training for the ministry) than in Technology. Women students of Science and Medicine were numerous enough to provoke a haughty letter from the house secretary of the men's Union to the Union newspaper in 1952, objecting to 'the number of misguided young females sat in Caf. wearing dirty lab. coats' and suggesting that they eat their meals in laboratories and dissecting rooms instead. Women applying to read Medicine could expect to have their claims closely scrutinised: was it particularly likely that they would soon choose to marry and have children and a doctor be lost to the profession after a long and expensive training, taking up one of a limited number of places? For all this they were more numerous in Medicine than in Science, for women accounted for about a quarter of all medical students, although they were less strong in Dentistry and Pharmacy. In the Science Faculty about one student in eight was a woman.

Although the Manchester students of the 1950s were far more numerous than their pre-war predecessors, many of them were conscious of forming part of a privileged minority and were anxious, on that account, to repay the trust reposed in them. Some of the earnest and appreciative statements published in *News Bulletin* would have seemed priggish or excessively deferential to a later generation which regarded access to higher education as a right. But there is no reason to think them hypocritical. 'There is tolerance here and clear thinking and free criticism. We are luckier than we realise to live and work in

such an open atmosphere', pronounced a leading article at the end of
the session in July 1953. 'Let us never claim money from the State as
a right, and expect that the very fact that we are students opens the
national coffers ... It's reported that only about three in a thousand
write to thank Education authorities for grants at the end of their
courses. H'mm ... ' Thus another such article, published on 1st
December 1955. When the new Arts Festival was launched at the end
of 1956, with a production of *Henry V* in the Free Trade Hall, the
men's Union President, Ian Kane, spoke of 'the desire of the students
to make some repayment for the money provided by the country
which keeps most people at the University.'

Perhaps such sentiments were to be expected of the kind of responsible student who was well accustomed to dealing with the University
authorities and absorbing something of their outlook. There undoubtedly was a more frivolous café – or cafeteria – society whose headquarters lay in the cavernous, deconsecrated Welsh chapel known as
Caf. The glitterati who spent hours chatting under its roof were unin-
fected by any nonconformist conscience lingering in the atmosphere
and liable to think that simply being at the University was more
important than slaving away for a good qualification. Get a good
degree and you might end up as a teacher or social worker; be a University sophisticate with an air of social aplomb and you might make
a fortune in business. But the desire to take nothing for granted and
to show responsibility to the community seems to have been widely
diffused.

For all its licensed buffoonery the University Rag, in which about
2,000 students took part in the early 1950s, had a strong social purpose and raised large sums of money for chosen charities. Children's
hospitals and clubs predominated among them; nineteen charities
benefited in 1951, twenty-three in 1955. In 1955 25 per cent of the
Rag takings went to five hospitals and 10 per cent to the University
Settlement. Founded in 1895, the Settlement in Ancoats embodied a
long-standing tradition of service to the community, for it enabled a
small number of students and graduates to live in one of the poorest
areas of Manchester, to study social conditions, and to attempt to give
practical help to their neighbours. This outpost of the University was
hard by the old workhouse, known as Part III Accommodation, for
people in need of shelter and some form of training. A student of
Social Administration, aged nineteen, might find herself (as Jean Taylor remembers) advising a woman with five children how to cook on
a stove. ' ... we were very aware that we were quite privileged and that

what we were doing was looking into the lives of other people who were not quite so privileged.' Some of the halls of residence practised good works unselfconsciously. At St Gabriel's, the Catholic women's hall, the title of the Marillac Society recalled the spiritual and corporal charity of the seventeenth century; its members undertook the task of visiting 'the aged and lonely poor'. Students residing at the Methodist Hartley Victoria College, a hall licensed by the University, took seventy poor children for a week's holiday at Staithes on the Yorkshire coast.

Former students who were at the University in the 1950s have spoken of another kind of privilege – the privilege of being alive. Sheila Griffiths, who as Sheila Chapman read history from 1954 to 1957 and lived in Ashburne Hall, remembers: 'I had a state scholarship, so I felt I had to compete. Also there was a great sense of privilege. After all we had been children during the war and we had survived. I think at that time many of us wondered whether we could survive in the future because there was a threat of atomic warfare and the Cold War and everything and you wondered about that.' Students apprehensively watched the ominous advance of Russian tanks into Hungary in 1956 on the one television set in Ashburne. 'We didn't know if the Russian tanks were going to go straight through Europe. We thought, "Today it's them and tomorrow it's us."' Despite the rigours of the examination system and the austerities of hall life, warmed by personal friendships rather than by efficient heating, 'It was just wonderful to be able to study what you wanted to study and to have that peep into an intellectual, academic world. To feel that there was that potential in your future, the things that you might do. It was just a wonderfully exciting time.' There was a sense that if Western society survived the world would be at one's feet. A Londoner, enjoying the adventure of living away from home, she found in Manchester 'a certain northern frugality and seriousness' to which she responded with sympathy and enthusiasm.

The financial support enjoyed by students varied a great deal, but they were seldom if ever driven to take jobs during term and work their way through college in the American manner. State scholars were few and relatively fortunate. Some students held University scholarships. By the session 1957–58 some really valuable major scholarships, not means-tested and worth about £350 a year, had been introduced; in February 1958, when for the first time candidates were allowed to sit the papers at their schools without coming to the strange environment of the University, the number of candidates rose

about threefold and reached about five hundred. Most students, however, were supported by local authorities and held so-called 'county
scholarships'. Some authorities were markedly more open-handed
than others. Blackpool, as Peter Taylor remembers, made part of its
allowances as grant and another part as a loan repayable after graduation; it was unwilling to recognise that students of Dentistry
attended throughout the year and did not enjoy the same vacations as
most others. Bolton, on the other hand, was willing to subsidise vacation placements for students of Social Administration, so long as the
Department declared these exercises essential to the course.

Many students were partially supported by parents proud of the
opportunities enjoyed by their children, who were often the first in
the family ever to attend a university. Since a majority of students
came from Lancashire and Cheshire, many of them lived at home and
kept up with school and neighbourhood friends. Two buses might be
needed for the journey from Droylsden, but there was good company
on board to make it pass quicker. Alan Tallentire, reading Pharmacy,
would catch the 7.31 from Burnley in the morning and the 5.12 back
home in the evening, but he could be sure of the company of fellow
students and they would do some of their swotting together on the
train. Only by keeping their sons and daughters under their own roofs
could some families support them throughout the longer courses,
such as those in Medicine.

However, the chances of vacation work were good, and the Union
acted as a useful employment agency for it; post office work at Christmas was a stand-by, and former National Servicemen had sometimes
managed to accumulate savings which provided some kind of a cush-
ion on which to subside for support. The pay of an officer contrasted
dramatically with the income of a student and even with the salary of
a junior academic.

Budgets could more or less balance because there was little conspicuous consumption and, in the early 1950s at least, not much of a
distinctive youth culture. Save on special occasions, beer was drunk in
half-pints and there was little of the pubbing and clubbing of later
decades; few would have chosen Manchester for its night-life rather
than its courses, though Saturday night dances were popular and the
Union, having few competitors, could afford to hire excellent bands.
Smoking was too expensive an indulgence for many, though it was
occasionally used for defensive purposes at work. Medical and dental
students smoked while dissecting to drown the stench of formalin,
and had to be admonished by Dr Torr, Lecturer in Anatomy, 'You do

not use the body, when you open it up, as an ashtray ... ' Personal computers and hi-fi systems were things of the distant future and television sets, owned by institutions rather than people, were watched in public rooms (women students could sometimes be found knitting and gazing at the adventures of Andy Pandy in their Union lounge). At most one might aspire to own a record-player, for these were becoming available and affordable about the year 1957. Drugs, if used at all, were taken not for pleasure but for stimulation in the examining season; Honorah Kenyon, who read English, remembers the circulation of tablets very similar to Speed, which made it possible to stay awake almost indefinitely and accomplish unheard-of feats of revision for exams.

Dress was conservative and inclined to be formal, founded on tweed jackets and ties for men and two-piece costumes for women. 'We were the last generation to dress like our parents', according to Norman Leece, who read Electrical Engineering and lived in St Anselm Hall from 1952 to 1955. Women students, as Pat Case remembers, 'wore a cheaper version of what middle-aged, middle-class women wore', and usually cut each other's hair, although they were skilful at adding livelier touches to their appearance – 'Earrings, we used to make them out of buttons and stick them on, we had some quite exotic earrings.' Femininity was greatly prized, for men seldom regarded women as their exact equivalent or treated them as honorary chaps; the Women's Union organised both talks on make-up by representatives of Yardley's and fashion parades in which students acted as mannequins. Men usually had haircuts once a fortnight, and their short-back-and-sides could be maintained unceremoniously within five minutes by Alf, the grumpy barber in the Union. At least for a time, University blazers were in vogue and worn with great pride. They were supplied by Wippell's, a shop in town which also kitted out the clergy and hired gowns and hoods to graduands about to collect degrees. Scarves were not only a form of insignia for the student population, but also smog masks for defence against the polluted air and protection against the deep chill of poorly heated buildings. Neat dress had its uses, especially in the professional schools – 'if I look as though I'm a doctor, patients won't mind me discussing their ailments and general condition'.

A few sophisticates attempted more raffish styles, if only by smoking cigarettes in long holders until the price of tobacco proved prohibitive. Some of the Caf set, as Derek Torrington recalls, 'were at pains to wear houndstooth sports jackets, waistcoats, and corduroy caps'. But an article on 'The new Elizabethans' by Arnold Hinchliffe in *The Serpent* for autumn 1953 complained that 'Students dress and live drably, and they seem to have lost the capacity for excitement … It is inevitable that the mood of students living on University Coffee and Nut Roast will tend to be grim. Moreover, the aesthetic soul, delicately burgeoning in our traditional rain with all the optimism of ignorance, will receive no encouragement from the monuments about it. Mock temples, slum tenements, converted chapels and the monstrous spires of Whitworth, come as a shock, and the best absorber, unfortunately, is indifference … Let us shock people, be sneered at, ridiculed, perhaps even admired; but let us never be ignored … '

Religious societies still exercised a strong influence over student life and customs, including sexual mores. Many students had been fed into the University by the Catholic grammar schools of the North West and the Catholics formed a fairly distinctive body. Sometimes they assembled conspicuously on great occasions, as at the Coronation mass in 1953, when the huge Church of the Holy Name was packed to the rafters. Some good Catholic families would still ask the bishop, through the parish priest, for permission to attend the University, which was usually granted on condition that the new arrival would join the Catholic Society. This was one of the largest and most powerful student organisations, complemented by the Student Christian Movement and by the much more aggressive and evangelical MIFCU (the Manchester Inter-Faculty Christian Union). Much of the political activity of the late 1950s was inspired by religious conviction; Gillian Hopkins, the president of the Nuclear Weapons Protest Committee, described herself as a Christian pacifist and sent to *News Bulletin* a description of an Aldermaston March entering and leaving Reading in the spring of 1958.

For whatever reasons, principled or pragmatic, sexual morality was strict, at least in discouraging promiscuity, and if there was much heavy petting there was little full sexual intercourse outside marriage. Opportunities for being alone together, away from the public gaze and secure against interruption, were restricted; when Ashburne girls, walking home down Oxford Road, showed too much affection for their boy friends they provoked public complaints and incurred reproof from their Senior Student. In the days before the Pill, contraception was harder to obtain without embarrassment. As one 1950s student puts it trenchantly, there was a 'morality of necessity' tinged with a good deal of 'self-frustration' and, on some girls' part, wearisome curiosity. Tongue-in-cheek advice circulating among former convent girls admonished them to avoid extra-marital sex 'for the love of Jesus, on account of venereal disease, and for fear of having a child'. Risqué communications to student journals were liable to earn lofty rebukes, especially if they came, or purported to come, from women. The innuendo in *Rag Rag*, the magazine sold annually during Rag Week to the partially unsuspecting people of Manchester, was the subject of recurrent controversy. Indeed, in November 1953, the chairmen of the Catholic Society and the Student Christian Movement combined to fulminate against 'the immoral character of past editions of the magazine *Rag Rag*. The magazine is a disgrace to the University, a blot on its good name and on that of the Rag itself.' But

'Clean up *Rag Rag*,' cry the pious,
'Fun without a sexy bias,'

mocked a couplet in *News Bulletin*.

In the late 1950s the Medical Faculty announced a course of lectures on 'homosexuality and other perversions'. Earlier in the decade a University Reader, Alan Turing, convicted of a homosexual offence, had escaped with probation only on condition that he 'submit for treatment by a duly qualified medical practitioner at Manchester Royal Infirmary', a process which involved the injection of female hormones to reduce his libido. Student attitudes towards what judges and magistrates treated as, at best, a curable disease were somewhat uncertain. After a visit to the Union by the film actress Greer Garson in 1953, *The Daily Express* reported that students had booed the name of a famous actor who had recently been fined for importuning. *News Bulletin* hastened to intervene, to point out that 'one or two students made what can be described only as a gasp, and the chief sounds were those of approbation of Miss Garson's references to Sir John' as one of her favourite stars. The student journalist took his lead from *The Observer* and declared that 'a large body of students in the University' would share that paper's opinion. 'Homosexuality is far less socially destructive than adultery, and criminal prosecution can claim no greater moral justification in one than the other. Publication in the popular Press that informed student opinion boos and jeers at a victim of this vindictive law does not facilitate sympathetic and emotionless thought on the subject, nor does it do credit to the supposed accuracy of the reporter.'

Student exuberance, fantasy and slapstick humour were allowed to have their day on two festive occasions each year – during the brief

Rag season and, for a time, at graduation ceremonies. Though once described by the Soviet journal *Pravda* as 'Manchester students rioting for bread', Rag was more carnival than insurrection. Culminating on Shrove Tuesday, it descended from those ancient festivals which briefly turned the world upside down and handed the sceptre to the Lord of Misrule, the gross carnal sins such as lechery and gluttony being brought to the surface and put on display the better to purge them during the rigours of Lent. The eggs, flour and water that should have been mixed into pancakes were flung with abandon into the midst of revellers and spectators. Rag ceremonies were tersely if superciliously summed up in 1955 as 'a Ball, a paper magazine, a carnival procession and systematic begging', which entailed holding the local population to ransom with collecting boxes and disrupting all the traffic. The procession consisted of tableaux, sometimes almost forty of them, usually borne on the backs of lorries, though during the petrol shortages after the Suez crisis steam traction engines were used instead, thereby adding to the prevailing murk and gloom. Not all students were amused. 'Mock funerals are an offence to good taste; overturning cars deserves severe legal punishments; and obscene vulgarity is degrading', warned a writer in *The Serpent* in the spring of 1954, arguing that only a minority of students were in favour of this tawdry festival.

Particularly objectionable to this critic were the so-called Rag stunts, daring or merely lunatic operations, sometimes carried out at the expense of other universities and designed to draw attention to the approach of Rag Day itself. Jolly japes and idiotic frolics by halls of residence or other groupings of students abounded and sometimes took on a rather tired appearance. The exploits of raiding parties might well attract censure from the Vice-Chancellor, particularly when in 1955 Architecture students succeeded in capturing as a trophy from Liverpool University a portrait by Augustus John worth over £2,000. More acceptably, it seemed in 1960 that the new hall of residence, Needham, intended to do nothing worse than roll a barrel of beer from Manchester to Sheffield, while the Jewish society were to 'make a survey of drains with regard to the introduction of a Manchester Underground service'. However, Montgomery House (whose patron was the Field Marshal himself) were said to have almost succeeded in capturing Chester Castle, much to the discomfiture of the regular soldiers supposed to be guarding the stronghold.

Female participation in some aspects of the Rag aroused misgivings in the minds of some adults, who managed to cling to the belief that young women were, or ought to be, more innocent than young men. When the Senate approved a request from the President of the Union in 1952 to be allowed to put on a Rag revue with an approved script, the University stipulated that 'strict measures would be taken to prevent rowdyism and women students under the age of 21 years would have to present to the producer written permission from their parents'. Eight years later the minister of the Church of the Nazarene in Ashton-under-Lyne was still perturbed by the vulgarity of *Rag Rag*: 'Fancy putting a paper like this in the hands of a girl. Nice girls who want to help the Rag, well, it's putting them in a difficult position.'

Since about 1921, Ragging students had been accustomed to collect money for Manchester and Salford hospitals. When these hospitals were on the verge of being taken over by the state in 1947, many had wondered whether Rag could continue in the old tradition, or whether it could survive at all. But in 1948 Stopford had advised that the National Health Service Act should not put an end to 'local interest, pride and the need for help'. This Act contained clauses which allowed gifts to be made to particular hospitals, in order to provide extra services and amenities and to promote research. In any case charities, especially children's charities, were always popular, and included not only the Settlement in Ancoats but also the Salford Poor Children's Holiday and the Cripples' Help Society (Mayor of Stockport's Appeal).

Perhaps the end – raising money for these good causes – did not always justify the means. But the 'systematic begging' was highly and painstakingly organised. Halls of residence, for example, were assigned specific areas of Greater Manchester to cover each year, by collecting or by selling the Rag magazine in pubs, sometimes in competition with the Salvation Army's chaster product. Fund-raising was sometimes very successful. In 1958 the Rag attracted public disapproval because the organisers had failed to cancel a stunt which coincided with the news of the disaster at Munich at which Manchester United players and their manager were injured and killed. But in that year the Union's newspaper was able to claim a 'Manchester first', a record for any British university, based not only on the high level of the takings in that year, but also on the low level of the expenses. Almost £18,000 had flowed in and expenses amounted to no more than 8.5 per cent. Manchester's closest rival, Bristol, had been obliged to deduct 15 per cent from the sum they had amassed. By way of a peace-offering, the organisers donated £1,200 to the Manchester United Disaster Fund.

Graduation ceremonies, the final rite of passage for students collecting their degrees, were not the decorous affairs that they subsequently became. Until 1959, when the summer term was shortened and graduation ceremonies began to be held outside it, degree days were liable to be held in the rowdy presence of undergraduates. If the graduands, in their gowns and hoods and subfusc clothing, took the performance seriously, their juniors did not; they assembled with missiles to hurl at the new graduates as they departed from the Whitworth Hall. Joan Wood (born Joan Keane), who read Physics and Chemistry and graduated in 1947, remembers that

'I was the unfortunate recipient of a direct hit with a brown paper bag filled with white chalk dust which took me about three weeks to get out of my hair and clothes. I was told later that it had been meant for Lord Woolton, who was Chancellor, but as he had been unable to attend, I got it. Perhaps I should have felt honoured, but I didn't. The cap and gown had been hired from Wippell's and I did not wait to hear their reaction when I returned them.'

Did the Rag Day carnival act as a form of social control, by providing a safety valve through which student discontent and iconoclasm could harmlessly escape? Be this unlikely theory as it may, it is true that before about 1958 student journalists were seldom openly disrespectful of authority or critical of teaching or discipline. They were sometimes, admittedly, troubled by a disappointing suspicion that, as the average age of students fell, the University was becoming increasingly like a glorified grammar school, that student life was over-regulated, that the longed-for change of status from adolescent to adult was not coming about as it should. Since the age of majority was still twenty-one, most undergraduates were still in an ambiguous state, neither schoolchildren nor fully-fledged grown-ups. This made them sensitive to any attempts by the University to behave like a parent without proper warning or consultation with representatives of the student body.

Towards the end of the decade *News Bulletin* ran a series of unsigned articles entitled 'Revolt at Redbrick'. One reporter created a brief sensation by quoting – no doubt, as was claimed, misquoting – certain dignitaries in the Chemistry Department as suggesting that students were incompetent to design their own experimental apparatus. This seeming slight provoked angry references by a group of third-years to 'professors who closed their minds to new facts 13 years ago, and teachers so engrossed in the mysteries of research as to be quite inept in the art of teaching'. It became almost commonplace to suggest in print that relations between staff and students were in a sorry state, that the quality of teaching was poor and excessively dependent on uninspiring and dully factual lectures, that students' written work was not taken seriously, that classes were not properly conducted, that research reigned supreme to the detriment of everything else.

In Manchester the relationship between lectures and tutorials was almost the reverse of that which prevailed in Oxford and Cambridge. Until the early 1960s proof of attendance at lectures rather than seminars was considered necessary to satisfying education authorities that the grants they paid were being properly used, and that a student's work and attendance were adequate. Attendance lists circulated for signature at lectures, although it was easy to falsify them, as witness a verse on the downfall of one unlucky Jim:

> Soon lectures ceased to interest Jim,
> He'd miss them on the slightest whim.
> His friends would sign his name instead
> While he remained in Caf or bed.

For these and other reasons lectures became a prime target for satire and complaint. Some lecturers, it seemed, failed to understand the differences between the written and the spoken word. Certain of their performances closely, perhaps exactly, reproduced the contents of books which the speaker had just published and which were generally available. Sometimes the lecturer appeared to be reading aloud the page proofs of some work about to break upon the world. The ominous word 'paternalism', to be so much used in the 1960s, broke the surface in the Education Department in 1957 when complaints about the 'excessive number and the quality of lectures' were coupled with resentment that graduates taking the teaching diploma were allegedly being 'pushed about like so many little children'.

Some students, however, were aware, or have since become aware, of encountering a new and unfamiliar situation. University professors and lecturers were not schoolteachers prepared to devote their lives to their pupils and their welfare; the primary interest of most of them lay in research. This was supposed incidentally to make them livelier and more inspiring teachers who would communicate to their students the excitement of discovery and awaken in their audience the desire to break new intellectual ground, to go always a little further into the unknown, rather than be content with received wisdom. Dr Burkhardt, the Science tutor, exhorted the students at the freshers'

conference in 1958 to believe that the whole of university life was
research. 'The students, knowing nothing of their subjects as yet, were
really researching into knowledge left by other students ... ' Ideals
apart, the careers of young lecturers depended heavily, not on their
excellence as teachers (which was seldom investigated systematically),
but on their ability to distinguish themselves and bring lustre to the
University by publishing the results of their research. These provided
more tangible evidence of ability, and could be examined by referees
and brought to the attention of committees concerned with promotion and tenure, whereas few persons in authority would be likely to
audition a junior colleague's lecture or tutorial.

A few years later, Leslie Brook, the Professor of English Language,
in a book on *The Modern University* (sent to press in 1964), would
argue that the hallmark of a university was the combination of teaching and research and that it made no sense to ask which was more
important. You might just as well ask which was more important to a
car – the engine or the wheels. But some tutors, at least in the view of
their students, had not achieved the right balance between the two,
and the emphasis upon research could become an excuse for slipshod
and unprofessional teaching. The engine might be roaring throatily,
but the tyres be bald and under-inflated. Samuel Alexander's essay of
1931, reproduced in Charlton's centenary volume, had accused
Oxford of spoon-feeding and of failing to contribute sufficiently to
the advancement of knowledge because it was given to 'excessive individual care of the students'. Some parts of the University of Manchester could hardly be convicted of this error.

Usually the complaint was that research drove out teaching, but
some departments, quite the other way, were so heavily committed to
communicating subjects which had been totally unfamiliar to sixth-
formers that they had little time to develop research. Pharmacy students spent five and a half days a week, including Saturday mornings,
in lecture rooms and laboratories. When Alan Tallentire was
appointed a full-time demonstrator in 1953 the job required him to
work alongside students for twenty-eight hours a week. Only in the
early 1960s, after glimpsing an utterly different world through a year
spent working on radiation biology at the Argonne National Laboratory in the United States, was he able to steer both himself and his
department towards a programme of systematic research, financed by
grants from sources outside the University.

Lectures, at their worst, might bore students, but at least they were
undemanding. Essay classes at their worst, in the view of a satirist

writing eloquently in *The Serpent,* chastened students with a sense of their own inadequacy, particularly by means of the 'terrible weapon of the Silence'. This followed the reading aloud of a sadly unoriginal essay, and arose at the dreaded moment when the tutor, after a few noncommittal remarks which nevertheless managed 'to convey the idea that the author of The Paper is either a scoundrel or an idiot', invited the comments of the uninformed and tongue-tied group.

Tutorials in History, as Sheila Griffiths remembers them, were indeed formidable experiences: 'No quarter was given.' Recollections of the English Department suggest a more kindly and tolerant atmosphere, at least for those encountering the younger lecturers, who were sometimes on first-name terms with their pupils. However stern the demands of Anglo-Saxon, one could be inspired by the tutor who had taken out a bank loan to purchase a first edition of Blake's *Heaven and Hell,* which he showed proudly to the students. He could not afford to become its permanent owner, for the loan would have to be repaid. But it was important to have had and held it for a time. In Social Administration, on the excellent course which was run by Barbara and Brian Rodgers, husband and wife, very close attention was paid to students as they worked their way from one department of the social services to another. In Jean Taylor's recollection, the staff 'were very much hands-on, you know. They arranged your practical work, they supervised you, they marked your papers, there were a lot of informal get-togethers ... '

In Medicine and in Dentistry it was difficult, particularly at the advanced level where students were walking the wards or operating on patients' teeth, to reconcile the demands of teaching with those of research and patient care. At the Dental Hospital most of the staff, apart from the professor, were not much older than the students and were engaged in the laboratories in working on their own higher degrees. Student dentists encountering problems with a patient in the chair would be compelled to go and disturb their supervisors at their more fascinating work. For all the slight differences in age, the staff appeared to be on another planet. The Medical Faculty paid some attention to students as individuals, as Rita Davies, formerly the Dean's personal assistant, remembers, because the personality of doctors was thought to be just as important as their academic attainments. In the memory of Leslie Turnberg, a medical student from 1952 to 1957, there were good and inspiring teachers of anatomy and physiology, in the pre-clinical part of the course. But the clinical teachers at the Manchester Royal Infirmary and elsewhere seemed, with rare and

splendid exceptions such as William Brockbank, the Dean of Clinical
Studies, to be more remote figures, inclined to regard students as an
encumbrance. It was all too easy for students to escape notice altogether throughout their time at the teaching hospitals.

In the Faculty of Economic and Social Studies as a whole the pattern of tutorial teaching was, in Derek Torrington's recollection,
extraordinarily variable, though the lecturing was often of high quality and in the hands of highly experienced academics. Standards in
Government were high, but in Economics 'a lot of the seminars never
ran at all, and of course the students didn't complain! They thought,
"Oh, we don't have to go" ... There were no seminars in Law. There
were certainly seminars in Statistics ... ' Seminars 'really were very,
very disorganised and casual, and it was all supported by the notion,
"Well, you know, you chaps, you come here to read for a degree. You
don't come here to get taught." And I think that, of course, was an
excuse which we carried on using until very recently. But it was pretty
slapdash.' He himself succumbed to the pleasures of Caf society and
acquired a thorough grounding in advanced bridge rather than work
at his books. However, after some years in industry and personnel
management he eventually returned to academic life. There, perhaps
uniquely, he became a professor in the University he had left without
taking a degree.

Norman Leece's memories of the methods used in the Electrical
Engineering Department are equally mixed, though in the end highly
favourable. There was nothing of the school about the place and relations with the staff were very distant. 'Schools teach. Universities present you with the information, and it's up to you then to imbibe as
much of it as you can from the eminent people who are talking to you,
absorb it, learn it, and keep it for future reference.' As in most science
departments' students devoted three afternoons a week to practical
work and were almost immediately called upon to carry out, using
much initiative, what was from their point of view original research.
'You were partnered up, you were given a sheet of paper describing
what the experiment was to do, and asked to produce results and con-
clusions.' He and his partner faced an unfamiliar machine, and 'we
were told how we had to conduct the experiment, but that was a hor-
rifying experience. We did suss it out eventually, but oh my goodness,
you really felt you were being dropped in at the deep end!' As Peter
Jones of the same department remembers, students seldom received
the hand-outs and potted aids to study which they later came to
expect. In the pre-xerox age, long before the advent of the personal

computer, the most they could hope for were handwritten examples sheets, churned out by a duplicator which rendered them in repulsive ink.

The standard of lecturing was generally poor. Lecturers chosen for their academic prowess were 'bloody awful teachers for the most part', arrogant, offhand and unwilling to answer questions. One lecturer in the new science of solid state electronics seemed wholly incapable of relating to students and did provoke face-to-face remonstration, although no complaint was made to his professor. A brilliant exception was Eric Laithwaite, later a professor at Imperial College London, who could be heard through the wall by a neighbour, Derek Whitehead, rehearsing his carefully prepared lectures. Laithwaite was for a time refused promotion by the professor, F.C. Williams, on the grounds that he was giving too much time to teaching and not enough to research. His protest, that he was employed as an assistant lecturer and not an assistant researcher, fell on deaf ears and he was goaded into embarking on his highly significant research into linear motors. Williams himself, a master of the plain style with a talent for epigram, incurred no charges of lecturing badly, and the students were greatly impressed by his willingness to give a course in basic electronics to the first-years. 'We were worshipping people's reputation, rather than, you know, them as people ... we were a necessary evil, we helped pay their salary!' In the end, however, the sense of involvement in research and discovery, instilled from the first year onwards, began to bear fruit when Norman Leece was involved in a project concerning the Manchester computer, Mark II, and proceeded after taking his degree to spend a lifetime working for Ferranti's. 'I came from what was really the cradle of the whole thing, a very inspiring place to work and be taught.'

The articles published in *News Bulletin* on 'Revolt at Redbrick' attacked excessive reliance on lectures which appeared to provide all the answers (this would not have been Norman Leece's complaint) and prevented students from discovering answers for themselves. 'Our Special Correspondent' called for '"massive re-thinking" about the purpose of a university'. Not very specifically, he complained that 'It is an article of faith that undergraduates cannot find their own sources of knowledge, but must be forcibly fed, if the sacred syllabus is to be covered in the prescribed time.' The purpose of university education, he argued (not with great originality), was to unsettle young people and get them answering questions. Instead, their days were cluttered with 'badly-delivered lectures and brief, overcrowded lecture classes'. There should be fewer lectures and more reading, especially on the part of Arts students, to encourage them to make discoveries for themselves. 'Good reasons are found for not having a tutorial system, but without such intimate tuition, the place ceases to be a university. There is not enough staff to go round, true – if we insist on a ten-to-four day ... Every student needs – as a right, not a favour – access to his teachers at stated times to discuss definite topics – and why shouldn't it end sometimes over a pint?'

It was perhaps not surprising that No. 327, Oxford Road should house the establishment of J.E. Grime, B.A., B.D., and V.J. Sansom, B.Sc., which was called the Manchester Tutorial College Ltd. and consisted of an association of thirty-five graduate tutors. It offered tutorial help for university students as well as coaching for university entrance, and proudly advertised its possession of six laboratories – two for chemistry, three for physics, and one for biology. Some of the deficiencies of university teaching could well be remedied by private enterprise, as well as by the growing self-reliance of the better students.

Many of the younger students of the 1950s felt, or were made to feel, that they were somewhat incidental to the main function of the University, which was to conduct research. The regime they experienced was liable to depend heavily on lectures, practical work and regular examinations, less so upon tutorials, essay-writing and discussion, less still upon any organised system of pastoral care or advice upon academic and personal problems. The experience of students in different disciplines could vary spectacularly, and some, as in Social Administration, were very well looked after. But there was no common code of practice extending across the whole University, no attempt to lay down rules which established the rights of students to a modicum of individual attention. In some respects the younger students were children continuing their schooldays, entering a seventh form at grammar school, many still living in their parents' houses or returning at weekends to nearby homes, never forming part of any independent student community, and dressing much as their parents did. But they were also expected to develop a certain self-sufficiency and resourcefulness, to make what they would of the information laid somewhat impersonally before them, without looking for a great deal of help. Most were, or professed to be, grateful for the experience, which few took for granted. Some were, as always, interested primarily in acquiring qualifications and were accused of being swots running away from life; others pursued a wider, less disciplined experience of student existence, setting the world to rights round the tables of Caf; others devoted themselves to running the Union or managing undergraduate societies. Outlandish and rumbustious behaviour was contained within strict limits, licensed to break loose on recognised occasions, when the sobriety of those who lived on small incomes in a dirty old town could for a short space be abandoned. Student journalists and correspondents of *News Bulletin* were not afraid of expressing high-minded sentiments or giving way to moral indignation. By the end of the 1950s they were becoming less reverent, more inclined to criticise openly the duller, more authoritarian aspects of the educational methods to which they were subjected. But 'revolt at Redbrick' remained a journalistic concept, and showed few signs of spreading to the student population at large.

4

Building and social relations

To accommodate the huge increase in the numbers of students and staff, to promote closer relations between them, and to maintain its own primacy in research, the University embarked on an ambitious building programme which was to continue for more than twenty years. This scheme set out first to provide classrooms, laboratories and an extension for the Library; secondly to house the Men's and Women's Unions in a more spacious modern building; thirdly to increase the University's stock of residential places for students. The first two undertakings were financed mainly by grants from the Treasury assigned to the University by the University Grants Committee, the last by an appeal to local business and commerce launched in the names of the Chancellor, Lord Woolton, and the Vice-Chancellor, Sir John Stopford.

About 1950 most of the University's premises, apart from the teaching hospitals and the out-stations, were concentrated on the western side of Oxford Road, bounded by Bridge Street (now Bridgeford Street) to the north, by Lloyd Street to the west, and by Leamington and Ackers Streets to the south. However, the University did not fill all the space within those boundaries, and had many close, non-academic neighbours. Only recently had it begun to colonise the quarter to the east of Oxford Road, where it had taken over the superannuated 1881 buildings of the Girls' High School in Dover Street, now deserted by pupils and mistresses, who had gone to seek elbow-room in Fallowfield. Here for a time could be found the Faculties of Education, Economics, Music and Law. Attached to the building was the Arthur Worthington Hall, a barely adequate venue for operas, concerts and plays. University buildings, many of them dingy and featuring the lavatorial tiles that frequently lined the walls of Victorian laboratories, were surrounded by streets of two-up, two-down 'terraced houses black as ink'. Here, too, were factories, garages, shops and churches. Some University departments were ensconced in dwelling-houses rather than specially constructed buildings; Law was at one time taught in a T-shaped one-storey hut scarcely worthy of its dignity. Oxford Road, the barrier between east and west, later to become the University's great divide, was a noisy thoroughfare and a tramway, dangerous to tangle with in the infamous Manchester fogs. A Professor of History, not a natural driver, was said to have turned out into it in the gloom and mounted a ramp on to the back of a brewer's dray, which was probably delivering to the College Hotel on the corner of Brunswick Street. A betting shop close to the back of the Dental Hospital attracted a large clientele from the University. Red light districts impinged on the University; the ill fame of both Dover Street and Hathersage Road lives on in the memories of those who knew the University well in the 1950s. Near by, too, were houses which offered cheap lodgings to theatrical folk.

Relations with the locals were cordial enough, if not particularly intimate; old ladies in clogs and aprons would cheerfully greet the University people as they passed. As Walter McCulloch remembers, the University had opened up its cellars for use as air-raid shelters during the war, perhaps creating some kind of a bond with its neighbours. For many students, however, the University was a cocoon, a self-contained world in the midst of a grim inner-city area, though some medical students working with midwives entered local houses and were surprised at what they found there. The College Hotel, better known as the College Arms and sometimes as Committee Room X, was a pub frequented both by academics and by local people, though the students were said to be deserting it in the later 1950s when the quality of Union beer began to improve. The Arts Building Extension overlooked the back yards of houses and their outside lavatories, on whose roofs the snow would accumulate to a depth of five or six inches, thus providing material for snowballs chucked by apprentice electricians on to the heads of householders emerging from the privy.

In 1946 the University had sought help in finding living room from the city planning authorities. The area was to be gradually cleared of dwellings, evacuated householders would be installed in superior accommodation on the city's new housing estates, and a zone devoted almost entirely to higher education, teaching hospitals and those who served them would eventually be created. It might even be possible to close to traffic the roads which partitioned the University's somewhat flat and featureless reservation. The most ambitious plan was to create a new Science Centre or Science Quadrangle to the east of Oxford Road. However, in the early 1950s, the first concerns were with an

extension to the Arts Library and with a new building in Coupland
Street, within the old area, for the Departments of Architecture and
Town and Country Planning. There was a successful move to concen-
trate all other Arts departments into one building by means of an Arts
Extension and to provide them with adequate lecture rooms and
other space.

A few years later, a trenchant article by Lionel Brett in *The Architectural Journal* for October 1957 was to discuss the plight of most
civic universities, bound as they were to stay in town and 'anchored
there sometimes by enormous and unsaleable Victorian buildings,
sometimes by a great teaching hospital, sometimes by convictions of
the moral and social value of being at the centre of things'. All these
considerations doubtless weighed with the University of Manchester.
The word 'campus' was sometimes loosely used, but the place was
unlikely to develop into a campus in the strict sense of the term, a
'university in a garden'. It was true that Stopford, a keen gardener,
had yearned for spacious lawns, shrubs and trees which might
improve the surroundings and had looked benignly on students sitting
out in Lime Grove in the summer. But the University reservation was
best called a 'Planner's Precinct', and Manchester's Master Plan was,
in the view of the ungracious Brett, 'two-dimensional', 'severely axial
and inflexible'.

Whatever the merits or flaws of the scheme, the University Council
and its agents energetically addressed the task of buying up sites for
development. Throughout the 1950s the Council's minutes were
punctuated by resolutions formally approving the actions of the Treasurer (no doubt guided by the Bursar) in acquiring items as the leases
fell in, usually with financial help from the UGC. Since many householders were happy enough to leave, the number of compulsory purchase orders used was limited. However, technicians from the
University Library were called upon to photograph certain properties
and provide evidence which could be used to support applications for
such orders. Occasionally local people did resist attempts to move
them; as Harry Cameron remembers, two old ladies impeded the
progress of the Arts Extension and it was necessary to leave in place
not only their house but the two adjoining ones which were holding
it up. Another elderly woman clung to a large house in Wright Street,
holding out for more money; on her death, as Walter McCulloch
recalls, thousands of pounds in banknotes were found amid the inde-
scribable squalor of the house in which she had been living in one
room. An article in *News Bulletin* for March 1959 spared a thought

for four houses at the end of Eldon Street, soon to be reduced to rubble by the inexorable progress of the Development Plan. It reported an interview with the sad but resigned Mrs Deardon, now sixty-eight, who had lived there for forty-three years. David Kirby, a student architect, pleaded in 1954 that the little houses within five minutes' walk of the University could conveniently be converted into tiny residential colleges for three or four students, with shared facilities and separate study bedrooms. He used the £200 prize he had won from *The Architect's Journal* for unorthodox ideas to begin work on the adaptation of 43 Ackers Street, off Oxford Road. Sadly, his house must have fallen victim to University expansion, for Ackers Street (now labelled Akers Street, but still Ackers in the *A to Z*) is today no more than an abortive cul-de-sac in the shadow of the Holy Name church and the dwellings have all disappeared.

Conditions were sometimes attached to the purchases made by the University. In 1954, for example, it acquired 375–7 Oxford Road for £4,500 on the understanding that the shop would be leased to Duncan and Foster Ltd for a period of seven years at an annual rental of £80, which was scarcely a high return on the capital. Many sites were sooner or later cleared, but some buildings survived and were adapted to new purposes. Acquired in 1952, the Methodist church and schools on Oxford Road were converted the following year into a club with recreational rooms for the University's support staff. This new institute bore the name of William Kay House, in honour of an outstanding technician who had been Steward of the Physical Laboratories and assistant to the great Ernest Rutherford in his Manchester days. It offered table tennis and snooker and a beautiful dance floor; the House's catering was good enough to give the Refectory cause for concern at the advent of a serious competitor. At 259–61 Oxford Road a former factory took on new life as a laboratory for nuclear engineers.

The grandest scheme in the 1950s set out to rehouse University science in spacious premises to the east of Oxford Road and the north of Dover Street. First to be erected was the new Electrical Engineering Laboratory, which was occupied during the session 1954–55. A year or two later operations began on new premises designed to be the temporary home of Mathematics and the permanent resting-place of Geology. It was named the Williamson Building, in honour of the Victorian polymath who had been Professor of Natural History at the inception of Owens College in 1851 and had served it for forty years. By the end of the decade other buildings were projected or actually in progress, designed to serve Engineering, Chemistry and Physics, together with a large block of classrooms and lecture theatres for teaching and examining, the future Roscoe Building. This edifice, erected in the Science zone, was intended to serve the whole University. Though once high on the list of priorities, the new Medical School appeared to have slipped dramatically towards the bottom – a tribute, perhaps, either to the Vice-Chancellor's impartiality, or to the UGC's determination to encourage investment in science and technology, or to both. The well-being of medical students cannot have benefited from the fire which broke out in their building in Coupland Street in May 1954, burning out the laboratory on the top floor and causing part of the roof to collapse.

To its first occupants, freed from their Victorian dungeon, the Electrical Engineering building represented unheard-of luxury. The Ferranti computer was duly installed on the top floor, like an oracle surrounded by priests and acolytes. Whatever the practical virtues of the building, however, it drew diatribes from student architects – perhaps the most outspoken critics of the University in the 1950s – for its unlovely exterior. Its brick boxes did not delight them. Since it seemed likely to set the tone for the entire science centre, it was doubly urgent to attack it. 'The "character" of the building from outside is a blank', complained one architect in 1953. 'The needs of students, of staff, and of the University as an institution have not been considered.' Michael Sharp, a fifth-year student architect, objected that 'On a virgin site … there has arisen this reactionary design, so lacking in any decisive character. And here is the danger, for it is likely that this building and its amorphic neo-Georgian will set the pattern, the visual guide from which the rest of this totally new area of building will be created.' He broadened the polemical front to include the design for the proposed new students' Union building, which was later to be condemned by other architects as a sorry specimen of 'a terrible neo-Fascist style'.

Lionel Brett's article of 1957, though more sophisticated and wide-ranging (for its target was all civic universities), reads like an elaboration of Manchester students' own criticisms. The University was not alone in offering a mixture of styles – 'convinced Victorian' (for the Waterhouse buildings did at least convey a sense of knowing what a University ought to be about) and 'scientific barracks' (which suggested no convictions at all). Manchester was responsible for four of the twelve bland post-war university buildings singled out for special derision, and these four items represented most of its programme to date. They were, said Mr Brett, 'the monumental record of the failure of nerve in academic patronage, envelopes of red brick and stone, enwrapping an entirely vacuous concept of who, what and where a university is.' Bold architecture was not the University's forte – though members of the Building Committee, if they read the piece, would surely have rejected the suggestion that they were unsure of the University's identity, function and purpose. Other utilitarian buildings reminiscent of barracks or warehouses were soon to dwarf the electrical engineers' headquarters and their different heights relieved the scene of monotony. However, since Brunswick Street continued to divide them and was never closed to traffic, they did not convey the impression of forming, as had been intended, a modern quadrangle which would balance the Victorian court on the other side of Oxford Road.

New buildings and social reorganisation went hand in hand, one leading to the other, especially with the new students' Union which made it impracticable to cling to the customary segregation of the sexes. From 1947 onwards the student officers hoped to create 'a utopian student paradise which would sweep away all memories of grimy, gloomy Burlington Street'. So wrote the historian of the old Unions' premises. From its foundation at the beginning of the century, the women students' Union had been separated from the men's. The internal construction of the buildings between Burlington Street and Lime Grove, on the site of today's Refectory, seemed calculated to discourage everyday contact between men and women and to give each sex the chance to manage its own affairs. It was true that the doors between the men's and women's debating halls could be opened to create a ballroom when dances were held; that mixed audiences were allowed to attend debates; and that there was an uninviting joint common room on the top floor, little used save by couples sitting out during dances and taking advantage of the dim light. But such concessions were grudgingly made, and Caf was the natural rendezvous for men and women students.

In the masculine sanctum some effort was made to create the atmosphere of a gentlemen's club. For a while, says Harry Cameron, it was stylishly attended by 'little coffee boys with little pill-box hats on, running about with trays and silver salvers'. At one time it contained a blackboard bearing a sketch by Amundsen of a cross-section of the ship used by the expedition which reached the South Pole ahead of Scott's party. A huge fire, capable of swallowing a hundredweight of coal at a single gulp, dispelled some of the gloom of a bitter Manchester morning; when the Corporation, ca. 1956, declared the Uni-

versity area a smokeless zone, students pleaded that kitsch electric
fires with glowing false logs should be purchased in the hope of creating an equally cosy atmosphere in the new Union building. But three
students from the London School of Economics who had hitched to
Manchester for the weekend were unimpressed by the dingy premises
and 'most intrigued' by the continued separation of the Unions. As a
porter told them with an air of finality, 'We just don't agree with
women oop 'ere, lass!'

No doubt this separation reflected a deep-seated instinct to build a
retreat safe from female influence where boys could be boys, and to
prolong the segregation which prevailed in many schools and made it
hard to be natural with young women. But there were some more
respectable arguments in favour of two Unions. It might be best to
represent constituencies and interests and not treat students as an
undifferentiated mass, ruled by the majority. So long as separate
Unions survived, the University would be obliged to seek the views of
women students through their representatives. They could claim to
speak for some 25 per cent of students at Owens, for a significant
minority whose opinions might otherwise be ignored. It was widely
believed that since men were more brash and aggressive they would
inevitably seize control of any organisation not protected from their
invasive presence. On the whole, however, the women's officers
argued a different case, sometimes by invoking economic rationality
and sometimes by proclaiming women's ability to hold their own in
open competition with men. 'If the incomes of the two Unions were
combined, many more improvements could be made', said Pat O'Gara
in May 1954. 'Every other University', maintained Margaret Griffiths, house secretary of the Women's Union, six months later, 'has
realised that it is far more reasonable and financially satisfactory to
run one student union in a university rather than two ... There are
two committees on either side of a brick wall running two similar
places, with the same general aims and interests.' Naturally, the task
of planning a new building prompted much debate on the possibility
of forming a jointly administered Union in which most amenities
would be shared. It would be practicable, at the same time, to reserve
some space to provide retreats for one sex or the other, and preserve
to some extent the distinct identities of the two Unions. These chose
to federate rather than to merge.

By November 1955 a majority of men attending a debate were
declaring themselves in favour of a jointly administered Union, speakers arguing earnestly for 'adequate experience of mixed social life in

preparation for life in the world after graduation' or pompously regretting 'that congenitally women are unable to sustain their own social life' and therefore holding that it would be chivalrous to provide them with masculine company. Nevertheless, the vote (389 in favour, 317 against) failed to secure the necessary two-thirds majority to authorise constitutional change. However, in May 1957, as the time for occupying the new building drew near, the result of a student questionnaire was announced. Three thousand circulars had been sent out and 1,860 returned. Of these 1,385 favoured one mixed administration and only 475 two separate administrations.

From this point onwards, argument shifted to the question of the number of places that should be reserved for women on the joint committee which would spread its wings over the Union – though some favoured a system of 'universal' or 'general' suffrage which would have allowed open competition for all positions. The plan under discussion in May 1957 was that the Union should be administered by a joint committee of sixteen men and six women. A confident woman held that 'The principle of the best person for the job regardless of sex should be recognised.' A fearful man, associating beauty with bimboism, warned that 'We don't want to leave ourselves open to the ghastly possibility of men voting for long eyelashes. Under universal suffrage the position could arise where the Union was completely in the hands of Marilyns and Brigittes.' The system of reserved places for women won the day. But it was possible for men and women to compete on equal terms for the presidency and vice-presidency of the jointly administered Union, and the first woman President, Elva Corrie, was elected in 1960.

Planning the Union building began in earnest in the early 1950s. Though gaining much space and material comfort, the Unions lost – or thought they were losing – some of their independence. The old building had been theirs. Now they became free tenants of the University, and they owed their new palace to public funding. A deed of 1951 bound the University Council to pay compensation, to the extent of £32,500, to the Trustees of the Union in exchange for resuming occupation of the old Unions' premises, the sum to be paid only when the new building was ready. Four years later the UGC made a grant of £380,000 towards the new building and the University lent the Unions £20,000 to pay for furniture.

At one point the generally cordial relations between the Union and the University authorities threatened to break down over practical questions connected with catering and specifically related to competi-

tion between the Refectory and the Union. It seemed that the UGC
had stipulated that the Union was not to offer the same services as the
Refectory. This condition was interpreted, at least by Rainford the
Bursar, as meaning that the Union should be confined to offering light
refreshments only and compelled to leave anything that involved serious cooking to the Refectory. Some Union catering had begun in
1928, and the Union had recently been making a profit out of under-
selling the Refectory. When the Union officers proposed to pay the
cost of installing kitchens, they were told that it was now too late to
alter the plans for the building. Fortunately, compromise was reached
and friction reduced when the University agreed to allow the Union
to provide hot snacks such as beans on toast after 4.00 p.m., to install
a cooker to provide meals for distinguished visitors, and to bring in
outside caterers for major events.

Much of the space in the new Union building was devoted to joint
accommodation – a main entrance hall, a main debating hall with
seats for 500, a large coffee bar on the ground floor, a joint common
room flanked by a soft drinks bar and a mixed bar. The last item
appeared 'revolutionary' in its intention to allow men and women to
drink together as a matter of course and not just on special occasions.
Only in January 1959 did the University Council, ever protective of
women students and concerned for their good behaviour in a naughty
world, grant permission to open a mixed bar every evening. This concession was described as 'the final step in the integration of the Men's
and Women's Unions'. When Harold Macmillan, the Prime Minister,
opened the new building on 1st November 1957, he had said: 'I am
not quite certain whether I am opening one Union or two ... but since
this is the University where Mrs Pankhurst's daughters were educated
the problem will no doubt be rapidly resolved.' The formal decision
to federate and to form a joint body under the title 'The University of
Manchester Union' was taken by both unions on 21st February 1958.
The Prime Minister might still have been perplexed, since legally
there were now three bodies in existence, the Men's, the Women's
and the federated Unions; only in 1967 would the Vice-Chancellor be
able to report to the University Council that there was now a single
Union in the eyes of the law.

Arrangements for students' welfare grew more elaborate during the
1950s and the new joint Union building was only the most prominent
example of them. About 1950, the University launched a student
health service. At first its main concern was with physical illness and
with the detection of tuberculosis, through mass X-rays and more

selective forms of screening. By the session 1955–56, however, some official notice was being taken of the anxiety and examination strain which seemed to be overtaking certain students. No statistics appeared in the Vice-Chancellor's annual report, but the level of stress seemed to be higher among students residing at home or in lodgings, markedly less among those who lived less isolated lives and formed part of integrated communities in halls of residence. This was one of many reasons for urging the University to increase the stock of residential places and to do something more than provide cheap beds for heads to lie on. Both Stopford, the Vice-Chancellor, and Woolton, the Chancellor, were enthusiastic. Stopford was to warn, in a farewell interview, that the University had a fine academic record, but its students were narrow, had little experience of life outside the classroom, and compared unfavourably at job interviews with candidates from Oxford and Cambridge. Could Oxford and Cambridge colleges be said to represent any true form of 'life'? Should something vaguely resembling them be introduced into Manchester on a larger scale, or were Manchester soot and Oxford spires destined to remain the symbols of two contrasting cultures? Would the growth of halls of residence, by creating other social centres, draw students away from the Union, which ought to be the natural place of resort in their leisure hours? Such questions were earnestly debated at intervals throughout the decade.

Some Manchester students lived at home; others lived in approved lodgings inspected by the lodgings officers; others still took unapproved lodgings or flats they had found for themselves; a few entered halls of residence licensed or owned by the University. No uniform discipline was imposed upon students, as in Oxford or Cambridge, where undergraduates were required to spend a specified number of nights in residence, to keep the same hours and to maintain the same distance from the opposite sex, whether they lived within college walls or not. Landladies were vital to the University, and the first event entered in the Vice-Chancellor's engagement diary was the landladies' tea party, at which he could be expected to move among them, clad in his robes, and make them a speech commending the sterling work that they did for the academic community.

Champions of the virtues of lodgings spoke of the relative liberalism of most landladies and of the cheapness of lodgings compared with halls of residence. During the long summer term, when examinations were over but the staff were still obsessively marking, students at home or in lodgings could begin to take vacation jobs, whereas wardens of halls compelled their charges to serve out their time until term ended with the graduation ceremonies. In 1957 Frank Taylor, the Grants and Welfare Secretary of the Union, carried out a survey which suggested that the annual cost of lodgings was only about £98, whereas hall fees might amount to anything between £140 and £160, and (he maintained) no attempt had been made to standardise their charges. However, not all landladies were equally enlightened, and low charges sometimes went with cheerless lodgings. Peter Taylor remembers a regime marked by a scanty coal ration expected to last all night, an allowance of one bath a week, lavatory paper consisting of 'cut-up pieces of newspaper on a piece of string', no keys to the house, a lounge shared by four residents, and a rule that everyone must be in by ten o'clock at night unless he could prove 'very special extenuating circumstances'. Gerard McKenna, who read Classics in the late 1950s, had an excellent landlady, but for five days of the week only; there was nothing for it but to go home at the weekend. Travel costs must often have been added to the costs of the lodgings themselves. Dismay struck students in 1959 when the University lodgings officer made what he termed 'suggestions' concerning the behaviour which landladies were entitled to expect of students in lodgings. Women students should be in by 11.00 p.m., men by 11.30, with extensions allowed until midnight on Saturdays. Since this unfortunate circular also proposed that 'any serious infringement of this principle should be reported to the Lodgings Officer without delay', it was difficult not to interpret the 'suggestions' as a new set of regulations, arbitrarily removing one of the main advantages of living in lodgings, and attempting to transform the rather bewildered landladies either into informers or into disciplinary officers.

Mr Smith, the lodgings officer, had a laborious task and was inevitably the target of much complaint. By 1957 he had been joined by a woman's lodgings warden, Miss Healey-Hunt. Only by 1959 had Smith's clerical staff expanded to the point at which he could write to all seekers of lodgings before they actually appeared at the University. Only in 1959–60 did the supply of available and accessible lodgings begin to exceed the number of students pursuing them. Hence a common sight on the first Saturday of the academical year was a sluggish queue snaking through the Main Building; the need to keep a place in it caused some new arrivals to miss the speeches of welcome and other entertainments laid on for them at the introductory Freshers' Conference. One or two preliminary nights in a hotel were sometimes needed and there were always unverified horror stories of freshmen sleeping like hoboes in telephone boxes or station waiting rooms. Lodging-houses sprawled over a wide area, which included Altrincham, Heaton Moor, Stockport, Droylsden, Prestwich and Swinton. Vacancies existed in Hazel Grove and Bramhall, but in 1957 they were said to be too remote from the University for anyone to want to fill them. Living in lodgings often bred a depressing sense of isolation. To combat this a brave attempt was made in 1957 to form an association of women students in lodgings, a form of 'ghost hall' equipped with a common room and a notice board, in the hope of providing them with 'some of the social activities that those who live in hall get as a matter of course'.

At the most optimistic estimate, there were no more than about 700 places in halls of residence for Manchester students in the early 1950s. Approximately half of these were reserved for women, so perhaps one woman in four and one man in twelve could obtain a hall place. Before 1956, only two halls, both for women, Ashburne and the much smaller Ellis Llwyd Jones, were owned by the University and administered through boards known as delegacies. Ellis Hall was in Old Trafford, next to the Royal Residential Schools for the Deaf, and reserved a number of places for students taking the course in deaf education in which the University had been a pioneer.

But the University also recognised, in another word licensed, halls which it did not own. Most of these had been founded independently by religious denominations for the benefit of young men or women attending the University, some of them as ordinands taking courses in the Faculty of Theology. It was the proud boast of Dalton Hall in Victoria Park, founded by the Society of Friends in 1876, that it was 'The oldest University Hall of Residence in England outside Oxford and Cambridge'. Hulme and St Anselm (for men) and Langdale (for women) were Anglican foundations. Uniquely, St Anselm had, since about 1922, been owned and administered from afar, 'in matters of high policy' rather than day-to-day affairs, by the central authority of the Church of England. St Gabriel's, run by the nuns of the Cross and Passion, was primarily for Catholic girls. Two Nonconformist theological establishments, the Unitarian College and the Lancashire Independent College, had spare capacity and made room for 'students of any faculty as well as theological students'. A third such college, the Methodist Hartley Victoria, approached the University Council in 1954 and after inspection duly obtained a licence.

Some residences offered variations on the theme of the conventional, single-sex hall confined to University students. Mr R.F. Torrington, the secretary of the local YMCA, persuaded the University in 1951–52 to recognise as a hall of residence the new and specially constructed war memorial hostel near the Hulme Grammar School. Field Marshal Montgomery himself would be the patron, lending his name to the establishment and occasionally visiting it to give talks under terse titles such as 'My Job' and 'Current Affairs'. About two-fifths of the hostel's residents were university students; the remainder were trainees in industry or the professions. Perhaps inevitably, given the prevailing passion for slangy abbreviation, Montgomery House soon became known as Moho. A small number of students and former students lived in the Settlement in Ancoats, at one end of Ancoats Hall; such discipline as it had was informal and enforced by the residents themselves, and it was not a licensed hall of residence.

Although many halls had originally been owned by religious denominations, they rarely if ever tried to confine recruitment to members of their own churches. They set out to provide some kind of communal, mutually supportive life which would overcome narrowly departmental loyalties and even bring Owens and the Tech together. They offered sports, plays, dances, concerts, collecting for Rag Days and a modicum of self-government by student committees. Students were expected to dine together in the evenings, and sometimes to wear gowns when doing so, a symbol of student status and allegiance to the hall, or (as some more earthily suggested) a form of protection against flying soup. The practice of 'twinning' male and female halls enabled them to get together over common enterprises such as plays or concerts and to hold joint dances. They created more opportunities for men and women students to meet – sometimes under the penetrating and vigilant gaze of the female wardens. Cast by men in the role of fire-dragons guarding hoards of treasure, these authorities were said, perhaps libellously, to keep a close eye on the distance between dancing partners and otherwise protect the innocence of their charges.

Critics of the halls saw them as a protraction of boarding school existence or a belated introduction to it. Their manners and customs were said to prolong adolescence in undesirable ways and to savour more of Billy Bunter's Greyfriars than of *Brideshead Revisited* or other epics of Oxford life. Some suggested that they represented feeble attempts at introducing into Manchester the incidentals – not the really valuable features – of Oxford and Cambridge colleges, thus offending against the proud native tradition of Manchester without any compensatory gains. It was undoubtedly true that at least two halls, Ashburne (called at its foundation in 1899 a 'younger sister of Newnham') and St Anselm, had in the past turned consciously to Oxford and Cambridge models. The name St Anselm Hall was probably an echo of St Edmund Hall, and in 1933 the President and Fellows of St Anselm had sent for a copy of the constitution of Keble College Oxford in the hope of obtaining from it information and guidance.

However, there was one major difference between Manchester halls and Oxbridge colleges, in that halls seldom if ever offered on their own account systematic teaching which could supplement, let alone supplant, that of academic departments. They educated students in the use of leisure and in civilised conduct rather than in academic subjects. Hall tutors' function was to give general guidance through the complexities of academic life, though if they happened to be in an appropriate subject they might give a little help to students in difficulties. Only one hall, Dalton, attempted to provide a range of tutors capable of covering most university subjects. Advertising in the University Calendar for 1951–52, Dalton Hall promised its students 'friendly oversight, tutorial assistance, and other educational and social advantages of College life'. Twenty-nine academics, all of whom held appointments at Owens or the Tech, were listed as tutors in addition to the Principal, George Sutherland, a former Senior Lecturer in Physics in the University of London. Only two of them, however, resided on the premises. Fees for Dalton were appropriately high – £160 for the session, compared with £135 for Hulme and £110 for St Gabriel's Hall.

Wardens of halls of residence were not, and did not pretend to be, hugely eminent academics crowning their careers with the mastership of a college, although they did include some future professors. They were sometimes lecturers in mid-career, sometimes part-time lecturers, sometimes semi-professional wardens with previous experience elsewhere (Miss Kathleen Gough of Ashburne, high-principled, a vegetarian, a Quaker, formidable but kind-hearted and endowed with a certain grim humour, had been warden of Rankin Hall in the University of Liverpool). Wardens would attend meetings of the governing bodies of their halls, but they did not generally preside over them in the style of an Oxford or Cambridge master or mistress, and they did not always have a vote in their deliberations.

Resident tutors were often, though not invariably, young academics holding assistant lectureships and perhaps seeking some means of overcoming their own loneliness in a strange city and compensating for their lack of money. Again, at least one Manchester academic was quick to disclaim any close parallels between the Manchester and the Oxbridge version of the tutorial office. Tom Lawrenson of the French Department, who wrote a lively history of St Anselm Hall, warned – or warned against – 'the Oxbridge graduate who cannot understand, or does not like, or even despises, the departmental system, and who thinks that by accepting a Hall Tutorship he is going, with promotion, back to the collegiate life he knew, this time in the quality of a don'. 'High Table will be full of recent graduates; he may have to help stoke the boilers; the food will be the same as in the body of the hall; the Hall tutorship won't influence his chances of academic promotion in any way.'

There was a strong religious presence in some halls, close attention to social decorum in others which had no associations with a particular creed. In St Gabriel's impeccable excuses were needed by anyone who did not wish to attend the Tuesday evening talks by the chaplain to the Catholic Society. Finding the priest concerned misogynistic and intellectually arrogant, quite untypical of his order, Pat O'Gara was driven by a desire to escape his homilies into a successful career in Union politics. Ashburne held formal dinners two or three times a week, preceded by a dressing bell which sounded half an hour before the meal began; students formed up in pairs outside the dining hall and solemnly processed in after the arrival of the High Table party. Should any student wish to leave before the meal had ended, etiquette demanded that she go to the trouble of catching the warden's eye and exchanging a bow with her. Should such premature departures happen frequently, the student might expect to receive a note enquiring: 'Is this a regular commitment that you have with your department?'

Most halls required their students (especially first-year women) to keep early hours, partly to encourage temperate habits and partly to control expense, since they wished neither to employ all-night porters nor to hand out keys. They also sought to regulate the conditions under which visitors of the opposite sex might be entertained on their premises. Most appeared to believe that immorality could be related to Greenwich mean time and associated with the late evening; the rhetorical question of a former Ashburne warden, 'Don't you know that men's passions rise after six o'clock?' still hung in the air. Somewhat illogically, regulations allowed greater latitude at weekends. At St Gabriel's male visitors who were not relatives could be received only in a visitors' parlour which had to be specially booked for the occasion. Here couples gazed upon an edifying picture of a newly canonised saint, Maria Goretti, who had died in 1902 defending her chastity against a would-be rapist and had thereby become a martyr, not for the Christian faith, but for the Christian life. Residents at Montgomery House chafed against the rule which forbade them to entertain women visitors anywhere on the premises other than in the spacious lounge, only to be told that this regulation was common to all YMCA hostels, and therefore could not be changed.

The 1950s saw two major developments in the field of student accommodation. First, the University began itself to take over the management of licensed halls of residence which were in financial difficulties and could no longer sustain independent life. Their residents were often too few to generate fees sufficient to pay the wardens' salaries and maintain the buildings and grounds; the halls had no capital to spend on enlarging their premises and increasing the numbers they admitted. Should the University take them over, the UGC, which was already contributing to the wardens' salaries, would also pay the rates. Although the Church of England still wished to influence the student community, it was inclined to do so through chaplaincies rather than halls of residence; indeed, in 1955 the Bishop of Manchester proposed to Council that an official University Chaplaincy should be erected, though it would not be an exclusively Anglican concern, and would contain 'rooms for Chaplains of Free Church denominations'. St Anselm became the first of the denominational halls to pass directly to the University, which it did on lst August 1956 after three years of negotiations. In 1953 the Hall had sheltered only sixty-three students; the UGC was willing to promise assistance only if the University of Manchester would double the number of residents. This was hardly consonant with Lawrenson's belief that the corporate life of a hall could only be kept up if it contained no more than eighty students. The new halls founded in the 1950s and 1960s were to be conceived on a much larger scale.

The second move took the form of increasingly ambitious schemes to build new residences. In 1946 the city's development plan had reserved sites for the University's residential accommodation: 18 acres to the west of Oxford Road, extending southwards to Whitworth Park and the Art Gallery, and 24 acres in Fallowfield, in the neighbourhood of Ashburne Hall, of the Vice-Chancellor's residence, and of the University's athletic grounds. At intervals the Treasurer and the Bursar would seize opportunities to buy up properties in Fallowfield – the Oak House Hotel for £9,000 in 1954, the premises of the Hollies School (which was moving out to Didsbury) for £50,000 in

1956. The Hollies, explained the Council minute which approved the purchase on the understanding that the UGC would put up the full amount, 'occupied the greater part of the island site bounded by Oak Drive and Wilmslow Road, Fallowfield. This school forms the central part of the site for projected Halls of Residence.'

The University was already sitting on one or two nest-eggs, money promised for halls. Some years earlier Lord Woolton's firm, Lewis's, had given a dinner to celebrate his election as Chancellor and voted the sum of £35,000 to the University to establish a hall in his honour. The family of the late Sir Christopher Needham, who had preceded Lord Simon as Chairman of Council, had for the same purpose presented the University with a house known as 'Fair Oak' in Didsbury. When a neighbouring house called 'Warley' also fell vacant in 1952 there were good prospects of combining the pair and building further to create a hall of residence in an outlying suburb, select, leafy and favoured by academics. This part of Didsbury, though desirable, lay twice as far from the University as the main site in Fallowfield.

In his annual report for the session 1954–55, Stopford castigated Manchester's slowness to provide such halls. 'Today Manchester can accommodate less than 20 per cent in halls whilst the figures for Reading are 64 per cent, Nottingham 37 per cent, Southampton 40 per cent, Hull 79 per cent, and the University College of North Staffordshire is fully residential for both students and staff.' An appeal for £1 million had been announced at Founder's Day and addressed in the first instance 'particularly to those industrial firms who employ our graduates and must be interested in the personal qualities and interests as well as the academic qualifications of those who pass out from the University'. A few months earlier Stopford had envisaged a target of no more than £300,000, when he advised Council that 'the University was free to erect new buildings without charge against the UGC's ration, provided that it financed them itself'. The appeal was launched by Stopford and Woolton, but for some reason did not carry the support of the Chairman of Council, Lord Simon. Caught between Woolton and Simon, the Treasurer, Sir Raymond Streat, confided to his diary in December 1955 that 'There is a nice little fire of intrigue and controversy burning at the University.' Streat wrote painstakingly to Simon, explaining his own reasons for supporting the appeal. The UGC would give for teaching buildings, but probably not for halls of residence; it would be better to seek funds for halls alone, rather than embark on an unfocused appeal for the general purposes of the University. An appeal in the names of two such famous men would be advantageous in every way, for it would add 'to the tradition of famous men associated with identifiable buildings, which always seems to me to build up the historical tradition and the morale of any institution'. Predictably, the question of competition with Oxford and Cambridge arose. In the Treasurer's view one could only recognise and accept the attractions of those ancient universities for 'brilliant students from schools throughout the country', but Manchester's charms would undoubtedly be enhanced by having more halls of residence. They would make the place less parochial and provincial. 'I think it is good for the bulk who must always be local boys and girls to have contemporaries from other parts of the country mingling with them.' Woolton, meanwhile, was nettled by Simon's disapproval and by the all-too-obvious fact that he was absenting himself as much as possible from University occasions at which the Chancellor would be present.

Despite this embarrassment the appeal proved largely successful and, though falling short of its target, raised a little over £800,000. Lewis's increased its original gift from £35,000 to £100,000, covenanted over a period of ten years; gifts flowed in from the industrial firms to which the appeal had been primarily addressed – from Turner and Newall, Mather and Platt, the Metropolitan-Vickers Electrical Co. Ltd, and many others. The names of firms which were later to supply the University with distinguished lay officers, such as Paterson Zochonis and William Kenyon and Sons, also figured in the increasingly long list of donors. Woolton himself took an active part in the campaign. Legend had it that he had tempted providence sorely by tearing up a friend's cheque and telling him that he could afford twice as much as the proffered sum. The Chancellor, however, was very persuasive and, at least on that occasion, got everything he wanted.

Fittingly enough, the most immediate fruits of the appeal were two new halls of residence organised along traditional lines, Woolton in Fallowfield and Needham in Didsbury. Since both were owned by the University, neither boasted a chapel and neither acknowledged any particular religious allegiance. The University announced a new policy of appointing full-time lecturers as wardens of halls wherever this was practicable, guaranteeing them 'the fullest technical assistance' in tutorial and bursarial matters. Both the new halls exceeded Tom Lawrenson's unofficial ceiling for an effective community; Needham opened with a full complement of 127 students, Woolton with 180 distributed among four residential blocks.

Although they were providing between them more than 300 new residential places, the new halls were far from solving the problem of ever-
increasing numbers. The ambition of Woolton and Stopford was,
realistically, only to provide enough places to enable every student to
spend at least one year in a hall of residence. Their intention was probably that this should be the first year, in which the hall would help to
acclimatise students to university life. However, as Lawrenson's book
argued, it would be impossible to run a traditional hall which contained
only first-year students, without the sobering influence and guidance of
more senior residents. It was fairly common practice for those who
entered halls to stay in them for all three undergraduate years. Woolton
Hall, indeed, met criticism at the outset from a student journalist,
partly on the grounds that the proportion of freshmen among the residents, amounting to two-thirds of the whole, was too large to make for
a balanced community. Neither of the new halls was cheap: at £171 a
session, Needham and Woolton were certainly more expensive than St
Anselm, Hulme, Dalton and Ashburne. Presumably they were offering
less battered premises in exchange for the money they took.

More radical solutions, departures from the traditions of the community hall, were contemplated towards the end of the 1950s. In the
interests of economy and rapid construction other ideas were floated.
These included the notion of an American-style dormitory, consisting
of 'blocks of flatlets with a capacity for one or two persons which contain the basic living requirements of students'. Such residences would
at first dispense with communal facilities, but they could be built in
rectangles, so that at a later date a central block might be inserted in
their midst and provide them with dining halls and recreation rooms.
Such an idea was considered in 1956 by the Council of the College of
Science and Technology, which was sure to provide a large proportion
of the new students. The desire of many students for greater freedom,
the University's desire for economy and rapid action, the need to
make effective use of cramped urban sites by building upwards: these
things could conveniently be combined, the tower blocks of the 1960s
replacing the quasi-collegiate halls of the Woolton–Stopford era.

In the light of later events the students of the 1950s may seem
almost passive in comparison with their successors in the late 1960s
and the 1970s. Certain sections of student opinion could, however, be
outspokenly critical of authority over specific, practical issues. Student architects robustly attacked the University's unenterprising taste
in the design of buildings. Any suggestion of encroachment on the
Union's autonomy, as in the matter of catering, was sure to arouse

indignation. So was any hint that students were being patronised and not properly consulted about their own interests. Much was done diplomatically, however, and compromises were usually hammered out. Pat O'Gara, as President of the Women's Union in 1953–54, felt that she was treated with courtesy and never forced to be aggressive: Union officers were being genuinely involved in building the new world of the expanding post-war University. There were, no doubt, many students who took no part in Union affairs and did not share her sense of involvement and participation.

Halls of residence marked a genuine and often effective attempt to break down the alienation of students from staff, the isolation of students in lodgings, and the barriers between academic departments. On the other hand their regulations and formalities constituted an easy target for student journalists. Speakers in the more intellectual debates on the topic taxed them with fostering a 'communal' spirit hostile to the 'individualism' which was, or ought to be, essential to a university. Charges of being paternalistic or perhaps matriarchal were not difficult to frame.

Unusually, early in 1959, students won sympathy from the national press on the grounds that the University was treating them discourteously and with a heavy hand. On this occasion the cause of the furore was, above all, the 'infamous Diggers' Guide' issued by the lodgings officer to the landladies. But there was also the fact that students' cars had suddenly been banned from the main quadrangle, and the fact that the dates of the summer term had been altered – in the hope of helping students, certainly, but without sounding their views. 'If the authorities always act in this arbitrary and discourteous manner they must not be surprised if students come to regard them as a mysterious and fearsome dictatorship. We are convinced that the University authorities have our best interests at heart. But it will not help Staff–Student relationships if they treat us like a lot of school children.' One of seven national newspapers which carried stories about the affair of the landladies remarked that 'this and other actions might have been arranged more diplomatically if the Unions had been consulted'. Somewhat lamely, Mansfield Cooper said that 'the authorities had not wished to implicate Union Council in the eyes of Union members', to which the Union's general secretary understandably replied: 'It will be a long time before the University authorities need to protect Union officials from Union members.' By later standards, it was a minor dispute which soon subsided. But it may seem, in retrospect, like a modest foretaste of things to come.

II
The 1960s

5

Before and after the Robbins Report

New decades tend to bring, like grandiose New Year resolutions, new slogans, new goals, new forms of debate, turmoil and protest. Higher education in the 1960s was dominated by the ambition to expand the universities of the United Kingdom in such a way as to increase the number of student places by almost 50 per cent over the quinquennium from 1962–63 to 1967–68; this would form part of a sustained process of expansion which would continue at least until 1980–81 when, having offered a mere 133,000 places in 1962–63, universities would provide 346,000 in the early 1980s.

Such were the recommendations of the Robbins Report of 1963, the most vigorous exhortation of those years to educational effort and generous public spending on higher learning. This goal was to be achieved partly by expanding the great regional universities. It was often assumed that Oxford and Cambridge had reached the limits of their growth, or would have done so when Churchill College and New Hall were completed, and that their supremacy ought now to be challenged by directing much of the student population to other, less ancient institutions. Growth would, however, also depend partly on the creation of new universities in smaller, more salubrious towns, old county capitals which had flourished before the industrial revolution, cathedral cities where green fields and cheaper building land were readily available. Graduates, too, could be multiplied partly by raising the status of existing institutions, especially the Colleges of Advanced Technology recognised in 1956, so that they too would become universities entitled to confer their own degrees.

Behind the process lay determination to get justice for the age-group long ago dubbed the 'bulge' – the extraordinary number of young people who would reach the age of eighteen in 1965 or thereabouts. They would become a kind of lost generation, their talents fruitlessly scattered, unless more places were hurriedly provided for them. There was also the conviction that the country contained great reservoirs of ability which existing institutions were failing to tap. Lord Robbins himself told the Lords in December 1963 that the proportion of young people entering higher education from the higher professional families was as much as 45 per cent, but no more than 4 per cent of the children of skilled manual workers were doing the same thing. There was, too, the belief that the country's economic future, its standard of living and its capacity to compete in international markets, depended on its ability to produce graduates, particularly in certain directly useful disciplines. An article in *Manchester Independent*, which had succeeded *News Bulletin* as the principal student paper, asked pertinently whether the real aim of expansion was to cater for the bulge, or to serve the needs of commercial and industrial capitalism. This question would be asked many times over in the years to come.

In 1963 Lord Robbins's committee enunciated the famous principle that no young men or women qualified to benefit from a university education should be refused it merely on the grounds that there were no places available for them. Much greater numbers of students could be admitted to universities without any reduction in the standards of entry. Critics grumbled, in the wake of the novelist Kingsley Amis, that more would mean worse; warned of the dangers of 'irresponsible expansion'; or called for firmer guarantees that the necessary resources would in fact be forthcoming. 'More is worse unless more is paid for', declared a tutor of the Faculty of Arts in March 1963. But others sympathised with the longing of thousands of families that their children should go to university and enjoy opportunities and experiences, both intellectual and social, that had lain far beyond their parents' expectations for themselves. The success of *University Challenge*, the televised quiz game, reflected a new public interest, not just in the rowing contests of ancient universities, but in the knowledge and wit displayed by a much greater variety of institutions.

Manchester University was no stranger to swift expansion and was already committed to it long before Robbins reported, although Robbins was to steepen the rising curve of students on the graph and ensure that the process would be prolonged. Already, in the late 1950s, the UGC had established a sub-committee to consider proposals for new universities; University College Sussex was already shaping up, and six others, which escaped the need to serve their time as university colleges, came into being in the first half of the 1960s. Robbins, though proposing yet more, also affirmed his faith in large urban universities, and suggested that they could profitably expand into the region of 8,000–10,000 students and begin to rival the great campuses of the United States.

Manchester had now to adjust its administrative machinery, its social relations, its arrangements for representation and communication, in order to accommodate an ever-growing and increasingly unionised body of teachers, students, administrators and supporting staff. It faced rivalry from new institutions which, though they lacked sufficient quantities of books and other amenities, could seem much freer of the oppressive weight of formality, tradition and narrow departmentalism. Hence they proved more than capable of luring away a large proportion of Manchester's ablest staff. There was a risk that the emigrants might have to be hastily replaced. There was a fear that the University might become vast, impersonal, soulless, encased in dull new buildings and forbidding tower blocks run up with undue speed to cater for increasing numbers. But to many lecturers of the 1960s, sensing unlooked-for prospects of mobility, unprecedented opportunities to overhaul constitutions and redistribute power, there seemed to be an extraordinary chance to flatten the old hierarchies and to create a more genuine community of scholars. For a short time, in Philip Larkin's words, lives became 'a brilliant breaking of the bank, a quite unlosable game'. Since students were encouraged to believe that their study was not just a means of self-betterment but a way to serving the country, some of them ceased to regard higher education as a privilege, financed by a form of public charity, which ought to be reserved to a grateful few. Why should they not be paid wages rather than grants and form trade unions, very different from the traditional students' unions, to pursue better conditions and demand their own version of industrial democracy in their workplace, the University? Inevitably the University itself was drawn into a system of national education within which it became increasingly difficult to maintain its autonomy and impossible to insist any longer on its freedom from the obligation to open its books to scrutiny by the Comptroller and Auditor General. There was much debate as to which of three forces constituted the greatest threat to the independence of universities: control by government, the needs of capitalism, or the demands of radical students in revolt.

Some changes occurred within the small band of influential officers, academic and lay, who headed the University's government and represented it to the world. The sages of mid-century, tireless, authoritative, enthusiastic, gave way as they approached or entered their eighties to a new generation which adopted different styles. Lord

Simon had been succeeded as Chairman of Council by Sir Raymond Streat, who held office from 1957 until 1965. It was said of him on his retirement that his 'manner of approach and his personal sensitivity prevented any comparisons being drawn' with his predecessor. Anna Ford, President of the students' Union from 1966 to 1967, remembers him as 'a great pro-student member of Council', 'a sort of mentor for me, and someone I could turn to later for advice. A very wise man.' Sir Raymond's own successor was Alan Symons, Chairman from 1965 to 1972 and thereafter Treasurer. Another textiles man and a former Chairman of Tootal, he had been a colleague of Sir Raymond on the Cotton Board, and was Chairman of the Bradford Dyers' Association from 1962 onwards and of Viyella International Ltd in 1969–70. He was later to explain, in an article in *Communication*, one of the University's new journals, his belief that the most useful lay officers were 'those who, having succeeded in their own occupation, felt a need to render some further service [in an institution] where there is no religious, racial or political prejudice'. He added reassuringly that 'Laymen are required for their understanding, sympathy and judgement, rather than for their fire, zest and other youthful qualities.' Sir Charles Renold, who had occupied the chair of the Buildings Committee since its inauguration in 1946, retired in 1962 with fifteen major projects completed and another four in various stages of realisation. He gave way to one of the younger industrialists, George Kenyon, an engineering graduate of the 1930s whose first-class degree gave him the confidence and sympathy necessary to understanding and holding his own with academics. His vision, energy and diplomatic skills were soon to be taxed to the utmost by the task of planning the great new Education Precinct of the 1960s.

In an article in *Encounter* for 1958, entitled with Mancunian panache 'The World's Cities. I. Manchester', the historian A.J.P. Taylor had portrayed Manchester as the last of the Hanse towns, a city-state created by traders with little regard either for the monarchy or for the landed aristocracy. Honourable exceptions, however, were generally made for the Earls of Derby and the Dukes of Devonshire. Seeking a successor to Lord Woolton, who died at the end of 1964, the body of Manchester graduates, Convocation, sent deputies to Chatsworth to offer the nominal headship of the University to Andrew Cavendish, eleventh Duke of Devonshire. A relative of the Cecils, he had served under Macmillan as a Minister for Foreign Affairs. Chancellorships (at Exeter, Liverpool, Leeds) ran in his gracious family, and his forebear, the seventh Duke, had been first Chancellor of the University in Victorian times. Courteous, charming and self-deprecating, he told a student journalist, 'My duty is to do as I am told', and politely declined to comment on a parallel development, the election of a Communist, Mike Costello, as President of the students' Union. Devonshire's was to be the last uncontested election of the century; in the 1980s and 1990s, in the absence of an equally natural successor to the throne, the University was to discover the excitement of a spirited open contest for the position of Chancellor, and to have the honour of voting on several candidates of high calibre.

Three of the University's chief professional administrators, Mansfield Cooper, Rainford and Knowles, continued to hold sway throughout the 1960s. Knowing the strong-minded Bursar personally was still the key to getting most things done of a practical-material nature. Rainford addressed the gargantuan task of administering the building programme and became deeply involved in national discussions of academic pension schemes. Modern art was not, perhaps, at the forefront of his interests, but on seeing a relief being hoisted into place on the wall of a new skyscraper, he correctly diagnosed that 'The bloody thing's upside down', and had it properly installed.

The Registrar was much involved in the new Universities Central Council for Admissions (UCCA). He continued to inspire in his younger colleagues a sense of the honour attached to being a university administrator, particularly one in Manchester. As he conceived it, he was the centre of a 'solar system' which enabled all his junior colleagues, unimpeded by line managers and other intermediaries, to have immediate access to him. Some of them longed to get together with counterparts in other universities and discuss common problems, with a view to adopting a more professional approach to their work and perhaps even organising some formal administrative training. Knowles himself adopted the attitude of 'benevolent neutrality' which enabled the process to gather speed. But some of his fellow Registrars were profoundly suspicious of the initiatives of the expanding Meeting of University Administrators, as it was cautiously termed. Were they trying to form some kind of trade union? A London Registrar, it was rumoured, had talked of 'mounting a white charger to scatter this rabble'. Hence Knowles felt obliged to request his colleagues not to use the University's official stationery for their correspondence. Arguably, however, these measures, so circumspectly undertaken, equipped the University's administrators more fully to meet the UGC's growing demands for statistical information, projections of student numbers and estimates of expenditure, and enabled them to adapt to an age of accountability in which resources had to be more carefully managed.

The fourth member of the 1950s quadrumvirate, Moses Tyson, the self-effacing, misogynistic, chain-smoking Librarian, retired in the mid-1960s and was succeeded by one of his former protégés, Fred Ratcliffe. A Germanist, Ratcliffe had started as an Assistant Cataloguer in 1954 and had since held high positions in the University Libraries of Glasgow and Newcastle. His ambition as University Librarian of Manchester was clear and simple – to develop in Manchester at this ripe time the biggest and best University Library in the country. ('It just happened that I was determined to get the books, and people were determined to give them to me! Well, in my Librarianship, never less than three major collections every year came into the Library, apart from what we spent, and we spent more than any other library on acquisitions. ... ') Between 1954 and his departure for Cambridge in 1980, the Library holdings expanded from 350,000 to 3.5 million volumes. Ratcliffe's most coveted prize, the John Rylands Library in Deansgate, rich in books and poor in money, was not to elude him, despite predictions that the Rylands trustees would never allow it to pass into the University's hands.

Mansfield Cooper, now a senior Vice-Chancellor much respected by his ever-growing assembly of colleagues, became Chairman of the Committee of Vice-Chancellors and Principals for 1961–62 and was knighted in 1963. A Lord Mayor of Manchester, who had been his childhood playmate, paused in her finery before his portrait in the Exhibition Hall and said, as well she might, 'Ee! That lad's done well for himself.' Mansfield Cooper was ready to launch his University into expansion so long as the means of supporting it were provided, but he was jealous of its autonomy. He was also suspicious of the intentions of government – both of its continued willingness to invest generously in higher education, and of its tendency to direct expenditure into the channels it considered most useful. Addressing the Staff Forum in 1965 he dissected a government spokesman's ominous definition of efficiency in terms of 'impact per pound spent'. In 1968 he spoke with misgiving to the Court of Governors of the UGC's new vocabulary of 'earmarking', 'indication' and 'co-operation', designed to ensure that funds within the University's block grant should not be used exactly as the University itself chose.

In January 1960, as though sounding the keynote for a new decade, Vivian Bowden, the Principal of the College of Science and Technology, published in *Universities Quarterly* (the journal sponsored by

Lord Simon) an article entitled 'Too few academic eggs'. It would be good if government expenditure on universities (£37.4 million the previous year) could at least be brought up to the same level as expenditure on the egg subsidy (£47.6 million). Drawing on figures provided by UNESCO, Bowden set out to prove that the United Kingdom contained almost the lowest proportion of university students of any civilised country in the Western world. Within a few months Lord Simon himself, nearing the end of his life but still girded for battle, launched a well-orchestrated debate in the Lords at which he called for a general inquiry into the state of higher education in Britain. Bowden's argument was cited in discussion and called by Lord Hailsham, then Lord Privy Seal and Minister for Science, 'a gross libel on English education', a piece of sophistry which had shamelessly exploited the fact that there was no world-wide agreement as to what did or did not constitute a university. But, uneasily accepting the main thrust of the campaign, the government did agree before the year was out to establish under the leonine economist Lord Robbins an inquiry of very wide scope into the shape of full-time higher education in Britain and its future development.

Bowden had proclaimed that 'Scientists and technologists are the missionaries of the modern age. The days when a man might qualify himself to govern the Empire by studying Greek and Latin verse are over. Few countries want us to administer them, but many want us to educate their young people so that they can mechanize their industries.' Honoured with a life peerage, Bowden, the herald of a new age of educated technocrats, was to join Harold Wilson's first administration as Minister of State for Higher Education. Indeed, a contributor to the first *Black Paper* on education in 1969 was to complain that government pressure was 'increasingly towards making all universities the Bowden Institute of Technology'.

If Bowden stood for one kind of idealism, another of Lord Simon's Manchester allies, Lord James of Rusholme, the High Master of Manchester Grammar School, articulated a different one in somewhat cloudier language. He spoke in the Simon debate of a more liberal and traditional concept of education, of the values which universities should continue to transmit. As he reminded the Lords, 'Coleridge used the word "clerisy" to mean the body of the most educated men, the men who, by reason of their high intelligence, their keenness of perception, their richness of imagination, would set standards of value for society. It is with the education of the clerisy that we are concerned today, and it is right that we should remind ourselves that from its members we demand not only technical skill, not only new knowledge, but, in the last resort, those judgments of value which can illumine the life of the whole community.' The fear that education might become narrowly utilitarian, the countervailing suspicion that universities might suffer because they failed to supply practical training as did the polytechnics: these were to enliven the debates of the 1960s at all levels.

As early as January 1960, universities had received a letter from Sir Keith Murray, the chairman of the UGC, inviting them to raise the targets towards which they had been working for the late 1960s and early 1970s. Unexpectedly large numbers of students would soon be clamouring at the gates and the existing universities would have to absorb most of them; several years would have to pass before new foundations were in any position to make significant contributions. Two-thirds of the additional places would be provided in science and technology, the remaining third in other subjects.

Within the next three months Manchester's University Council agreed to expand the future limits of the student population from the 6,000 agreed in 1957 to a total of 7,500 (neither figure included the Faculty of Technology). No precise date was set for the achievement of the goal, but it was probably assumed to lie at least ten years ahead. At the same time the University endeavoured to lay down four conditions. New buildings should be constructed, and old ones extended, in such a way as to maintain an adequate standard of accommodation for departments (the Vice-Chancellor urged the UGC to provide all the academic staff with rooms of their own). It should be made possible to receive all the 1,500 extra students into halls of residence or other forms of accommodation offered by the University itself. Additional staff should be appointed in proportion to the increases in student numbers in such a way as to preserve the low staff–student ratio. And the central facilities of the University – the Library, the students' Union, the administrative offices, the catering arrangements, the sporting facilities, the central lecture and examination rooms – should all be maintained 'at a proper level'.

The path towards expansion was never smooth, since the government was soon convicted of failing to give the necessary financial support. At the start of the new quinquennium, 1962–67, the Treasury declined for the first time to meet the demands of the UGC and the salaries of university teachers suffered unluckily from a pay-pause imposed by the Chancellor of the Exchequer. As the Vice-Chancellor explained to Council, the University could now expect to receive over the next five years only about 50 per cent of the additional sum it had requested. In May 1962 he presided over a gloomy and indignant meeting of University staff in the Arts theatre, which resolved that 'Having thus committed ourselves to expansion we consider that we have been deceived.' The Senate instructed admissions tutors, who had been overshooting the mark, to curb their enthusiasm and hold the numbers where they were; overcrowding afflicted certain departments, including Architecture, whose students' discontent found forceful expression in an article in *Manchester Independent*.

However, with the approach of the Robbins Report in autumn 1963, optimism renewed itself and additions to the recurrent grant began to be made in recognition of increased university costs. The total recurrent grant for the quinquennium had at first been estimated at about £14.8 million., spread over the five years; but the University eventually received a little over £20 million, that sum including an increase of about 36.2 per cent. Generating a new missionary spirit, the Robbins Report called for another big push over the top. To fail to receive the 'superabundant candidates', pleaded Lord Robbins, 'would be the very bankruptcy of academic resource and invention – to say nothing of the injustice to the young people and to their parents, whose absence on military service is responsible for the abnormality of the subsequent discontinuity in marriage- and birth-rates'. The text of the report conveyed a clear message. None of the older universities could be compelled to expand, but those which declined to do so should not complain if benefits flowed to those of their brothers and sisters who co-operated in the great venture. No one ever suggested that Oxford and Cambridge were too large. Could not all the older civic universities grow to the same dimensions? There was no mention of the fact that they did not possess, and could not quickly develop, a series of smaller collegiate communities to break up the mass of students and retain their loyalty. Fearful of becoming ill-favoured backwaters, most universities responded willingly, and were if anything inclined to overdo the exercise. In Manchester in October 1963 the Deans of the Faculties were called upon at short notice – with assistance from Vincent Knowles's civil service – to make new estimates of the distance to which they were prepared to go. They plucked the figures from somewhere. On receiving them the University Development Committee concluded that if conditions were favourable the targets could be raised to 8,890 in 1967–68 and to 10,530 in 1971–72. Postgraduates would account for just over one-fifth of those students. The Robbins Report had stressed the importance of providing by this means a supply of university teachers to staff the expanding institutions, which would then be able to take off into self-sustaining growth.

The additional recurrent grants soon promised for the years 1964-67 seem to have rested on the assumption that the University would expand to 8,500 students by the end of the quinquennium. In fact, over the decade from 1959–60 to 1969–70, the numbers rose from 5,142 students at Owens to 8,809 (an increase of 71.3 per cent), with another seventy-seven students in the newly established Business School; numbers in the Faculty of Technology had almost exactly doubled over the same period, rising as they did from 1,643 at the end of the 1950s to 3,298 at the end of the 1960s. Counting the Faculty of Technology, the University was now over 12,000 strong. During the new quinquennium, 1967–72, a breathing-space was expected, but there were also ominous signs of increasing financial stringency, of government demands for greater productivity, of tussles concerning overseas students' fees, of proposals to replace student grants with loans, of greater *dirigisme* on the part of the UGC.

Penry Williams, a historian, assistant tutor to the Faculty of Arts, wrote in the new journal *Staff Comment* for January 1964 a 'Manchester Retrospect'. Enjoying the freedom of expression permitted to one about to depart for the University of Oxford, he charged the University with failing or actively refusing to adapt to its increase in size and to changes in the composition and attitudes, though not the intelligence, of the student population. 'In structure', he wrote, 'this is still the Victorian University, while in numbers it has already been dragged, with scarcely a kick or scream, into the Robbins epoch ... As a degree becomes established as the essential passport to professional life, more and more students are coming to us without any very firm commitment to learning. At the same time the proportion of first-generation and working-class students is rising, bringing many who feel strange in the middle-class world of the university. These students in particular do not easily find guide-lines in a community already so large that many of us have "no common sense of belonging". They may easily fall into the habit of regarding their studies as something shut off from the rest of their lives, so that we come near to producing, or at least to tolerating, a dichotomy between the academic and the social ... From this alienation between study and the rest of life, there may easily come in time a rejection of university values ... ' In this trenchant and prescient article, he pleaded for a greater effort to develop 'departmental communities', smaller, more manageable units within the University, and for the University's architects to show more imagination and recognise that 'a community is moulded by the spaces in which it is housed'. 'Perhaps', he admitted, 'the university's power elite is bursting with radical schemes of its own and still anxious to nurture the ideas of the humblest lecturer. All I can say is that this is not how it looks from below, and that I have not been alone in feeling depressed and demoralised by the apparent resistance in some of our higher echelons to any new idea. If we are to transform our university, some encouragement must be given to those who are prepared to commit time and energy to solving our complex and urgent problems. Unless such encouragement is given, a lively, concerned and intelligent section of our community will either become embittered and withdrawn or will migrate to more dynamic institutions.'

There was indeed a danger that academics would start to play a great game of general post. Manchester could no longer count on a static labour force, which regarded Manchester as the only conceivable place of employment. New universities with virgin slates to write upon and old, prestigious ones with a stronger democratic tradition or a metropolitan location would inevitably beckon to promising academics. Prospects of promotion in Manchester were not especially good, as the post-war generation of lecturers became at the end of the 1950s old enough and experienced enough to aspire to senior lectureships and readerships. In December 1959 the Vice-Chancellor revealed that twice the usual number of applications for such promotion had been made. At all times the number of senior positions available was constrained by the UGC rule that in general it would only pay for a certain proportion of such posts: at first its rule was that there should only be two senior lectureships or readerships among every nine members of the academic staff below the rank of professor, and then, by 1967, that professors, readers and senior lecturers together were not to constitute more than 35 per cent of the whole academic staff (the proportion was raised to 40 per cent in 1972). There were attempts in 1962–64 to make the process of advancement from within the University to a personal chair less capricious and less dependent on the initiative of the existing professor or professors in the department. But the criterion established, the 'quite outstanding and widely acknowledged distinction in scholarship of the person concerned', seemed to put the personal chair well out of the reach of most academics in mid-career.

In leaving Manchester some sought promotion, others just the chance to begin afresh at the same level and work with different people and within another institutional framework. Charles Carter, a versatile applied economist who held the chair of Political Economy, became the founding Vice-Chancellor of the University of Lancaster. He had, wrote the author of his appreciation, 'ranged from the measurement of production movements, through the impact of uncertainty on investment decisions to the problems of applying science to industry'. Professor Marcus Cunliffe, the founder of the Honours School of American Studies in Manchester, a historian who had dashed off a successful Pelican book on *The Literature of the United States*, left for Sussex. Professor Tottle of Metallurgy moved in 1967 to a newly promoted College of Advanced Technology and endured stoically many tedious jokes about his Bath chair. Frank Kermode, the distinguished critic, chose to head for Bristol, whereupon his colleague, the Professor of English Language, never spoke to him again. The departure for London of Edward Ullendorff, Professor of Semitic Languages and Literature from 1959 to 1964, prompted the reflection that since 1st October students 'have no longer been able to obtain instruction in Amharic, Tigrinya, Tigre, Gurague, Argobba or epigraphic South Arabian'. Gerald Aylmer, a Lecturer in History, armed with a big book on the King's servants in the reign of Charles I, became a founding Professor of History at the University of York. A colleague, the social historian Harold Perkin, who could 'see no future for his subject in the interstices of the Manchester history school', left for Lancaster and was soon afterwards elevated to a chair. An outstanding large-scale exporter, however, was the Department of Government. Here the presiding genius, W.J.M. Mackenzie, had consistently advised his younger colleagues how to make their mark and helped them to identify the most promising areas in which to embark on research and publication. 'If one of Mackenzie's men should lift a corner of the curtain of ignorance, Mackenzie would push him through the gap,' proclaimed Mackenzie's eulogist, not altogether felicitously, to Council and Senate. Most of his first-generation appointments went to foundation chairs in other universities. When Mackenzie himself moved to Glasgow in 1966 it was said that 'This last session the Department of Government here has provided British and Commonwealth Universities with five professors, four lecturers, and eleven assistant lecturers.' 'To leave behind a Department which can with equanimity send forth from itself the equivalent of a Department larger than any other in this country is an achievement of almost historic proportions.'

During the session 1965–66 the University received 250 resignations; in March 1965 the academic and senior administrative staff of the University had numbered something over 1,000, including 870 full-timers. This could be a source of justifiable pride, in that Manchester had clearly nurtured so many academics coveted by other institutions. It was also a source of unease, a threat to Manchester's intellectual pre-eminence, a reflection, even, of its inability to command loyalty. Pessimists thought it a portent of relative decline in a greatly enlarged and increasingly competitive university world. One writer in *Manchester Independent* warned of 'Manchester's fading reputation', a condition attributed to the burden of bureaucracy and the weight of frustrating regulations encountered in an old-fashioned civic university. Manchester, he suggested, 'is the technical centre of the north but her arts and humanities disciplines are trailing far behind the new universities'.

This was not an altogether just comment, but it contained an element of truth. The University, it could have been added, was undoubtedly establishing new enterprises in the 1960s – the Business School, the new course entitled Liberal Studies in Science, the Hester Adrian Centre for the Study of Learning Processes in the Mentally Handicapped – and there were also new ventures in the arts. Prominent among them were the new Drama Department and the new University Theatre; John White's successful renovation and promotion of the Whitworth Art Gallery; the new interdisciplinary honours schools of American Studies and Medieval Studies. But there was a danger of ossification in those very departments, such as History, which had once enjoyed the highest reputation and built up a great tradition which was sometimes too obstinately protected by the more conservative professors. Michael Rose, a social historian who arrived from Oxford in the 1960s, suggests that the effect of the exodus to the new universities was to remove the mediators between the older generation of professors and the younger generation of assistant lecturers. It was as if the mid-field, vitally important in football, and perhaps in scholarly communities too, had disappeared from the scene. 'Every time a vacancy came up the tendency was to appoint somebody who would fill the gap that person had left, rather than thinking about new areas like social history or gender history or oral history, which were coming on to the agenda in the late 1960s, early 1970s.' The problem was not peculiar to History. In the words of Christopher Driver, the author of *The Exploding University*, 'A somewhat similar temper reigns in the English department, where young men with bright ideas are apt to be told, "that's the sort of thing Kermode would have suggested" – the reference being to a well-known and prolific scholar

who once held a Chair in Manchester but did not stay very long.'
Compulsory Old English exerted a strong influence upon a rigid syllabus, although the younger professors of literature, Jump and Cox,
were striving to give students a greater range of choice.

Faced in 1963 with further requests to expand, the University
Council had not at first envisaged the need to make great numbers of
junior appointments in order to provide teaching for the influx of students. They had contemplated recruiting part-timers, deferring retire-
ments beyond the normal age (which was now sixty-seven), and even
encouraging 'by all appropriate means' the return to the country of
university teachers who had accepted posts overseas. How they proposed to compete with American salaries was not clear. Eager to
encourage collaboration between universities and government
research establishments, the UGC drew attention to the presence of
scientists of the highest distinction in government laboratories, and
urged the universities to engage them as visiting lecturers who would
shoulder some of the burden of teaching. Since there were few large
theatres capable of accommodating the audiences that could now be
expected to attend the general lectures addressed to first- and second-
year students, it would almost certainly prove necessary to repeat
both lectures and complicated demonstrations. This was one of several reasons for applying in 1965 for Grants Committee funding in
order to introduce facilities for video-recording. With the aid of professional producers and properly equipped studios it might prove possible to provide adequate substitutes for live lectures, and thereby free
lecturers for more tutorial work with small groups of students.

However, since the staff–student ratio must not be allowed to dete-
riorate but kept in the region of 1:8, and since the Robbins Report had
extolled the virtues of the tutorial, there was no real alternative to
recruiting at high speed very large numbers of junior staff. This would
have to be done before the expanded system began to provide much
larger numbers of suitable graduates. There was a risk that it would be
comparatively easy to become a university teacher in the 1960s, when
something like one-fifth of all new graduates would be needed to staff
universities, and a good deal more difficult thereafter. For the number
of highly qualified graduates would multiply, the number of posts
available to them shrink, especially if the 1960s generation were
granted tenure and allowed to dig in.

Since universities were competing for able recruits with the civil
service, the professions and industrial and commercial employment,
the terms of service had to be made as attractive as possible, and there

was little question of trying to engage large numbers of staff on short-term contracts. If anything, tenure was granted more readily. It meant, or appeared to mean, a guarantee of secure employment until the retiring age, except for those few who lapsed into gross inefficiency or indulged in blatant impropriety. It offered protection against dismissal for voicing unpopular opinions, and was seen by many, not as a shield for laziness or mediocrity, but as a vital defence for academic freedom. Under the prevailing system at Manchester most new arrivals had served three or four years on probation as Assistant Lecturers, and had then spent a further three years in the grade of Lecturer before being appointed to the retiring age. The likelihood of dismissal, never very strong, receded rapidly, until a lectureship or higher office became, like a Church of England living, a virtual freehold. In 1970 the Assistant Lecturer's grade was abolished, and new university teachers were required to serve an average of only three or four years before being granted tenure, as they almost always were. Academic freedom had been safeguarded, and some very able people enlisted, as in other decades, in the University's service; but there was inevitably a danger that the 1960s generation, all growing old together, would occupy until the year 2000 a disproportionate number of posts. Since expansion could not continue indefinitely at the same pace, they would partially block the gangways to a great many potentially able teachers and researchers, who would have much less chance of embarking on the academic liner.

The University had responded swiftly, and some said too willingly, to external demands that it should promote the country's well-being and the good of individuals by opening its gates to greater and greater numbers of students. Decisions rapidly taken in a near-emergency were to produce enduring and far-reaching results, for neither temporary buildings nor temporary appointments were seriously contemplated. Prompt accommodation to outside forces seemed, however, to be combined with excessive caution in domestic reform, for to many critics the University seemed desperately slow to abandon its attachment to professorial oligarchy, its liking for secrecy, the rigidity of its departmental structures, the seeming indifference in some quarters to the value of teaching and the importance of personal relationships with pupils. Out of this tension between a war of movement on one front and trench warfare on another, out of the conflict between an old and an unusually large younger generation of university teachers, out of the appearance on the scene of a new generation of students who regarded higher education as a citizen's right, came much of the unrest that began to shake the University in the late 1960s – though in Manchester it took the form of earth tremors, light shuddering in the region of a geological fault, rather than seismic shocks that registered high on the Richter scale.

6

Education Precinct and Student Village

The University Council and the Bursar now faced the formidable task of providing on an ever-larger scale buildings for the studies, investigations, amusements, social intercourse and residence of an ever-growing population of students, academics, administrators, secretaries, technicians and others. The Grants Committee now exercised immense direct power over universities, not so much through recurrent block grants as through the Committee's decisions to give or deny finance to the numerous building plans submitted for its approval. Year after year the Council put forward a list of buildings which it hoped to see started or taken to a further stage in two to four years' time, arranging them in order of priority. Long-term planning, the Vice-Chancellor explained in 1965, was hampered by the unpredictability of such capital grants, since it could never be assumed that the Grants Committee would succeed in extracting from the Treasury all the money that it sought.

Since all institutions of higher education in the city were responding to the call to expand, the City Council was prevailed upon to make additional grants of land to the north of the University, in the region of All Saints, which would now be densely settled by the University itself, by the College of Science and Technology, by the Northern College of Music, and by the City Colleges. These, the Regional College of Art, the John Dalton College of Technology and the Adult Education College, would eventually be grouped together to form the new Polytechnic, founded in 1970. A new body, resoundingly called the Joint Committee for the Comprehensive Planning of an Education Precinct, was established with the Vice-Chancellor as chairman, and was designed to promote collaboration and resist piecemeal growths. Seats were filled by Principal Bowden, by members of the University Council, by city aldermen and councillors. Successive town clerks acted as honorary secretaries, and the bursars of the University and the College of Science and Technology as their assistants. Most active on behalf of the University was George Kenyon, the chairman of the Buildings Committee, who recalls that 'the University was first off the mark with its detailed plans; and because its expansion was so urgent nationally and it got its UGC funds so quickly, each project following the next in rapid succession, the University became the natural leader of the whole operation and this position was sustained throughout'.

Some things were impracticable. There was no prospect of engaging a super-architect, since UGC policy precluded prestige buildings. But a master-mind was needed, and town-planners were engaged to co-ordinate the operation and to produce a comprehensive design which would determine the landscaping of the site and the general disposition of buildings, their masses, heights, materials and colours, and the extent of the open spaces between them. Within the limits which the plan established, individual architects were free to design their own buildings. 'It could have been totally disastrous to have settled for one architect', writes Sir George. 'The 1960s were not a happy decade for building in England.' The planners engaged were Hugh Wilson and Lewis Womersley. Wilson had been responsible for Cumbernauld, a Glasgow overspill town modelled on Scandinavian lines, and was also supervising the construction of a Lancashire development, the new town at Skelmersdale; Womersley had designed the King's Heath shopping centre at Northampton, and the Park Hill flats in Sheffield. Arguably they were better planners than architects, for their notions of building were severely functional and utilitarian. Nevertheless they were commissioned to design the shopping precinct which now spans Oxford Road like a bridge-restaurant on a motorway, and conveys to southbound drivers a certain sense of crossing a frontier into a special reservation.

Crucial to their plans were several principles which were revealed to a wide audience by their interim report of 1964. So far as possible pedestrians ought to be separated from motor vehicles throughout the site. Where new buildings were to be erected in the immediate neighbourhood of major roads, ramps and walkways should be provided to enable people to walk above the traffic. Today, as a result of these plans, pedestrians can ascend a ramp to the west of Oxford Road en route for the shopping centre, cross the road through a roofed-in concourse and enter the region of the Chaplaincy, skirt the upstairs courtyard of the Computer Building, and descend by another ramp to the foot of the Mathematics tower on the eastern side of the road. Ideally, Oxford Road itself, somewhat diverted from its all-too-straight and divisive course between science and arts, should be closed to all but service traffic. So should Brunswick Street to the east, and Burlington Street to the west, which between them formed a dangerous staggered crossing of Oxford Road. A ring road was to pass to the south of the University in the region of Grafton Street. There was much talk of moving people without resorting to motors of any kind, as if the University were an airport served by horizontal escalators. Roy Kantorowich, the Professor of Town and Country Planning, received a grant from Council to explore, among other things, 'the possibility of a system of Travelators to connect key parts of the educational sector of the city with the Oxford Road and Piccadilly Stations and with the Hospitals and neighbouring development'.

It had been said that the older universities would all have to struggle against a 'trifurcation', a division of sites into the University's teaching and research headquarters, the premises of the central students' Union, and the halls of residence. Because they were starting from scratch, the newer universities would be able to avoid creating this undesirable division. To some extent the planners and their masters tried to avoid perpetuating it, though there was no discarding the arrangements already in place. It was important to them that the Precinct should not become dead and deserted at night or hopelessly underpopulated during vacations. Some students, rather than be relegated to the halls in Victoria Park or the more distant Fallowfield site, should live in the Precinct itself, not only in the recently erected Refectory Residence Tower, but also in the region of Whitworth Park or in the newly designated Student Quarter to the north-east of the University. Members of the University staff, and people from the city who had nothing to do with the University, should be encouraged to live in the Precinct. It was most desirable that the Education Precinct should not be cut off from the town. If it became isolated the people of Manchester, remembering what had been demolished in order to make it, might become indifferent or hostile towards what had once been their University. Rather, the Precinct Centre should, as the planners put it in 1967, 'become the focus of a variety of activities catering for both town and gown'. It might include, not only shops, offices and banks of interest to everyone, but 'a new Student Health Centre, a public library, a small police station to replace the existing one in Ormond Street, and housing accommodation for staff, married students and people working within the city.'

George Kenyon's vision for the University was captured in an imaginative document submitted to the Joint Committee in 1963. Well aware that 'public money is being used so markedly for a mere increase in numbers, irrespective of the atmosphere of the resulting community', he was anxious that the Precinct should not decline into a wilderness of lecture rooms, laboratories and study-bedrooms set in bleak and uninviting surroundings. As he pleaded, almost lyrically, 'it is the nature, the spirit, the atmosphere of the University that matters. Academic standards above everything, but backing this up a mental relaxation in pleasant surroundings - arcades and galleries, suited to the soft rain which encourages the green growth to light the eye and to insulate the ear.' In his opinion the greatest need was for more points at which informal social exchanges could take place and brief spells of leisure be pleasantly spent. Kenyon had served an apprenticeship as Chairman of the Radiological Protection Committee. Since many people were potentially exposed to invisible noxious emissions, he had made the acquaintance of a large number of academics and realised the importance of consultation (he calculated in 1965 that he had transacted business with 85 out of 130 professors in the University). He and his colleagues were a trifle wearied, however, by some of the concerns of those consulted. 'Just as the subject which always leads to passionate discussion in any committee is car parking, the canteen or the colour of paint on the cloakroom walls, so we found ourselves resisting the demand for 75 or so departmental libraries or tea-making cubby holes or rest-rooms instead of having our minds and spirits elevated by the opportunity to expand the quality and breadth of the British first degree ... '

Unavoidably, perhaps, a common complaint about the parsimoniously constructed individual buildings in the years to come was that they failed to create for their inhabitants any real sense of community. They lacked common rooms and were indeed without 'tea-making cubby holes', losing the intimacy of the cramped houses which they had often replaced with their purpose-built austerity. Rooms, designed to be offices, were geared to the status of their occupants and the dimensions of their filing cabinets rather than the likely size of their classes; architecture emphasised hierarchy. 'The architects and planners have pronounced our doom: it is to spend the rest of our days in this university (which I for one hope are numbered) in identical cells, for ever wandering down long, dark tunnels, lurching against doors that will always open the other way, searching for the numbers that alone will distinguish one cell from another and one floor from another ... Does seminar room have to be ranged alongside seminar room, professor alongside professor, lecturer alongside lecturer, shelved according to size like books in a library?' Thus a letter to the editor of *Staff Comment* from Brian Manning, historian of the people in the English Civil War, in 1965. In the recollection of Jeffrey Denton, who arrived in Manchester in the same year as an assistant lecturer, 'what struck me then about Manchester University was that it was very much part of the commercial development of the city. So this University always seemed to me like sets of offices ... with not a nine-to-five regime, that's too many for a good gentlemen's club, it was a ten to three-thirty regime', and the buildings encouraged few people to stay on the premises any longer than they had to.

During the 1960s the University site became, in the words of a visiting schoolteacher who envied the amounts of money being poured into higher education, an empire on which the concrete never set. It was a land of vacant lots and devastated areas, a waste of water and mud out of which rose starkly the girders and cranes which heralded the new order. Would-be conservationists defended a few buildings of character, especially the King's Hotel at 278 Oxford Road on the corner of Devas Street, which was threatened with destruction for the purpose of providing a car park. Geoffrey Nowell-Smith of the Italian Department saw its impending demise as symbolic of the inexorable progress of the academic ghetto, for the King's, with its superb interior, was a good pub and a good building, 'needed by the people who use it, staff, students and the (often neglected) population of Chorlton-on-Medlock'. The Vice-Chancellor received a petition and passed it on to the Building Committee, but, invoking the boring voice of common sense, commented that it had long proved impossible to manage the King's Hotel profitably, and that the losses it sustained had made it all the easier for the University to acquire it cheaply. Aesthetic and social considerations yielded to economic arguments, and the King's Hotel was duly reduced to rubble. However, some older buildings escaped the prevailing doom because they could be successfully adapted to academic uses, especially in the performing arts. The Rivoli Cinema in Denmark Road, although it needed better sound-proofing, successfully absorbed the Faculty of Music; a German church became a studio for the new Department of Drama.

Student officers objected to the plan because it made no provision for a greatly enlarged Union. Their building was a new one, but it had been constructed for a student population of about 4,200, and one twice that size was now in view. Already it was making 'a sardine tin seem empty', or so the Union President claimed in 1964. Hence the student officers were moved to compile a painstaking report entitled 'Bursting at the Seams', in which they called for Union buildings divided into several units grouped around a central quadrangle, in such a way as to allow room for further development. But the general thrust of official planning was towards providing amenities for students in other places, rather than concentrating them in the Union and either extending it on the ground or providing an additional floor. When Sir Raymond Streat retired from the chairmanship of Council in 1965, it seemed that one of his greatest achievements had been to persuade the students' representatives to accept this system of 'dispersed amenities', and to do so without interpreting it as an attempt to undermine the Union.

Some student journalists gleefully took up the theme of the 'academic ghetto', seeing the planning of universities either as a form of social control or as a neglect of social control which could lead to an explosion. Post-Robbins policy generally, argued a leading article in *Manchester Independent* in October 1967, had been to locate universities away from the largest centres of population, and also to divide them domestically into smaller units, often in the form of colleges. In Manchester, however, 'The University and the City are combining to create a situation comparable to that of a Negro ghetto in a North American city. The ingredients are the same - a large influx of population, mostly disorientated, lack of adequate social facilities, lack of communication between the ghetto and the rest of the city - one cannot prove by analogy, one can only warn and wait.'

This warning was over-dramatic. Even in the years to come the largest and most vociferous student protests could never compare with a race riot. But high-speed planning and construction, spurred on by pressing demand and reined in by the availability of public money, were unlikely to produce the most appealing results or the warmest consideration for users of buildings. Some buildings contributed to the impression that the University was not merely serving the needs of industrial capitalism but importing its architectural forms in order to house a 'knowledge factory' in office blocks, towers and warehouses, with a drably clad student labour force pouring in and out of its doors, like figures in a Lowry drawing, at set hours of the day.

In October 1963 the shopping list of buildings approved by the University Council for submission to the UGC began with a new Medical School, to be constructed in three phases, benefiting pre-clinical, para-clinical and clinical subjects respectively, and occupying a 'net usable area' of 358,200 square feet, six or seven times as much as most other items. It was followed by a new Mathematics Building; a further extension to the Arts Building; new premises for Metallurgy; new accommodation for Architecture and Town Planning (which, for the greater good, had surrendered its premises to the Dental Hospital); a small communal building for the purpose of handling high levels of radio-activity; additional premises for Electrical Engineering, which had had the misfortune to receive favours too soon in the 1950s, and was now outgrowing the much maligned building of those years; a new building for Law and Economic and Social Studies, which, with a 'net usable area' of 130,000 square feet, was destined to be a little more than one-third the size of the proposed new Medical School. A Humanities Building, which was not quite the same as an overspill from Arts, and was intended among other things to house the Faculty of Education, was already in progress. By 1965 Computer Science, too, was making its first serious financial demands on the Grants Committee's benevolence. At intervals the need for large-scale student accommodation would figure in the University's petitions for capital grants. By 1966 Drama, Audio-Visual Aids and the University Library were also pressing claims.

Tower building was favoured, at least until the sensational film *Towering Inferno* fuelled misgivings. 'Everyone knows that mathematics is penetrating more and more into the research techniques of many disciplines, and its power is to be vertically demonstrated for all to see', observed the urban geographer T.W. Freeman. The Mathematics Tower of nineteen storeys was the only building of the 1960s entrusted to Londoners, rather than to local architects. Its relative boldness and authority as it soared darkly above Oxford Road made it the most conspicuous landmark of the new order. The School of Medicine, too, would have liked a tower, despite the difficulty of expanding such premises in response to unforeseen needs. However, after numerous visits by the Executive Dean, Dr Beswick, and the architect, Harry Fairhurst, to Continental universities in search of warning and inspiration, the doctors were persuaded to settle for a tower lying on its side, which had first been sketched by the architect when returning from Finland by air.

The new Medical School, long identified as the highest overall priority, was almost the last great undertaking of the 1960s. It had once, in 1961, been dropped by the UGC from the list presented to it. Medical schools generally had suffered from the verdict in the late 1950s of the Willink Committee, which had concluded that they were producing more doctors than the country needed and recommended a slowing down. Hence the Medical School declined from a total of 662 students in 1953–54 to 528 in 1960–61, while the rest of the University was expanding. But the Willink Committee had received misleading information about the extent of probable population increases. It had not anticipated either the extent to which doctors could be expected to leave the country (especially for lucrative jobs in Canada and the United States) or the tendency of doctors, particularly in hospitals, to devote more time to their patients so that more doctors would be needed. Although Robbins, doubtless to the Treasury's relief, had said little about the expansion of medical education, the climate changed in the 1960s and gave rise to a Robbins-like demand for rapid growth in this quarter too.

Between 1964 and 1967 the Grants Committee showed a new interest in financing increased intakes of medical students. For once the reorganisation of universities brought tangible benefits to Manchester, new opportunities to bring in students of high calibre. When Dundee separated from St Andrews in 1967 and received its own charter, it no longer felt able to accept St Andrews medical students for clinical education in its teaching hospitals. Instead a number of St Andrews students came by invitation to Manchester, which in the early 1970s agreed to accept them all. In 1968 the Commission on Medical Education chaired by Lord Todd recommended sharp increases in the number of medical students, to be achieved mainly by enlarging existing medical schools rather than founding new ones. Even before Todd reported, the University's bargaining power with the UGC was growing. It was well placed to obtain its vast new medical building and also to promote the development of new teaching hospitals, a process which would also call for building operations (these, however, would be carried out some distance away from the Precinct, at Withington Hospital in South Manchester and at Hope Hospital in Salford). Annual intakes into the pre-clinical school, which had sunk to a mere eighty to eighty-five students in the late 1950s, rose to 105 in 1964 and 160 in 1968. They were scheduled to reach 200 by 1975. Other new enterprises, particularly the development of degree rather than diploma courses in Nursing, were to swell the numbers of the Faculty of Medicine as a whole.

Hitherto, University medical departments had been housed some distance away from the teaching hospitals, most of them in the old Medical School to the west of the main buildings on Oxford Road, built partly in 1874 and partly in 1894. This School, in the early 1960s, housed Anatomy, Physiology, Pharmacology and Psychology; other departments, including Bacteriology and Pathology, lay nearer the hospitals, in York Place. As the move to new premises proceeded and medical disciplines became concentrated in their new mansion to the east of Oxford Road, relics of past medical practice, such as a Lister spray used for dispensing carbolic acid in early antiseptic surgery, and a Dr Cruise's endoscope of 1865, ominously illuminated by a paraffin lamp, were rescued, labelled and placed in showcases by Charlotte Beswick, the Executive Dean's wife. An elegant display of these items in the entrance hall of the new building, named after Sir John Stopford (who had died Lord Stopford of Fallowfield in 1961), served as a symbol of continuity between the old regime and the new. Much of the Medical Library remained behind in the old Medical School, until it found a new home in the newly extended University Library of the 1980s; only materials relating to pre-clinical subjects made an appearance on the top floor of the Stopford Building, which guaranteed them safety from noxious fluids leaking through the floor. Much effort was made to preserve the initials of famous doctors carved in their student days on the desks of the old lecture rooms, though attempts on the part of students to establish similar customs in the new building were treated as acts of vandalism deserving of withering rebuke.

There had been thoughts of linking the new Medical School to the nearest teaching hospital, the Infirmary, by a bridge which would span the new ring road at Grafton Street. But, since the plans for reshaping the local traffic system eventually came to very little, the bridge was never built. As Dr Beswick now explains, concerning the building which he helped to commission, 'The Ackers Street side by the Holy Name, all the pillars, the whole building, has a gap in it right the way through, top to bottom, filled with cork. So that on that side, there are all the things that shake, like the air conditioning, the workshops, students who are working for exams, and all that sort of thing! And the middle bit and the rest of the building are absolutely still, and you can put anything in there. You can take all the walls out, put anything in, an electron microscope, whatever, that mustn't have any movement at all, and you can put it anywhere in that part of the building ... you have to be able to bring your services up from somewhere underneath, you have the lights on the ceiling, and you have all the wet things in the floor. The troughs that they're in lean back to the risers, so the building can't flood, because all the risers go down from the building, and they all drain into the river Medlock.' A group of Saudi Arabian visitors could not understand why the Faculty should have wished to leave anything so picturesque as the cramped old Coupland building with its sinister basements, but to most users of the new premises the answer was perfectly clear.

The Electrical Engineering building had played host to a series of increasingly powerful computers - to Ferranti Mark I in 1951, to Mercury in 1958, and in 1962 to Atlas, whose strength was about 2,500 times greater than that of Mark I. Since the University had at first been unable to use them to their full capacity, they had in large measure been able to pay for themselves by having their services offered to industrial concerns and government departments. Because University staff were mainly responsible for designing Atlas, the machine's owners, International Computers & Tabulators Ltd (ICT), were prepared to make half its time available to the University, free of charge, until the end of 1970. However, the demands of the University and of the College of Science and Technology had become so much more voluminous and exacting (punchcards were now used in registering students) that by 1967 even the mighty Atlas would be unable to go on taking the world upon its shoulders. A new discipline, Computer Science, had developed under Tom Kilburn, Freddie Williams's former assistant, who was appointed the first Professor of Computer Engineering in 1960. The department which practised it was due to receive its first undergraduates in October 1965. Expected to house this new department and to provide a base for a growing computer service, the Electrical Engineering building had become overcrowded. Hence the demands of computing on the Grants Committee were beginning to intensify. It was claimed in 1964 that a new building would be needed in order to house the computer itself, the Department of Computing, and the Computer Service (which would in future be administered by a professor at the College, Gordon Black, and run by a staff of eighty). The estimated cost of the premises, with a 'net usable area' of between 80,000 and 100,000 square feet, would be £1 million, and a new machine ought to be ordered before December 1967, allowing two years for delivery. Estimates of the annual running cost of the computer service were in the region of £365,000. Since the University had now lost its near-monopoly of such machinery, and commercially organised computing services had developed elsewhere, it was now 'impossible that any substantial part of this annual cost can continue to be met out of earnings'.

Work began on the Computer Building, whose eventual cost proved to be in the region of £1.5 million, in September 1969, and finished, a month or two behind schedule, in 1972. The inner courtyard was pleasantly embellished with a 'water feature', in other words a concrete fountain for the pond which the architect (Mr Baines of the Building Design Partnership) and the contractors (Pochin Ltd) presented 'without additional cost to the contract'. Still larger grants were made towards the cost of the sophisticated machinery housed in the building. The sum of £2.6 million came from the Department of Education and Science, by way of the Computer Board for Universities and Research Councils, to pay for the 7600 computer of the Control Data Corporation of America, and this was linked with the 1906A, a product of International Computers Ltd., a British firm based at Gorton. Together they would form a complex equivalent in power and capability to more than twenty Atlases, and would serve the needs of the Computer Service. This had now evolved into one of three regional computer centres in the country, the others being in London and Edinburgh, and was designed to serve, not Manchester alone, but northern universities in general, and some others outside the region altogether.

Almost miraculously, the new University Theatre in Devas Street, opened in October 1965 by Dame Sybil Thorndike, escaped most of the obloquy heaped on the greater part of the University's new buildings and earned lavish praise for the modernity and technical proficiency of its auditorium, dressing rooms and stage machinery. 'In the wilderness of undesign and unarchitecture which is Owens campus', rhapsodised a student journalist, 'the theatre stands out like a Corbusier amongst a collection of council houses.' Addressing the staff forum, Stephen Joseph, who lectured in the new Drama Department and was also director of Theatre-in-the-Round at Scarborough, had complained of the inability of most architects to understand the function and purpose of the theatre, of their tendency, especially, 'to place lighting fixtures in the traditional positions appropriate to candles but not to electricity.' This theatre, however, was designed in such a way as to create new, intimate, reciprocal relationships between actors and audience, to enable actors to speak and not shout or rant their lines. Two mobile platforms, operated by lifts, made it possible to set up as many as five entirely different stages, suitable to the varied and unconventional programme now in prospect (the three plays of the opening festival were Dion Boucicault's *The Shaughraun*, Ben Jonson's *The Silent Woman* and Albert Camus's *Caligula*). A simple proscenium, a thrust stage, an apron stage, a concert stage, or a very large open stage: all these things were available. Lighting and sound controls were concentrated in a glass-fronted observation room at the back of the auditorium.

Triumphantly replacing the old Arthur Worthington Hall on Dover Street, the theatre had arisen in the wake of the new Drama Department and was directed by its first professor, Hugh Hunt, who had been Director of the Australian Elizabethan Theatre Trust and in that role responsible for forming opera, ballet and drama companies throughout Australia. A Lecturer in Drama acted as theatre manager. But the theatre was not intended solely for the Department's use, or designed to turn inwards towards the University itself. Rather, it was designed, as was the Whitworth Gallery under John White's direction, to appeal to audiences from the city and break down the threatened isolation of the academic quarter from its surroundings. It was to be used partly by a resident professional company, partly by departments which taught or sponsored drama or opera, partly by University dramatic or musical societies, and partly by organisations which did not belong to the University. Fearing that the development of television might deprive young people of any experience of live theatre, Hugh Hunt eventually decided to create a young people's theatre company. Established in 1972 with support both from the Arts Council and from the City Council, the company took the name Contact. It moved in when Sixty-Nine Theatre terminated its contract and found a permanent home in the city at the Royal Exchange. Contact had a nucleus of ten players and was to work in Manchester throughout the year. When not performing at the theatre it would present special programmes to schools, colleges and youth clubs, aimed at audiences of young people aged between about fifteen and twenty-five, who might otherwise never be tempted to enter a theatre at all. In the words of Dennis Welland, the Professor of American Literature who was one of the original trustees, it was not to be 'theatre in education' so much as 'education in theatre'. Contact opened towards the end of 1972 with a modernised version of Francis Beaumont's *The Knight of the Burning Pestle*.

Equally pressing was the task of housing the expanding student population, of providing it with something more than beds to lie on. To the Robbins Committee it was vital that young people should enjoy the experience of living away from home as if it were a rite of passage into responsible adulthood. Ideally all universities ought to be of national standing, not just of regional or provincial importance. Only then could they begin to rival the great cosmopolitan and residential universities of Oxford and Cambridge. Other commentators thought it particularly likely that head-teachers would advise girls to live away from home, lest they suffer continual distraction from requests to help with domestic chores. The Robbins Committee had anticipated a growing shortage of lodgings: as opportunities for female employment rose, the need and the desire to earn extra money by letting out rooms to students would very likely diminish. Clearly, then, it was vital that universities themselves should provide the accommodation, rather than merely approve and license lodgings situated within an ever-lengthening distance of the lecture rooms, libraries and laboratories.

In Manchester the problems of distant lodgings were aggravated in the 1960s by an unpopular rule obliging all first-year students under the age of twenty-one, unless they were in halls of residence, to live in approved lodgings and not in flats of their choice - a protective measure abandoned only in 1969, in the face of recommendations from a government committee that the legal age of majority should be lowered to eighteen. Anecdotal evidence told of women students living as far out as Wilmslow in Cheshire, 'the gateway to the south', as some of its reluctant inhabitants described that pleasant town. Students had long been accustomed to club together and take shared flats in which they lived communally. But there were ominous signs of a reduction in the number of large flats suitable for such treatment, as landlords realised that higher profits could be made by subdividing them into self-contained flatlets which would tend to isolate their single tenants and condemn them to loneliness.

The future now seemed to lie with forms of university residence which would be cheaper to build and could be constructed on a much more generous scale than the traditional halls. These new establishments would accord with the students' own desire for freedom from excessive regulation and from attempts to force upon them an *esprit de corps* which some were disinclined to share (one thinks of the practice in one hall of shackling to a radiator those who refused to conform and join in hall activities with sufficient zest). In June 1963 the University Council resolved to extend 'provided accommodation' in such a way as to include 40 per cent of the total student population, only to have their ace trumped by the UGC, which wanted the figure increased to 50 per cent. Statistics vouchsafed by the Registrar's department to *Manchester Independent* suggested that in 1962–63 4,692 students lived in lodgings or flats (56.3 per cent of the whole student body, including the Faculty of Technology); 1,691 in University hostels (20.3 per cent); and 1,950, including 412 women, at home (23.4 per cent). In November 1967 the Accommodation Office estimated that 53 per cent of students were now occupying lodgings or flats, whilst 31 per cent had places in University residences, and 16 per cent were living at home. Within five years, therefore, there had been a marked shift towards living in University accommodation, although it still fell far short of supplying the requisite 50 per cent of places.

To some extent the stock of places was increased by the old methods - by theological colleges and denominational establishments offering to make rooms available to University students or seeking licences as University halls or hostels. Greygarth, run by the vigorous Catholic movement Opus Dei, became a licensed hall in 1965, the local Baptist College in 1966. As a mark of the friendship between Mansfield Cooper and the Bishop, George Andrew Beck, the Roman Catholic diocese of Salford built Allen Hall on the Wilmslow Road in Fallowfield and applied to the University for a licence. Non-Catholics were admitted in the interests of establishing a heterogeneous community appropriate to a University, and a University Lecturer in Greek and Latin, D.M. Leahy, became the first warden when the hall opened in 1961. Hulme Hall, the largest Anglican foundation, followed St Anselm and Langdale into University ownership in 1962, and its accommodation was greatly extended and improved in the course of the next five or six years.

Less conventionally, the Essex Hotel, opposite the Infirmary on Oxford Road, all bedrooms equipped with washbasins and running water (a luxury by the standards of the time), acquired the new name of Grove House and from October 1964 began to offer accommodation to seventy-one students, postgraduates and undergraduates of at least three years' standing. It may well have been the most short-lived University residence on record, for it fell at the end of the session 1972–73 to make way for the so-called Southern Area development of student flats. But while it lasted it was run very successfully by its managers, Mr and Mrs Jack Lever, for an international student clientele, and more than twenty nations were represented among its residents at the time of its demise.

There was at least one generous private initiative, undertaken when in 1962 members of the Economics Faculty, concerned for the welfare of their many overseas students, clubbed together and contributed a substantial sum of money. When a donation from Lady Simon was added, this amounted to about £3,000 and was devoted to purchasing a row of old houses on Moss Lane East and refurbishing them in such a way as to create a small University residence, called Sunningdale. The British Council donated a further £9,000 to the scheme, and the hostel received at its inception about twenty-five students, including five married couples, one with a child. Optimists claimed another 'Manchester first', the first mixed hall of residence in the country, but the claim collapsed in the face of the information that Crombie Hall at Aberdeen had been mixed since it opened a few years before.

There was one loss to set against these and other gains, since Montgomery House, the YMCA hostel, felt obliged to surrender its licence at the end of the session 1965–66. For economic reasons its management had been driven to reduce the number of rooms rented to University students from about a hundred to about forty, and to let the rest to other kinds of resident who were in a position to pay a higher weekly fee and to occupy their rooms throughout the calendar year. Overtaken by more modern halls of residence, the management were attracting fewer conferences to fill their rooms during vacations, and could now repair their finances only by ceasing to be a University residence.

High-rise building, designed to make the maximum use of a site by piling floor after floor of bed-sitting rooms, bathrooms, sanitation and other amenities upon the smallest possible concentration of valuable urban land, accounted for the largest additions to the stock of available places. Plans for the Refectory Residence Tower (afterwards named the Moberly Tower) and for the Fallowfield Student Village (renamed Owens Park) preceded the Robbins call for expansion, but helped to contain its results. The Moberly was very much a dormitory and nothing more; its occupants, who were postgraduates and senior undergraduates, were expected to descend to the refectory in search of meals and to the nearby Union in search of entertainment and other comforts. By contrast the Student Village was consciously planned as an experiment in a new way of living for students and their mentors, a compromise between the community life of a traditional hall and the unsupervised freedom of a flat. True, the name seemed incongruous, since villages generally sprawl on the ground, and the most prominent landmark in Fallowfield was now to be a tower of nineteen storeys which looked from certain angles like a gigantic robot standing sentinel over the surrounding suburb. It was far more domineering than the spire of any parish church. It could be said that Fallowfield itself was the village, and Owens Park an urban intrusion upon its character. Better provided with trees, parks and gardens than were most Manchester suburbs, Fallowfield had been strongly connected with education before the brash tower was erected. It included the High School for Girls, the Grammar School, Withington Girls' School (then in Mauldeth Road), the famous Princess Christian College for smart nursery nurses, and Ashburne Hall, the senior women's residence of the University. Whereas, when expanding on the Oxford Road site, the University had grown largely at the expense of streets of run-down housing, in Fallowfield it displaced, to the distress of local people, some gracious houses and gardens. It also paved the way towards new and not altogether welcome developments almost entirely geared to the convenience of young people who would reside in the place for only about half the year.

Plans drawn up by George Grenfell Baines, the founder of the Building Design Partnership, first received wide publicity in 1960. They provoked some gloomy predictions that the social life of the University would suffer from the creation of alternative foci away from its principal centre of gravity. 'Overall, the effect would be to further disperse students into conflicting academic and social units', grumbled a columnist in News Bulletin. There was some muttering about the authorities' supposed fondness for 'white-tiled Oxbridges', giving voice to a fear that if Fallowfield succeeded these outposts might begin to spread.

For all this the Village had little in common with any college in an ancient university. It embodied a number of radical ideas. Although divided into separate blocks for men and women, it could be described as a mixed hall. There would be up to five canteens, each offering a different menu, and no question of everyone sitting down simultaneously after hearing a grace said. There would be resident tutors, but no warden in the conventional sense, as there was even in the Moberly Tower. Instead, there would be a Chairman of Tutors, and the administration would be based, like the American constitution, on a separation of powers: the Manager would be directly responsible to the University's Bursar, the Chairman of Tutors to the Senate, and neither would be in charge of the other. Intended as a male preserve, the tower block was designed to accommodate 388 men students and eight tutors. Also included in the first stage of the project was a quadrangle surrounded by a more squat and conventional four-storey building for 276 women students and six tutors. Other buildings, including offices, an assembly hall and a library, were to serve the whole site. Further residential blocks were to be added in such a way as to increase the capacity of the Village to 1,400 students. To soften this move towards a mass society, students were to be divided into small, manageable units, grouped around kitchens, bathrooms, lavatories, and pantries for boiling kettles and making snacks. A large group of about forty to fifty students would form a 'house', looked after by a tutor, or a married couple, in an adjacent flat, living among them not as housemasters or housemistresses in a public school, but as firsts among equals. Tutors would not necessarily be academics: young professional people who were graduates of the University working in the city would do just as well. Since male and female students were allowed to visit each other until midnight, cynics slanderously dubbed the place the largest licensed brothel in Europe.

The spirit of Owens Park, which opened in October 1964, was frankly experimental, and opinions differed as to how far these unconventional arrangements could hope to create a sense of community out of such vast numbers. One optimist, writing in *Staff Comment*, felt that a communal spirit was at last beginning to hatch when the warm weather arrived in the summer of 1965 'and the student body entered into its heritage, sunbathing on the lawns and - regrettably - spilling over on to those of Ashburne next door'. Most students were contented enough, though the great tower lent itself to imaginative and sometimes pessimistic interpretation. It could well be portrayed as a disturbing symbol of the transformation of the University itself into a mechanical institute for higher mass education and professional or vocational training, in which individual sensibilities might all too easily be drowned. One reaction, admitted not to be typical, was reported as follows to *Manchester Independent*: 'I stayed in Fallowfield Tower for almost a year, near the top. Some mornings I would look out over the village and watch the buses going up to University, and students pouring out of the building with their briefcases … When I turned round, saw the cube I lived in, heard the sounds of a hundred others getting up, it made me feel like a piece of regulated machinery … When you find yourself inserted into a little niche like that, you want to crumble it all up in your hands, the whole damn knowledge factory, the lot … '

As on Oxford Road, there were architectural and social casualties on the Fallowfield site, symbolic of the passing of the old order. Somewhat to its embarrassment, in 1966 the University found itself demolishing Barcombe House, which had been built by its own Victorian architect, Alfred Waterhouse, for his own occupation. In response to belated protests, it rescued certain portrait busts from the threatened structure. Building plans also levelled Donner House, a Victorian residence beloved of University bachelors, male and female, confirmed or otherwise. As Joyce Boucher, long a resident of Fallowfield, remembers, Sir Edward Donner had been a popular local figure in the

1930s, much given to inviting passers-by to come in and admire his beautiful garden. Occupants of Donner House were told that if they still hankered after the communal life it was open to them to become tutors in a hall of residence; some of them did so, but others preferred to form a housing trust with a view to purchasing another place of their own, near Needham Hall in Didsbury. Among the stalwarts of Donner House, as the geologist Jack Zussman recalls from his own experience of living there, were the economic historian T.S. Willan and a mathematician, Professor Mahler, themselves monumental figures. Willan, a considerable scholar who made his name as a historian of early modern transport, liked to boast that he had once been the longest-serving assistant lecturer in the University's history, and that during the war he had taught every course in the History Department. Mahler's motto, lugubrious and tinged with foreboding, was 'All change is for the worse.'

For better or for worse, responding with the most honourable intentions to strongly stated national need, the University had embarked on a period of rapid change and been carried forward by currents not of its own making, on which it did its best to float. Much of its physical appearance had changed beyond recognition, being transformed into something more hygienic, more sterile, more forbidding, further distanced both physically and psychologically from the city which surrounded it. Sheer increases in numbers, changes in the age structure of the academic body, the advent of many people at all levels who had not been imbued with the traditional values of a university community and regarded the place as stuffy, remote and impersonal: all these things seemed to demand drastic changes of attitude and organisation as the University adapted to enforced changes of scale and struggled to maintain its intellectual eminence in a world now densely populated with competing institutions.

7

Innovation and reform

Since the Robbins Committee had been empowered to range across the whole field of higher education, their report proved to be much more than a series of statistical projections and exhortations to accept more students. They took positions on most of the issues which were most strenuously debated during the 1960s: on the importance of teaching in relation to research, on that of tutorials, of broader under-graduate courses, of communication and consultation, of the role in making policy of academics who were not professors. Most of their attitudes were liberal and progressive but not radical. They declared their faith in a stratified academic society, in the value of lectures, in the importance of retaining lay majorities on university councils, in the role of the UGC as a buffer between government and universities. Though determined to increase the number of young people receiving higher education, they held to the principle that access to it should still be regarded as a privilege. Students, they said, 'are under the obligation to make the best of their three or four years and to remember, as Milton did, that "Ease and leisure is given thee for thy retired thoughts out of other men's sweat"'. Though seeking to bring about moderate increases in the proportion of students reading science and engineering, they did enter a brief defence of the humanities. Weaken those more traditional disciplines, and the 'intellectual and spiritual life of the country' would suffer with them.

Particularly relevant to the University of Manchester were three recommendations of the report. It called, though not successfully, for the recognition of five favoured institutions to be called SISTERS, of which the College of Science and Technology would be one. It called for the foundation of two Business Schools, which would be attached to universities. On the strength of another report, compiled by Lord Franks, the Provost of Worcester College Oxford, one of those institutions was established in Manchester. And the Committee expressed a desire that some particularly able students in teachers' training colleges should take advantage of their colleges' affiliation to universities by embarking on four-year degree courses which their universities would oversee, and not contenting themselves with less prestigious qualifications. Teaching would become, increasingly, a graduate profession, and begowned and belettered masters and mistresses would no longer be largely confined to public and grammar schools.

SISTERS was an acronym for Special Institutions for Scientific and Technological Education and Research. Inspired by Sir Patrick Linstead, the Rector of Imperial College, who formed part of the highly effectual inner ring within the Robbins Committee, they would have been the United Kingdom's equivalent to such prestigious establishments as the Massachusetts Institute of Technology or the Technical High Schools of Zurich and Delft. Three of them would have been developed from existing colleges in Manchester, London and Glasgow. But the Association of University Teachers, the academics' professional union, was soon questioning the wisdom of concentrating investment in this way and voicing its fears that the famous five would drain away postgraduates from elsewhere. Post-Robbins euphoria was beginning to evaporate by the beginning of 1965, by which time it was clear that SISTERS had been still-born. In an address delivered at the Manchester College of Science and Technology in March, Lord Robbins himself lamented the government's inconsistency in refusing 'to suggest that in any institution the quality of instruction and research may be superior to any other' – a sentiment wholly at odds with the fact that they still regarded teachers' training colleges as second-rate institutions. Unwilling to remain a mere college when so many others were becoming universities, Bowden's institution sought a new title and came close to acquiring the somewhat plaintive name of MUIST, which might have suggested a newly discovered Scottish island. From this fate it was rescued by Vincent Knowles's insistence, backed by a Privy Council official, that the proper title of the University of Manchester be used and it become UMIST instead: the University of Manchester Institute of Science and Technology. The concordat of 1905 would continue to govern the relationship between the two establishments and they would continue to use and jointly develop 'special facilities and resources'. Some members of the Science Faculty disliked the implication in the title that this was a more advanced concern than their own and one exclusively concerned with graduate education. But they did not press their objection. Fortunately, perhaps, the same principle was not consistently applied in devising names; Manchester University Press, for example, escaped the obligation to call itself UMP.

Like technical institutes, business schools were designed to be directly useful to economic development. Their aim, as Lord Franks defined it, was 'to increase competence in managers or those who will be managers'. They originated in the belief on the part of industrialists and traders that practical experience gathered in the course of doing a job was not enough. Business schools, argued Franks, should be located in universities, which alone could guarantee them the necessary academic respectability. Since the Middle Ages the universities of Europe had been providing vocational training for the professions, for lawyers, physicians, and (he might well have added) clergymen: why not, then, for the managers of the late twentieth century? Robbins recommended that business schools should be erected in old-established universities and not in new ones, Franks that they be placed in thriving centres of industry and commerce and not secreted, like the Administrative Staff College at Henley, in country houses. Business schools should provide 'framework knowledge' in the form of applied economics, sociology and psychology, and they should also concentrate directly on developing the skills and techniques of management, on 'logical methods of analysing and presenting information for decision'. Franks himself entertained no illusions about the natural compatibility of businessmen with university teachers, since businessmen were fearful that universities, left to themselves, would turn out 'scholars and not men better fitted for management'. Businessmen would naturally prefer short and intensive courses which would remove their employees from their places of work for the shortest possible time; academics could not, in the short time available, pretend to work miracles. 'This mutual uneasiness, if unchecked and not cured,' warned Franks, 'could spread through a Business School like dry rot through timber.' Industrialists would wish a school to concentrate on people, generally aged between about twenty-eight and thirty-five, who already had some experience; universities would naturally think in terms of longer courses for recent graduates. It was important that a school should make a success of both, and be prepared to accept on both types of course aspirants who had never taken a first degree.

The University of Manchester was a strong candidate for the honour of establishing a business school. It already possessed a centre for business research, established in the Economics Faculty and involving such firms as ICI, Unilever and Shell-Mex. This unit was designed to study

some of the major decisions of business, including those on investment; to examine methods of acquiring the information on which
those decisions relied; to consider the possible uses of mathematical
and statistical techniques in arriving at them. Supra-departmental and
supra-faculty organisations, often called schools, were becoming fashionable. By the beginning of 1963 the University had established one,
styled MANSMAN (the Manchester School of Management and
Administration), which was designed to co-ordinate activities in the
Faculties of Economics and of Technology. Negotiations proceeded
between the Federation of British Industries, the British Institute of
Management, and the Treasury concerning the establishment of business schools which would be financed partly through the University
Grants Committee and partly through contributions from business
itself. A working party appealed for not less than £3 million By October 1964 it was possible to report to the University Senate that £4.6
million had already been raised; the figure was expected to pass £5 million by the time that the appeal closed in December.

Somewhat uneasily, the School, officially known from 1967 as the
Faculty of Business Administration, was established neither as an ordinary faculty of the University nor as an institution related to it, as was
UMIST, by concordat. A strange hybrid, it was, or became within a
few years, a faculty equipped with a Council presided over by the
Vice-Chancellor and consisting of eight members of the Senate and
eight representatives of industrial employers. The businessmen
involved would not necessarily be local or regional figures, who had
acclimatised themselves gradually, as had a Streat, a Kenyon or a
Symons, to the foibles of academics. Rather, they were people of
national standing who might well become impatient with the University's manner of conducting affairs. It remained to be seen whether
business and university interests could be reconciled and Lord
Franks's dry rot be forestalled in such a way as to allow a genuine partnership between an odd couple to develop and flourish. By the
autumn of 1967 the degree of Master in Business Administration had
been established. In the autumn of 1968 the School registered fifty-
five students. It was, and remained, an essentially masculine concern.
Only three women were enrolled as students in 1968–69, and that
number remained pretty constant from year to year while the number
of men students continued to grow. In 1972–73, 149 men were
enrolled to three women.

In the years to come the Business School was in the University but
not quite of it, though a Registrar's man, Mike Buckley, a graduate in

Economics who had worked in insurance and industry, was sent to keep an eye on the School. Grigor McClelland, the first Director of the School, had been managing director of a chain of supermarkets in the North East, Laws Stores, and had recently held a Senior Research Fellowship in Management Studies at Balliol College Oxford. Established at first in Hilton House, near Piccadilly, the Business School moved in the early 1970s to specially designed premises at the north of the Education Precinct, flanking Booth Street West. Since the building had been paid for out of funds raised by the original appeal, nobody knew for certain whether it belonged to the University or the School, and a case could be made out for either proposition. Some members of the institution would have liked to develop it as a limited company which would keep its own profits and award its own degrees.

As Mike Buckley remembers, the School found it hard to content itself with the modest support which the University provided. It provoked resentment by demanding the right to employ high-powered personal assistants and pay them more generously than secretaries in other parts of the University. Problems arose over promotions. The Business School wanted its prodigies to be given accelerated advancement, often on the strength of work not regarded as grounds for promotion in other parts of the University. Leading lights of the Business School were not researchers and publishers in the normal sense, but people who had risen in industry and then taken to teaching in order to communicate to others the benefits of their experience. Solutions, however, were found when the Business School succeeded in devising titles of its own, by appointing various kinds of Fellow and by moving individuals from one kind of Fellowship to another which would carry higher rewards and status, or by creating additional part-time posts, each dignified by a suitable title and rewarded by a generous honorarium. To speak of fellowship was quite appropriate, for the Business School's building was designed very differently from others, and was intended to enable teachers and students to eat and drink with each other, social life merging with academic life, and to build up a rapport appropriate to a graduate school.

The Robbins Report was concerned, not only with scientific, technological and business education, but also with increasing the proportion of graduate teachers. In the early 1960s the normal way of becoming a graduate teacher was to take an honours or general degree at the University and then spend a fourth year pursuing a postgraduate certificate in the Department of Education. Should not those who had enrolled in teachers' training colleges – now to be styled Colleges of Education – enjoy similar opportunities? The University would still be the guardian of degree standards, and would still stop short of granting an honours degree to those who had trained in the School of Education – an organisation which, by 1957, comprised ten affiliated colleges and 6,000 students. Proposals approved by Senate in 1966 introduced a new four-year course leading to the degree of Bachelor of Education, which was to be constructed on much the same lines as the general degree in Arts. No First, Second or Third Classes would be awarded, but exceptionally good candidates would receive distinctions. Promising students at the colleges could be recognised as degree candidates at any time up to the end of their first year. They would study Education throughout the course; the rest of their time would in large measure be devoted to subjects already taught in the Faculties of Arts and Science. But syllabuses, reflecting the capabilities and interests of teachers in the colleges, would have to be specially designed for them. University teachers were to be involved for several years to come in approving proposed courses and the University would be expected to provide its own assessors to work with the colleges' examiners and ensure that they were applying proper standards. There were certain difficulties. Were subjects such as Rural Studies, Housecraft, and Art and Design, which were taught in the colleges and essential to many teachers, really appropriate to a university degree course? It was decided that they should not be taught and examined in the final, degree-giving year, but could be offered at earlier stages of the course. Physical Education enjoyed a more honourable status, and survived as an option in the final year.

If all the interests involved in the degree were to be properly represented, it would be necessary to create a huge Board of Studies with no less than forty-five members and lengthy meetings would ensue. The University would exercise influence over the colleges through representation on their governing bodies, through some control over appointments and promotions, through the power to give or withhold recognition of departments as fit to supervise degree work. Like some local version of the Grants Committee, the University would conduct 'visitations' of the colleges every three to five years. These were not to be inspections, but rather opportunities to meet staff and students, to discuss problems, and to collaborate over future plans.

One complaint concerning the new arrangements, which surfaced within the first five years, was that the colleges were not ruthless enough in selecting their degree candidates. Out of charity, or sloppiness, or incurable optimism, or a mixture of all three, they allowed too many indifferent candidates to have a go – a form of indulgence not entirely at odds with the spirit of Robbins, but very time-consuming for the University teachers who had to oversee the process. Peter Lowe, a conscientious historian, wrote that at the outset no more than 10 per cent of students in the colleges were supposed to attempt degree work, but some colleges had bumped up the proportion to 25 per cent. The failure rate was high, and University teachers in popular subjects such as History carried a heavy burden. Lowe estimated in 1970–71 that approximately 20 per cent of his time during term had to be devoted to the examining process in the colleges, and understandably complained that neither he nor his fellow assessors received recognition for the work they did – not even in the form of relief from other tasks.

The University might be exercising control over teachers' training. But it could be said uncharitably that the University itself consisted in part of a large corpus of professional academics who had never received any formal training in the difficult art of presenting lectures or conducting tutorials, and had, like managers in the days before business schools, learnt everything they knew, or failed to learn what they obviously did not know, by practising the job. There was also a body of students, seven or eight times as large, who treated the 'staff' warily and kept their distance, but dreamed at intervals of closer and friendlier relations. As the historian Penry Williams remarked, the very phrase 'staff–student relations', so much part of Manchester's vocabulary, implied something tense and uneasy, perhaps even, like 'industrial relations', a modified form of class war between workers and management.

It had, perhaps, been generally assumed, in Manchester more than in Oxford, that the primary purpose of the University was to add to knowledge. But the great expansion of the 1960s brought funding to universities on the assumption that they would devote much of their energy to educating young people, and called for competent undergraduate teaching. Short training courses for new university lecturers were contemplated during the 1960s and actually introduced towards the end of the decade. One of the functions of the new Audio-visual Service, planned in 1965, was to bring university lecturers (and students of education and drama) face to face with video recordings of their public performances. These, it was hoped, would make them aware of their more disconcerting mannerisms and their more glaring deficiencies of technique. Those who habitually stood on one leg and mumbled at the blackboard would at least know they were doing it, even if they did little to kick the habit. Official training for new arrivals was not very prolonged, but at least an effort was made where there had been none before. Training was to consist of a 'residential session' or 'conference' which would last for two or three days at the start of the academic year. Attenders would form 'syndicates' of ten or fifteen persons, and meet together monthly during the Michaelmas and Lent terms to compare notes and discuss such matters as voice production and the use of overhead projectors.

Robbins and his colleagues attached much importance to tutorials – not the one-to-one encounters between don and undergraduate favoured by Oxford and by some Cambridge colleges, but small discussion groups involving only a few students. Their report called for written work to be regularly presented, criticised and returned, and for students to be taught to think rather than crammed with specialised information which they were then required to regurgitate. Indeed, the committee favoured the introduction of broader courses, which in their view were often more demanding than sharply focused single honours degrees, and the recognition of such courses as equally prestigious undertakings. Much of the most detailed and complex information could more appropriately be acquired through postgraduate studies. If students learnt to be mentally agile and adaptable, and learnt how to learn, the country need not fear the unemployed graduate. Furthermore, the Robbins Committee advised that universities should, in their promotion exercises, recognise distinction in teaching and not make every kind of advancement depend on research and publication. The status and material rewards bestowed upon a Reader, distinguished in research, should not be greater than those enjoyed by a Senior Lecturer, whose achievements might lie in another field.

Tutorials in Manchester had occurred patchily; they were favoured and well organised by some departments and not by others. Lectures had reigned as the supreme form of 'instruction' (to use the official, somewhat authoritarian term, which conjured up visions of physical or military training), and the compulsion to attend them had given rise to unedifying scenes. Sam Moore, who took a part-time degree in the Economics Faculty in the early 1960s, remembers the dogged performer who droned on inexorably for exactly fifty-five minutes while his audience, unable to absent themselves, ostentatiously read their copies of *The Guardian*. Impervious to disrespect, he would stop almost in mid-sentence when his time expired and resume at precisely the same point in his notes a couple of days later. In 1962, however, on the recommendation of a Senate committee, the compulsory lecture fell from its throne, in as much as departments were now permitted to decide 'whether they wish to require their staff to record lecture attendances or prefer to adopt other methods for making reports on the work and progress of students'.

Two years later, a University Education Research Project carried out a survey of teaching methods within the University. It was to include studies in depth of the teaching of languages and of statistics, and also of 'student motivation and problems'. Responses to the investigators' questionnaires suggested that all faculties retained their faith in the usefulness of lecturing, though only 75 per cent of respondents in Economic and Social Studies were in favour of it, as compared with well over 90 per cent in Science, Technology, and Arts. Most respondents applauded the notion that there ought to be tutorial groups of between one and four members meeting once a week. They were less convinced of the effectiveness of larger classes, though in practice these remained fairly common and departments could reasonably be suspected of not acting on their convictions and of dismissing the ideal as impracticable. An article by Martin Southwold, a social anthropologist, in *Staff Comment* for 1967 stated that classes of eight, 'miscalled tutorials', still prevailed throughout his own faculty and seemed to be common elsewhere. Between 60 per cent and 70 per cent of respondents replied 'Yes' to the question 'Are there adequate facilities for student–lecturer interaction in your present system?', with 24–8 per cent of them returning a firm 'No'. Between 87 per cent and 93 per cent approved of the principle that students ought to have advisers to assist them both with academic and with personal problems, only a minority believing that the same person should advise a student in both capacities. Those academics who were conscientious enough to return questionnaires seemed, therefore, to be affirming their faith in small discussion groups and in the importance of pastoral care. Arguably, the staff–student ratio was sufficiently favourable for both these things to be established if the will to do so existed.

It was perhaps unusual for students to have tutorials in all their courses and in all their years. But the tutorial spread gradually and became a shade more sophisticated and egalitarian. In History, for example, the essay class at its most traditional had consisted of several students intoning their essays in turn, with only the most perfunctory tutorial comments by way of *entr'acte*. One medievalist was notorious for opening and even answering his correspondence to beguile the time while this depressing ritual unfolded around him. But the practice of meeting to discuss a topic became more common, even if the planned tutorial, with prescribed reading lists and questions given out in advance for students to consider, still lay in the distant future. Academics with experience of Oxford and Cambridge inspired a strong tutorial system in the Physics Department. Lecturing brightened and gained in spontaneity after the arrival of Brian Flowers, formerly a civil servant at the Atomic Energy Research Establishment at Harwell. Finding to his alarm that one lecture course had been running in exactly the same form for fourteen years, the new professor established the principle that no one should lecture on the same topic for more than three years at a stretch. He himself lectured to the first year in a frankly experimental spirit, feeling his way as he went and inviting comment and criticism from his audience. Student verdicts on lectures were sought in the Physics Department and, to the horror of much of the rest of the University, published on notice-boards (comments on tutorials were to be invited only at a much later date, in the late 1980s). Tutorials spread to other parts of the Faculty of Science, reaching Electrical Engineering, for example, when a new joint degree with Physics was set up; it would hardly have been possible to arrange tutorials in one department and not the other.

Law teaching aimed consciously at making students articulate and combative, at enabling them to think on their feet and develop the skills of advocates. One of the Law professors, Harry Street, introduced a method of teaching into his course on torts which was common in prestigious American law schools but seldom found in England. As Margaret Brazier, who was a law student in the late 1960s, recalls, 'You were given cases to go and read before each lecture, and then he picked on students to analyse, debate and pull the cases apart, which was frightening but enjoyable!' She remembers, too, the advice given by Peter Bromley to members of debating societies: 'Always try and represent the side you don't agree with, so that you get used to doing that.' One medical student was astounded to discover that law students might actually be commended for disagreeing with their professors, so long as they proved able to defend their opinions. In the Law Faculty generally there came to be more emphasis on jurisprudence and the theoretical aspects of law, and less on the kind of law normally practised from day to day by solicitors.

When David Purdy arrived in 1968 as one of three new Assistant Lecturers in Economics, all of them fresh from the M.Sc. course at LSE, he was allotted only four hours' teaching a week. Three of them were spent with the same group of first-year students, and he had the task of taking them through the assigned textbook from beginning to end. This was 'an excellent system of getting the basics of economics into students', so long as it could be afforded, as for a brief time it could (it was abandoned three or four years later in favour of one or two lectures a week plus a weekly tutorial).

Manchester students' rights to a system of personal supervision, which would bring out to the full their personal capabilities, were passionately upheld by Martin Southwold. He objected at length to the opinion of his 'learned seniors' that 'Manchester students are much inferior academically to Cambridge students; that our students are mostly II.2s; that they mostly come from working-class homes; and that therefore the supervision system is not suitable for our students.' Even if this were true – and it was not – these points were irrelevant, because supervision was the best form of education 'for II.2s, and indeed any students', and it would be reprehensible to perpetuate the legendary superiority of Oxford and Cambridge by contriving to ensure that Manchester students continued to seem inferior. 'Arguments produced in defence of our system remind me very much of those produced in defence of South Africa's Bantu Education Act. In both cases the alleged inferiority of certain kinds of people is produced as grounds for giving them inferior education … '

University education, its aims and techniques, were eagerly debated during the 1960s by voluntary organisations such as the University Dialogue Society, which drew on all levels of the hierarchy and attracted newly arrived professors, such as the sociologist Peter Worsley from Hull and the botanist David Valentine from Durham. Another such body was the University Teachers' Group, which had grown out of the Christian Frontier Council and the Student Christian Movement. One of their recorded discussions appeared – despite the policies pursued in the Physics Department – to reveal strikingly different opinions concerning teacher–student relations in an Arts and in a Science Faculty. For the scientists felt that the teacher–student relationship which existed in schools rested upon an adult–child relationship which could not be repeated at a university. In their opinion only a tiny proportion of students gained from close contact with a teacher, and it would not be practicable to reform teaching methods for the sake of so small a minority. Arts academics, quite the other way, held that the best teaching depended on the creation of a person-to-person relationship (not to be confused with an adult–child relationship), and that learning could only be pursued in an environment in which student problems of every kind received attention. Arts people saw a close connection between the learning process and that of becoming socially mature. Scientists did not; what counted for them was intellectual maturity, and in disciplines such as mathematics this quality bore no relation to social maturity. In Arts eyes there was no advantage in a close link between the subjects taught and the later careers of students, but Arts folk held that 'the general attainment of literacy is a factor of great social importance, and thus must be taken into account in assessing the success of any course'. Scientists held more prosaically that few if any would take a science subject at a university 'just for the attainment of numeracy', and that almost all student in the field would look to their subjects to advance their careers. Scientists, therefore, were inclined to believe that the impersonality of teaching was actually a virtue, and not merely a sorry consequence of the size of the University.

Sporadic action followed the endless debates about methods of improving relationships between teachers and students. Some believed that increased social contact would help to foster relaxed intellectual relationships, while others groaned at the prospect of small talk over sherry or, more likely, coffee between embarrassed, tongue-tied students and dutiful but ill-at-ease academics. Professor and Mrs Flowers, who disposed of half a large house, had children close to student age and knew their musical tastes, were able to entertain the student physicists in style and get them after the party to hoover up the mess they had made. In a friendly article in *News Bulletin,* Peter Campbell of the Department of Government urged that invitations should not flow only in one direction. Students should treat lecturers as equals and invite them on to their own ground: if their flats were sordid, they might prove to be an added attraction, for '*la nostalgie de la boue* is widespread even among respectable family men'. He added, however, that people got to know one another effectively not through superficial social contacts but by working together, not just in academic situations but also in such enterprises as society meetings. There was much confusion as to whether 'staff' and 'students' were allowed to eat together in those upper rooms of the Refectory to which they were both admitted: if they sat on opposite sides of the restaurant, was it simply a matter of custom or the consequence of a rule enforced or perhaps invented by the Refectory staff, who had their own ideas about who should eat with whom?

There had long been an Adviser to Women Students whose responsibilities extended across the whole University, and the University was slow to abandon the principle that all women students must be interviewed by her, even if they had no specific problem to discuss. Like most good counsellors, Margaret Young sat and listened to those in difficulties, and heard about homesickness, money problems, and the sad experience of being jilted. The system of advice from a central point was to be extended to men only in the early 1970s, when the Central Academic Advisory Service was set up and Geoffrey North, the former Warden of St Anselm Hall, was appointed to join Dr Young. Meanwhile, some departments had begun to make more effort to provide advice on academic and personal difficulties, or just to take a wider interest in the students in their charge.

'Moral tutors' or 'supervisors', charged with taking a general interest in the well-being of the students assigned to them, appeared in some parts of the University – in Social Sciences, in the honours school of Politics and Modern History which spanned Oxford Road, in the Department of History itself. Here Albert Goodwin, the gentle Professor of Modern History, had wept at the news that a student in his department had died and that nobody had realised the fact. Some holders of tutorial office were a trifle too eager to demonstrate their worldliness and liberalism, others a shade too sardonic. 'Don't tell me. I know – you're pregnant!' cried a tutor in Social Anthropology, called upon by Anna Ford and ready for high drama. 'No, I just wanted to ask if I could change a course.' A tutor telephoned a student in an Arts department: 'I'm meant to be your Moral Tutor. Are you still a virgin? I'm not sure what sort of questions I'm meant to ask you.' These remarks produced what may have been the desired effect – after that, says the pupil thirty years later, 'I wouldn't have gone to him with a splinter in my finger.'

Whatever the virtues or faults of their formal arrangements, some departments managed to create within their own boundaries a strong sense of community which embraced everyone. As Pip Cotterill remembers, most of the teachers in American Studies were only five to seven years older than their students, who were still few in numbers, and very ready to mix with them socially. Anna Ford, arriving in 1963 to read Social Anthropology, was delighted to experience in Dover Street a sense of joining an intellectual family: 'If you'd been given a place here, you were a very special person ... there was not a great deal of talk about how we were going to be expected to work, but just that you were immediately part of a community of people interested in economics, politics, sociology, anthropology, and treated as an equal straight away.' Having heard a bright American student swear picturesquely at the tutor who had dared to award a B for her essay, and seen that the victim rather took to the woman who had cursed him, she concluded happily that 'this is grown-up life ... you can say what you like and be what you want to be'. There was pride, too, in joining an enterprise which was 'thinking about what was going on in life today', and making, for example, a study of Manchester United supporters, 'who, they felt, after the Munich air crash in '58, had a particular sort of loyalty which lasted through any form of crisis, be it being bottom of the Division or losing all their players'.

It might have seemed, to put it crudely, that scientists were primarily researchers and Arts people primarily teachers, while social scientists managed to combine the two. Could certain parts of Arts, particularly those concerned with the appreciation of literature, be expected to break new ground in the same fashion as the research teams at their laboratory benches to the east of Oxford Road, or as the red-scarved fieldworkers following a football team? Was literary criticism comparable with scientific discovery? A moving obituary of Desmond Patrick Costello, Professor of Russian Studies, who had died suddenly in 1964, said of him that 'his idea of happiness was and always had been to make his students see the greatness of certain great writers; if these happened to be Russian writers rather than Latin or French or Italian, it was because he felt there was room in this sphere for someone who was interested in books as books and not as documents ... He never thought of himself except as an intermediary between the great and the young – between the uniqueness of a solitary genius and the untrained enthusiastic minds entrusted to our care.' His motto, recalled a colleague in the Arts Faculty, recognising in him a fine classicist as well as a Slavonic scholar, was 'that if people do not enjoy what you are teaching, you may as well give up'. Brian Cox, who joined the English Department as a professor in 1966, believes that his own greatest achievements lay in teaching and extramural work – in running the journal *Critical Quarterly*, famous in the late 1960s for outspoken comments on the fashionable educational theories which allegedly undermined educational standards in the country; in using the journal to organise huge Sixth Form conferences; in founding the Poetry Centre, which brought Auden, Hughes and others to Manchester to give readings of their work. 'I saw my job,' he recalls, as being 'to help my students to understand and enjoy great literature more than they did when they arrived.' Bob Burchell, who joined the Department of American Studies in 1965, remembers spending about five years in the University before becoming involved in the research which eventually led him to a chair. The delights of being a tutor in St Anselm Hall, a source of at least a dozen lasting friendships ('like having another student life without any essays'), proved to be more alluring. Some of his colleagues never developed the habit of producing scholarly books or articles, although they included, in Richard Francis, a distinguished novelist who also became a teacher of creative writing.

The impression could easily arise that Arts academics were at best scholars rather than researchers. This reputation was likely to cost them dear in the future in a system of financing universities where research was highly rewarded. However, the Arts Faculty was so mis-cellaneous as to defy glib generalisation. The Professors of Philosophy, Dorothy Emmet, the architect of the post-war department, and Arthur Prior, the world-famous logician, were prolific writers. History was a disciplined subject in which new discoveries could constantly be made. Even here, however, the professors did not urge junior col-leagues to publish in the way that Mackenzie of Government had done. Inclined to keep government and administration firmly in their own hands, they were remarkably *laissez-faire* in their attitudes to the interests of assistant lecturers, whom they had appointed primarily to teach certain courses. During the 1960s academics indifferent to pro-motion could and did neglect publication. Since some subjects were more popular than others with undergraduates, and left their practi-tioners less time for research, there was an understandable desire that good teaching should contribute to promotion – though few people had clear ideas of how to measure it, save in a highly impressionistic way. There was no applause for an inept attempt by a national body, the Prices and Incomes Board, in 1969, to introduce special salary awards as a monetary consolation prize for those who were good at teaching but not at research. Winston Barnes, the former Vice-Chan-cellor of Liverpool University, who had resigned over the issue and become a hero of the AUT, alighted briefly on a Manchester perch as Sir Samuel Hall Professor of Philosophy. It was considered very wrong to treat teaching as an activity which deserved only extra money and not enhanced status.

Throughout the 1960s universities were urged to serve the national interest by increasing the number of places in science and engineering. But student demand did not always lie in this direction, and it was now not the natural but the social sciences that appealed most strongly to prospective students. Aspirants with good A-levels competed for places in Arts in Manchester while vacancies occurred in Science, Engineer-ing and Technology. Norman Atkinson, an active member of the

Labour Party who had been chief designer in the Engineering Department at Manchester, publicly regretted the fact in his maiden speech in the Commons in 1964, after his election as member for Tottenham, and called upon careers teachers to take note and remedy the situation. Senate in 1965 heard the suggestion that prospective applicants might perhaps be deterred from attempting to read science in Manchester by a new requirement to pass an examination in the use of English. But, as a report of Senate proceedings phrased it, 'After being assured that those who failed plumbed depths of illiteracy which awed their examiners, Senate was not inclined to regret the new requirement.' As John Willmott (then Director of the Physical Laboratories) suggests, one reason for the lower level of accomplishment on the part of applicants to read Physics was the retirement of a generation of brilliant science teachers; these had entered school teaching between about 1929 and 1935, when opportunities to teach at higher levels were few indeed. Their successors proved less good at the job of preparing their pupils to embark on the journey towards degrees.

Student preferences aroused some disquiet. In 1967 the UGC disarmingly conceded 'that a University has other objectives besides providing Industry with ready-made recruits', but nevertheless urged universities to make 'a further deliberate and determined attempt to gear a larger part of their "output" to the economic and industrial needs of the nation'. Lord Bowden seemed to have absorbed some of the fashionable theories about the role of 'alienated intellectuals' in bringing about revolutions or introducing totalitarian regimes. In a speech to the governors of UMIST in 1968 he warned of a possible decline in manufacturing industry and a countervailing growth in the number of unemployable, vocal and discontented graduates in social studies, who might well find themselves with no economy to study, argue about or administer, and seek consolation in extremist political activity, whether of the Left or of the Right.

During the 1960s two powerful figures in the Science Faculty, Brian Flowers and the distinguished chemist Geoffrey Gee, attempted to bridge the gulf between two cultures – if not between science and the humanities, then between science and the social sciences. Since science and technology were expected to make so vital a contribution to the regeneration of the national economy, those who dominated politics, administration or the media should have a genuine understanding of them and of the social and economic implications of scientific advances and undertakings. Such people should not be learned specialists in a particular science. Rather they should represent a new kind of generalist who knew how scientists thought and could act as 'intellectual brokers' between specialists and laymen. The country needed an alternative to the old-style Oxford Greats scholar, educated in ancient languages, literature and philosophy, and perhaps even to the new-style student of 'Modern Greats', exposed to philosophy, politics and economics. Both should give room to a new race of pundits who had read what was unofficially termed Science Greats and officially Liberal Studies in Science. As Flowers told a meeting of Staff Forum in 1964, 'There would be a growing need for speakers, publicists, journalists and civil servants, teachers and industrial managers to interpret a technological society to itself ... Briefly, they would be people capable of reasoning, using the scientific method.' It was important to establish a balanced and integrated course, which did not consist simply of juxtaposed fragments from different disciplines. As the Professor of Liberal Studies in Science, F.R. Jevons, explained after the admission of the first batch of a dozen students in October 1966, 'Slightly more than half the time is devoted to the content of science. For the rest, science is regarded as an object of enquiry in itself. It has to be looked at in a number of ways, including the economic, sociological, historical and philosophical.'

'Science Greats' embodied many of the 1960s ideals captured in the Robbins Report – especially the desire for broader courses, based heavily on tutorials, essay-writing and discussion, which would overcome the constraints of rigid departmentalism and teach students how to think. It proved to be a qualified success and ran for several years before being converted into a postgraduate activity. One flaw, perhaps the most serious, was the fact that most of the students never succeeded in acquiring a deep enough understanding of science: it was easier to write about it glibly than to display any real knowledge of it. 'I know that I found the essay writing very irritating because they were writing about scientific subjects and they just didn't know science,' as Lord Flowers, now Chancellor of the University, recalls. Had they been inspired by the scientific teaching, they would probably have wanted to dedicate themselves entirely to the study of science. The prestige of specialism and the persistence of distinctive, mutually exclusive cultures in British universities were difficult to eradicate. But in February 1970 two contributors to *Manchester Independent* pleaded for the introduction of courses on 'Science and Society' into all degrees in the Faculty of Science.

During the 1960s the University had demonstrated beyond doubt its willingness to be adventurous in certain intellectual areas and to exploit its position as a seasoned institution located in a great centre of business and commerce. Some enthusiasts would praise the increasing range and variety of subjects taught by universities, the increasing number of degrees conferred under their auspices; some critics would argue that these very things resulted in a loss of identity and direction on the part of universities themselves, an uncertainty of the values they were supposed to be promoting and defending. Other observers looked askance at the increasing emphasis on the social utility of universities and their domination by the needs of 'Industry', a term which appeared to refer to industrial capitalists and not to trade unions. Manchester University, since it was now the home of a Business School and still owed a great deal to the advice and expertise of industrialists serving on its own Council, was vulnerable to left-wing radical charges of propping up a capitalist world order and reflecting a corrupt society.

During the 1960s, too, genuine attempts had been made in several parts of the University to render teaching more inspiring and less pontifical, to make it less dependent on one-way communication and more so upon discussion and exchanges of views between teachers and taught. Many departments had been willing to adopt a less one-dimensional view of students, to see them as people who might have personal or social problems as well as academic difficulties. Ironically, perhaps, the strongest sense of community between lecturers and students tended to develop in those areas (the social sciences, the interdisciplinary courses) which the higher university authorities regarded with the deepest suspicion. Certain experiments in education tended, in the Vice-Chancellor's eyes, to produce instability in the University. He told the UGC, on a quinquennial visit in the late 1960s, that much student unrest had surely sprung from 'the attack on the traditional honours school and the advocacy of multi-disciplinary courses ... The traditional honours school in Manchester had not merely been a method of organising teaching. It had been much more. It had been a focus of loyalty, a centre of leadership; it had helped to keep impersonalisation at bay and it had fulfilled in a civic university some of the functions which in Oxbridge had been fulfilled by the Colleges.' It seemed that the price of innovation and expansion, even in an older university which retained much of its traditional machinery, might prove to be the shaking of the structures of authority and power in the University – not just the questioning of orthodoxy within the confines of a seminar.

8

Communication and constitutional changes

If the expanded University of the 1960s were to retain any sense of common identity, it had somehow to improve communication between high and low places and across the boundaries between faculties and departments. It must arrange for those who were not professors to enjoy representation on the organs which shaped University policy, and at least have the opportunity to hear their discussions. Towards 1960 the students were better placed than their teachers, in that they possessed a lively newspaper of their own, increasingly disrespectful and on the point of becoming libellous. But in 1959 a man of ideas, Samuel Devons, the Langworthy Professor of Physics, suggested persuasively to Senate that a monthly bulletin should be published for the purpose of disseminating 'information' of more than departmental interest to senior members of the University.

From the Devons proposal there emerged a journal called *Staff Comment*, designed for circulation to members of the academic staff and lay members of Council. It carried essays and reviews; accounts of their own more recondite activities by academics and administrators (from examinations officers to town planners and paper scientists); reports of the deliberations of Council and Senate, so long as anyone could be found to write them; summaries of addresses delivered to discussion groups and societies; résumés of the latest pronouncements of the AUT and the UGC; mutinous comments on and defences of the official positions on car parking and on the planning of the Precinct; and a lively correspondence on the proper meaning of the word 'sophisticated'. As in a school magazine, institutional absurdities could be satirised acceptably by resorting to parody. *Staff Comment* ran a series of Swiftian pieces, purporting to be the lately discovered correspondence of Lemuel Gulliver with his friend the Master of Judas College Cambridge, penned while visiting an academy which, though not wholly unlike the Academy of Projectors in *Gulliver's Travels*, bore a stronger resemblance to the University of

Manchester. The identity of the satirist was not disclosed. But when the tone of the magazine became increasingly acerbic, it published some outspoken criticisms of the University hierarchy and its doings which their authors were brave enough to sign. However, it could not claim to be a newspaper. As the editors explained in June 1967, there was an understanding 'that *Staff Comment* should never publish material in advance of any press release that might be made on the same subject', and members of the University were therefore more likely to receive information through the national press than through any University publication. As a monthly periodical, issued only in term time, the journal was unlikely to make any scoops.

Much of the uncertainty and bewilderment rife in the late 1960s was blamed on poor communication. There seemed to be no organised way of presenting the University's case or of informing the 'staff' how the 'authorities' (the senior administrators) were coping with student grievances and protests. In July 1967 the General Board (the assembly of all members of faculties) urged the University to establish an Information Service which would communicate both with Manchester academics and with the press, both local and national. For some time the University Development Committee invoked financial stringency and refused the request, to the General Board's 'profound disappointment'. By 1968, however, events were demonstrating the importance of putting out accurate press statements to save the University from misrepresentation concerning such matters as its alleged involvement in research for military purposes. Parsimonious optimists dreamed as usual of tackling the problem of communication without spending more money, but in October 1969 the Senate agreed to approve in principle 'a University newspaper to be edited professionally and to be produced at least fortnightly in term time'. The cost would be about £15,000 a year, less any revenue that might be raised from sales and advertising. By this time Senate was inclining to the view 'that it would be preferable to have a newspaper of lesser quality than to have no newspaper'. Philip Radcliffe, an experienced journalist who was then a producer in the University and UMIST Television Service, was appointed Communications Officer with effect from the beginning of 1971, and, as will be shown later, launched both a weekly news-sheet and a handsomely produced features magazine with the straightforward title *Communication*. It was desirable that good news about the University should reach the press and if possible drive out the bad news. Mansfield Cooper had long dreaded the ill-effects of student protest and student journalism upon public opinion, although he had lacked effective means of influencing the public's view of universities.

In the course of its investigations the Robbins Committee had received innumerable complaints about the excessive power of the professoriate and of its constitutional organ, the Senate, in civic universities. Manchester, which was not unique, maintained a caste-like division into professorial and non-professorial teaching staff. Professors enjoyed a virtual monopoly both of senatorial places and of middle management, in that they alone had final responsibility for running academic departments. Discontent, pronounced Robbins and his colleagues, was in part the product of growth. The ratio of senior to junior staff had once been much more even, but in 1961–62 only 12 per cent of the academic staff of universities were professors, and the prospect of attaining seniority oneself had become more remote. Some tasks undoubtedly ought to remain with professors, including the allocation of routine duties, appointments, promotions, and recommendations about individual salaries. But there was 'a large residue of matters, ranging from broad questions of policy and general methods of instruction to questions of syllabuses, on which there is no special reason to assume that the holders of chairs have a monopoly of wisdom ... '

One Manchester lecturer, the historian Gerald Aylmer, had put the case against the rigid stratification of academics in civic universities in Lord Simon's journal, *University Quarterly*, for 1958–59. He argued that professorial power as such was not the whole problem, for many professors never penetrated to the heart of an oligarchic system which depended on 'the complicated overlapping membership of committees, with certain professors' names recurring on most of the important ones'. Regrettable products of this system were unnecessary secrecy, empire-building (the enlargement of one's own department without regard to the general interests of the University) and log-rolling (the practice of trading favour for favour between colluding oligarchs who sat on the same committees). Students became aware of lecturers' ignorance of and inability to influence University policy. Lecturers, who were not introduced to responsibility gradually, were ill-fitted to take it up when they eventually secured their chairs in middle age. 'Some may have been schooled by their long apprenticeship and be safe men ... others may be all too eager to gratify the pent-up frustration of decades ... '

Levels of discontent with professorial rule varied dramatically from department to department in accordance with the professor's personality, age and inclinations, and to some extent with the nature of the subject. If the department was small, intimate, given to meeting daily over coffee or tea, and involved in fieldwork and collaborative enterprises, as in Geography, Geology or Archaeology, relations were often pleasingly informal. Kopal, the astronomer, did not gather his colleagues together and ask them what should be done next, but, as his secretary, Ellen Carling, remembers, he mucked in with them and asked no one to do things he would not do himself. Should a professor be seen on a dig emerging from a sleeping bag in a string vest (as was Barri Jones, 'Jones the trowel', made Professor of Archaeology a few years later), he lost no respect and was unlikely to be regarded as remote and unapproachable. Others, differently situated, successfully adopted a more grave and courtly style, as did Ben Wortley, an international lawyer attired for professorial duties in a barrister's black coat and striped trousers. Sam Moore remembers his own early days in a department of about a dozen academics. Here Jack Johnston, the first Professor of Econometrics in the University, 'wasn't a natural democrat, but generally speaking he got on with everybody and he would consult, but it was a bit hit-and-miss. If you happened to be in the corridor when he wanted your view then he would ask you. There wasn't any formality of departmental boards, that came a little bit later. We had no gripes.' Ian Smith, now Professor of Geotechnics, remembers that when resources were plentiful, as they were in the 1960s, and the Professors of Engineering under Jack Diamond's presidency were ready to vote on the spot whatever money was needed to finance a project, there was little inclination to complain or to call for a democratic structure. Under Brian Flowers and his colleagues the large Physics Department was run by a steering committee of professors, readers and senior lecturers, and newly arrived professors were expected to make an impression by the cogency of their arguments and not by trying to pull rank.

Practice could vary considerably even within the same multi-professorial department, should it be divided into sections responsible to different professors. Under the mild Albert Goodwin the modern historians reached decisions democratically about their teaching. The effort of driving a car took so much out of Goodwin that it acted upon him like a truth drug, and Iori Prothero, the young lecturer whom he regularly transported home to Heaton Moor, could get him to divulge almost any secret of state. Goodwin was astonished that nobody appeared to be surprised at the official announcement in 1967 that the new Professor of Modern History would be M.R.D. Foot. On the retirement in 1966 of Eugène Vinaver, who had built up the largest Department of French Studies in the country and helped to create the first Department of Comparative Literature in England, it was said of him that he treated students and junior colleagues 'as his equals, not with condescension, but in a genuine belief that age does not make any wiser and that youth is no obstacle to the possession of wisdom ... ' The ropes of power in the French Department were always close to his hand, but few would have wished it otherwise. Margaret Young says of Vinaver, 'I served him always with pleasure; he was always very nice to me. He was not always easy; he was Byzantine in his cleverness; he always got what he wanted from the hierarchy, but they didn't love him ... '

Many examples of benevolent and humane rule could be cited, but it was natural that members of the University should look for guarantees against petty despotism and indifference to progress. There was nothing in the University's constitution to compel a professor to consult. A small, one-professor department headed for thirty years by the same incumbent could easily sink into intellectual decline, especially if its lord became an administrator rather than an active scholar. Early in 1968, H.H. Huxley, fresh from a year spent in the more enlightened atmosphere of an American university, published in *Staff Comment* vigorous criticism of the Departments of Greek and Latin. Initiatives, he said, were being stifled by professorial vetoes exercised in a sadly unimaginative fashion, publication had declined, and students had ceased to pursue doctorates in Manchester. The departments were eccentrically run as separate entities, with the bizarre result that senior lecturers and readers were permitted to lecture in only one of the two languages, however great their accomplishment in both might be. A.S. Lodge, of the Department of Mathematics in UMIST, hastened to support Huxley and warned of the 'Feet-on-the-Mantelpiece Effect' which would surely result if no provision were made for rotating the headship of a department and if the members of that department had no say in selecting their chief. 'If, for decade after decade, initiative is discouraged and real responsibility denied, even the most vigorous are apt to lose heart and to become cynical, especially when they see no sign that any extra-departmental hierarchy will make any move to alter an impossible situation. Moreover, the head himself, whether from a feeling that he has lost the confidence of his staff or from an unjustified but nevertheless real feeling of inferiority born of his own declining research activity, is liable to react in increasingly arbitrary and autocratic ways.'

It was true that the presence of several professors in the same department was a partial safeguard against decay, and it was sometimes argued that a remedy lay in making more professorial appointments, with a view to rotating the headship. As Iori Prothero observes, 'Oligarchy is not the same as dictatorship.' However, rivalry and mutual dislike, an over-developed sense of territory or an outbreak of intergenerational conflict between entrenched professors and new arrivals could soon bring a department into grave disrepute. There was a strong case for constitutional reforms which would provide safeguards against misguided autocracy, give official standing to staff meetings in departments, and alter, albeit cautiously, the composition of the Senate. Though unjust to many professors, the images of the 'mediocrity in authority', mired in unchallengeable inertia, and of the silent, sycophantic senior academic, ever ready to endorse the Vice-Chancellor's proposals in Senate, were sufficiently plausible to need to be dispelled.

In the words of Lemuel, the satirist of *Staff Comment*, 'the cries of those who thought themselves oppressed were heard beyond the walls, a Visitation followed and, the government of the Academy being found directly contrary to that of the Kingdom as a whole, the Senate was charged to admit some of less than Professorial rank to its counsels'. He was doubtless referring to a broad hint dropped by Sir Keith Murray, the chairman of the UGC, on a visitation in 1961. In June 1962 the Senate approved proposals for effecting this modest concession to academic democracy. Henceforth one-fifth of the seats in Senate would be assigned to elected members. Holders of probationary appointments would still be excluded from the process, and would be entitled neither to stand for election nor yet to vote. Six constituencies were created, based on faculties and groups of faculties, and seats allocated to them in proportion to the size of the electorate in each group. The last old-style meeting of the Senate, virtually confined to professors, took place on 30th September 1963, when fifty-nine persons attended. Twenty-nine non-professorial members, including the Librarian, Moses Tyson, appeared at the next meeting of ninety-five Senators on 31st October, at which they heard an account of the new targets set for universities by Robbins. If the Vice-Chancellor made them a speech of welcome, his remarks were not recorded in the minutes. However, it was later suggested that a treat be arranged, 'in view of the increased and increasing membership of Senate', in the form of a buffet supper after the January meeting. The promise of refreshment resulted in a large turnout, and the same hospitality was offered in subsequent years.

Manchester's Gulliver was privileged to witness the first entry to the Council Chamber of 'these fledgling Nestors'. 'I had seen them clustered thick about the chamber door, like Country Members at the cry of "Who goes home?" banded together for fear of swaggerers and bully-boys, whilst law-givers of more ancient standing swept by them to their accustomed seats. And within the door there stood a sort of Cerberus, a skulking fellow who pricked the members off upon a list as they passed him by, looking hard upon the newly-elect as though he thought them come there to purloin the plate.' Was it possible, they began to ask themselves, that the real seat of power lay not in the Senate itself, but rather in the Great Cabal, the Standing Committee of Senate to which so many contentious matters were referred? The proportion of elected members was not generous, and did little to alter the principle that grey heads should sway and green heads obey. But it was almost certainly true that in the years to come the elected members would exercise over Senate an influence disproportionate to their numbers. Moved by a sense of responsibility to their constituents, they would assemble in advance of Senate meetings to concert their efforts. They would also attend more regularly than did many professors. Some of these had become blasé, inclined to plead pressing engagements elsewhere rather than sit through the flowery compliments, the arguments over acquiring for the Council Chamber Willem Wissing's irrelevant portrait of Queen Mary II, and other rituals and rigmaroles that enlivened Senate meetings.

Alterations in Senate's composition called for changes in the University's charter. Early in 1963 a joint committee of Senate and Council was established and charged to embark on the lengthy process of overhauling the charter and statutes of 1903. The principal targets of would-be reformers were, not only professorial oligarchy, but also lay dominance of the University, exercised principally through the lay majority on Council and through its powerful honorary officers. Academics imbued with the values of Oxford and Cambridge dreamed of establishing a self-governing community of scholars; left-wingers dreamed of purifying the University of the influence of industrial and commercial capitalism, as though doubting that the lay officers of the University could ever be truly altruistic or philanthropic or politically neutral.

Almost ten years were to pass before the reformed charter and statutes, duly approved by the Privy Council, became law. The committee for their revision consisted of the Chairman of Council, the Treasurer and the Vice-Chancellor, all by virtue of their offices; of three other lay members of Council; of three persons chosen by Senate (all professors of at least nine years' standing, Brook of English, Mackenzie of Government and Street of Law); and of three representatives of the non-professorial academic body, John Mills (a physiologist), Harold Perkin (a social historian) and A.G. Rose (of the Department of Social Administration). The last three were chosen by the representatives on Court and Council of the non-professorial teaching staff. As it happened, two of them, Mills and Perkin, became professors (Perkin at Lancaster) before the deliberations on the charter were concluded. Mills, who was for some time one of the three editors of *Staff Comment*, admitted ruefully that 'having consistently and vigorously pleaded the rights and responsibilities of non-professors, I now find myself propelled into the professorial oligarchy'.

A committee so constituted was unlikely to propose radical changes, though it could hardly be said that its more senior members were all reactionaries. Harry Street, for example, was famous for his concern with civil liberties. For all this it was claimed that 'the laymen and the professors have been judge and jury in their own case' and that the committee was mainly concerned to defend the entrenched privileges of laymen and professors. Charges of merely tinkering with the engines and passing up a great opportunity to think boldly were quick to surface when the draft proposals were first published to the University and exposed for comment at the end of 1965.

There was no lack of rival schemes. An unofficial working party, which included one eminent professor (Vinaver), the secretary of the Staff Forum (Eric Cahm of the French Department) and one of the editors of *Staff Comment* (Louis Quesnel, a bacteriologist), had gathered after a meeting of Staff Forum. Two documents emerged from its deliberations: first, a general statement of principle, eventually signed by 250 members of staff, including five professors; and secondly, a more detailed attempt at rethinking the University's constitution, endorsed by 100 members of staff, including a professor. The detailed proposal was submitted to the official committee, which for the most part politely rejected it. This document argued that it was not possible to separate financial decisions from academic policy, and that both should therefore fall to a single Council of about forty members, performing the functions of the present Council and Senate. It would consist both of academics and of laymen, but with an academic majority, and it would be responsible to a Congregation consisting of all the permanent members of the academic staff and a few representatives of Convocation (the body of graduates). In effect the Congregation would replace the Court of Governors as the sovereign body in the University. Congregation would elect the academic members of the Council, Court the laymen, for the Court would still survive, but essentially as a consultative body, representing 'the legitimate interest of society at large in the academic working of the University'. Each department should have an elected head; departmental meetings should be held regularly for the transaction of departmental business; and 'no proposal or other action in the name of the department should proceed without the approval of such a meeting'. The general statement of principle declared, among much else, that 'One of the most powerful limitations on academic freedom at the present time is the power a professor has over the careers of those members of staff who are responsible to him in the first instance for the performance of their duties. It should be the right of every member of staff to be able, without fear of penalty, to signify publicly his disagreement with his seniors; this is not always effective in practice.'

Less radically, the AUT proposed that the existing structure of Senate, Council and Court should be maintained. But their membership should be modified, so as to allow academics more places on Council and Court (where seats should be evenly divided between academics and laymen) and to allocate a larger proportion of seats in Senate to elected members. Well aware of the increasing unwieldiness of Senate as its numbers increased, the AUT suggested that a greater part of its business should be delegated to a Standing Committee on which the non-professorial members of Senate would enjoy proportional membership. They proposed that departments should be transformed into faculties in their own right, which would presumably have given much more authority to meetings of their staff, and that faculties should be headed by elected deans chosen from among their more senior members. The AUT had their own ideas about a Congregation, but stopped short of proposing that it should replace the Court of Governors. Instead they suggested that it should replace the General Board of the Faculties and have largely advisory powers.

Not surprisingly, the official committee inclined more nearly to the AUT's reformist view than to that of the more radical unofficial working party, though the committee did not grant the AUT the equal representation of academics and laymen which they craved and was determined to maintain a lay majority on Court and Council. The Charter Committee made much of a paper from Lord Bowden, written before he became a member of the government, to the effect that the future independence of the University would be jeopardised if lay dominance on Council and Court were abolished. Such a move 'could only result in increasing direction from the central government both of the University's finances and its development'. This sentiment accorded with an observation of the Robbins Committee in favour of retaining lay majorities, on the grounds that it was wrong that 'the spending of university funds should be wholly in the hands of the users'; the public would be readier to respect academic autonomy if it could be assured that universities had access to 'independent lay advice and criticism'. Although the University had been drawn into a national system and although its finances depended overwhelmingly upon the Treasury and no longer upon local philanthropy, local businessmen were not to be displaced. At a hostile but rather small meeting of Staff Forum, Professor Vinaver challenged the committee's representatives to cite one single example of the lay majority actually serving to block the advance of state control. None was forthcoming. But the Charter Committee held firmly to its proposal that there should be on Council eighteen lay members elected by the Court, and twelve academics elected by the Senate (an increase of three).

On the subject of professorial authority, the Charter Committee resolved that the proportion of elected members in Senate should be increased from one-fifth to one-quarter. They were much persuaded by the submission of a retired Professor of Inorganic Chemistry, Fred Fairbrother, to the effect that 'Professorial power entails professorial obligation to non-professorial staff. Any reduction in the power of Professors could result in a lessening of their sense of obligation to their non-professorial colleagues.' On this assumption that power would somehow always be linked with a proper sense of responsibility and that the other ranks could not do without professorial leadership, the committee recommended the creation of departmental boards. At the same time it stated a firm conviction that these bodies should have only advisory and not executive powers: 'the power of decision and direction should, we consider, remain with the professors, who are responsible to the University, through Senate and Council, for the effectiveness of their departments ... But the existence of the board with its right to be consulted will ensure that decisions are not taken in ignorance of possible repercussions in the department.' The committee assumed that the head of the department and the chairman of the board would normally be different people, and that it might sometimes be the duty of a board chairman to put forward a view which differed from that of the professors.

1 Sir John Stopford, afterwards Lord Stopford of Fallowfield, Vice-Chancellor 1934–56.

2 Sir William Mansfield Cooper, Vice-Chancellor 1956–70, as represented by the student publication *Insitter*.

3 Sir Arthur Armitage, Vice-Chancellor 1970–80.

4 The visit of Queen Elizabeth during the centenary celebrations, 1951.

5 The Pharmacy Department, 1958.

6 Mr Patrick Gordon Walker (Secretary of State for Education), Professor George Wedell (Professor of Adult Education) and the leader of a student demonstration on 1st March 1968, when Mr Gordon Walker's extra-mural lecture was disrupted (*Manchester Guardian*, 2nd March 1968).

'Maison Longarse'
The Woodlands,
Little Neasden,
Rutland.

14th March 1970

My Dear Arthur,

I am not a little concerned with what I've been seeing in
the press about this sit-in nonsense, particularly with that Photograph
of you andthat brick. Your mother was most upset. Now, I am not against
protest,but I do **NOT** approve of this totally irresponsible action . Its
about time you students dunn settled down to an honest days work(If you
still know the meaning of the word). While I agree there might be a case
regarding files, it does not merit this outlandish behaviour. Anyway, you're
only there for three years so what can you know about the running of a
university, and anyway what does it matter if a man is an Anarchixist
Roman catholic, United supporter. Such facts are irrelevant anyway.
When I was a youth, people were big enough to stand up and shout and
not hide behind noisy, dirty revolutionary nit-wits, in a mob.

Quite frankly,your lazy student friends should have their grants
stopped, they are nothing but parasites on society. What they need is a
few months in the army.

Best regards

Your father.

Arthur Longarse Senior

P.S. *I do hope you've had your
haircut, your mother was most
upset, by the photo.*

7 'My dear Arthur', spoof letter from a student's father at the time of occupation
of the University buildings in February–March 1970.

8 The Great Charter, 1967 (*Staff Comment*, November 1967). Discussion of the University's new Charter and Statutes continued for the greater part of ten years, from 1963 to 1973.

9 '... students with young children must make their own arrangements' (*Staff Comment*, June 1968). The question of a Day Nursery was a controversial subject for many years in the 1960s and 1970s.

"... students with young children must make their own arrangements " (see letter)

"Low productivity, Dr. Smith!
Only 80% understood your lectures!
Salary reduced by 20%."

(Of historical interest only?)

10 'Low productivity, Dr Smith' (*Staff Comment*, February 1969). The proposals of the Prices and Incomes Board to reward good teaching by additional salary payments were highly unpopular in the University.

"He's never been the same since he got elected to Senate"

11 'He's never been the same since he got elected to Senate' (*Communication*, November 1973). Elected members were first admitted to Senate in October 1963.

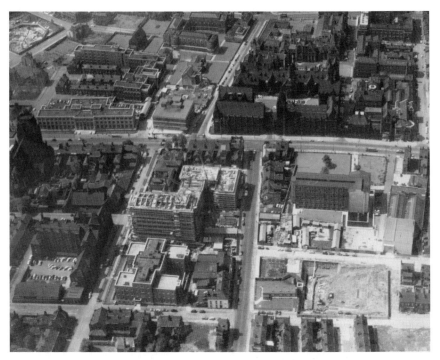

12 Buildings of the new Science Centre to the east of Oxford Road.

13 Manchester Refectory Building – phase 2.

14 One of the last traditional Halls of Residence: Woolton Hall (opened 1959).

15 A new style of student residence: the Owens Park Tower (opened 1964).

16 The Stopford Building.

17 The Moberly Tower

18 Self-catered, loan-financed accommodation: the Oak House Flats.

19 The Waterhouse Buildings, with the old Dental Hospital (afterwards the Department of Metallurgy) in the foreground.

20 The Mathematics Tower and the Precinct Centre ramp.

21 The Computer Building.

Although the name of Congregation was thought unsuitable, the official committee proposed the establishment of a consultative body to be called the Assembly, roughly on the lines proposed by the AUT. It was to replace the existing General Board of the Faculties. The Assembly would have a wider membership, which would extend to assistant lecturers, demonstrators, fellows and research associates, and it would have greater powers to initiate discussion rather than wait for matters to be referred to it from above. It would meet at least once a year to hear a report from the Vice-Chancellor and would be available to be consulted and to express opinions, but it would not, as the more thoroughgoing reformers would have wished, be the sovereign body of academics with ultimate responsibility for the government of the University.

Notions of academic freedom were closely tied to the concept of security of tenure, which gave lecturers and above who had been appointed to the retiring age protection against dismissal for anything other than scandalous misconduct or gross inefficiency. The Charter Revision Committee noted that 'So far as their contractual terms are concerned, non-professorial staff can be dismissed at a few months' notice without cause assigned', but acknowledged that in practice 'the security of tenure is very high'. One case in 1955 (to which they did not refer) had suggested the extremes to which an academic had to go in order to earn dismissal: a lecturer had been 'intemperate in his habits' for several years, had been twice fined and disqualified by magistrates for driving under the influence of drink, had failed in both teaching and research, and, in a consummate act of Lucky Jimmery, embarrassed the University by causing 'much comment' at an international academic congress. A more recent affair in 1960, referred to in Council minutes only in the most mysterious general terms, had resulted in the dismissal of 'a senior established member of the non-professorial staff', after which it was agreed on Senate's recommendation that in future anyone so dismissed would have the right to appeal to an independent tribunal. Taking note of this case, the Joint Committee for the Revision of the Charter concluded that a hearing before dismissal, perhaps under a legally qualified chairman, would be preferable to an appeal after it. At some point in the proceedings it was suggested, however, that it might prove necessary one day to dismiss staff on the grounds of 'redundancy or financial stringency'. Someone in high places was clearly aware that the government might withdraw its relatively generous financial support for universities; since salaries accounted for so large a proportion of the University's expenditure it would face bankruptcy unless it succeeded in shedding staff by one means or another. In such circumstances, what price tenure?

In 1966 the Senate pronounced on the official Joint Committee's Interim Report. Standing Committee of Senate had received a wide range of remarks on the subject of departmental boards. Despots opposed them utterly as a potential nuisance 'likely to interfere with the proper discharge of university business', democrats wanted them endowed with full executive powers. The most radical critics, perhaps inspired by the interdisciplinary schools established in the newest universities, took the view that departments themselves were outmoded. It would therefore be wrong to enshrine them in a new charter and strengthen them by creating boards to help them run, particularly as the old charter had never mentioned them at all, and their existence appeared to rest on custom rather than on constitutional law. But Senate agreed that the University should provide by statute for organisation by departments, although it conceded vaguely that some academics and some University activities might be organised in a different manner. It did not welcome the possibility that some kind of tribune of the people might arise within a department, with the chairman of a departmental board setting himself up against the professoriate, and recommended more strongly than the Charter Committee itself that a professor should normally chair such a board; only the professors themselves or the Vice-Chancellor should make exceptions to this rule. Such a view, one might think, raised awkward questions. If a professor served as chairman, he would have the right to control the agenda and rule on points of order. But could a chairman veto the recommendations of a meeting over which he had himself presided, and could he avoid being bound by its decisions? Senate preferred to evade the issues of financial stringency and redundancy, by suggesting that it was unnecessary to legislate for exceptional circumstances, and adding somewhat foggily 'that the question of redundancy will increasingly be the concern of national policy'.

In the words of the new Gulliver, 'this mountain, some cynic wag suggested, would bring forth a minuscule mouse and all things in their governance remain as they were before'. ' ... there all was much as it had ever been: laymen to pull the pursestrings, professors to wield the power in academic governance, and but a poor cabal to check them in abuse, a mere talking-shop without authority'. Be this as it might, the Draft Supplemental Charter, not substantially altered in principle in subsequent drafts, was redrafted as though for submission to the Privy

Council in July 1968. Departmental boards, the subject of much controversy, were empowered 'To discuss and declare an opinion on any matter relating to the work of the Department', and transmit this to the professoriate and if need be to the board of the faculty (which could presumably overrule the professors if it saw fit); the Senate would be the final arbiter. Nothing was said about the chairmanship of departmental boards. Grounds for dismissal were stated as 'grave or persistent misconduct, physical or mental incapacity or continued inefficiency or continued failure to perform the duties of the office ...'. There was no mention of redundancy.

As will appear later, for various reasons the University did not submit the new Charter and Statutes to the Privy Council until the autumn of 1971. Among much else, the events of 1968 raised the possibility of student representation on the principal legislative and executive bodies of universities; much work had still to be done on the ordinances and general regulations which elaborated in detail on the Charter and Statutes; and some points were still in dispute. The new Charter came into effect on 12th February 1973, save that one part of it – the increase in the proportion of elected members of Senate from one-fifth to one-quarter of the whole – was introduced by ordinance in 1970. The AUT had asked that 'steps be taken to make the academic body less a hierarchy of rank and more a community of scholars', and that members of Senate be authorised to communicate information about Senate proceedings much more freely to other members of the University.

Clearly the changes to the constitution had been cautiously made and root-and-branch reformers had been deeply disappointed. Much would depend on the spirit, liberal or otherwise, in which individuals interpreted the Charter and on the desire of professors to retain the goodwill and support of their colleagues. It was possible that the Charter might, if the right to be consulted were properly respected, secrecy modified and mutual suspicion disarmed, provide the framework for better working relationships between professors and their so-called junior colleagues. Much, as always, would depend on departmental custom and tradition, on personal relationships and not on enacted law.

Equally significant, though not so publicly debated, were the steps taken in the late 1960s by the University to establish more efficient formal machinery for the control of resources and the promotion of academic developments. These had nothing to do with academic democracy, and it seemed that many of the most important decisions in future would be taken, not by Senate and Council, but by a cluster of non-representative and (it was hoped) disinterested resource committees ultimately responsible to both bodies. Some participants in the constitutional debate had urged that financial and academic decisions could not be separated; they were now to come together, but not quite in the way which the reformers had advocated.

Public accountability and economy measures began to weigh heavily upon all universities from the end of 1966. During the next quinquennium, 1967–72, or so the UGC warned, universities could expect only modest increases in recurrent grant. They were invited to go slow on new developments, to make more intensive use of their buildings and costly equipment, to improve collaboration with other universities, to develop (as always) co-operation with industry, to give priority to undergraduate activities rather than to the further growth of postgraduate education. Universities had now lost their long-standing immunity from the obligation to open their account books and records to teams responsible to the Comptroller and Auditor General. Since government expenditure on universities had swollen over the last twenty years from about £4 million annually to well over £200 million, neither they nor the UGC could continue to escape scrutiny. The Secretary of State for Education and Science gave assurances that the Comptroller would not question policy decisions, and the Comptroller himself assured an anxious meeting of the Committee of Vice-Chancellors and Principals that his staff might well seek to establish what a University's policy was, but they would not presume to question the policy itself.

For all this the facts remained that the University's financial procedures would now be liable to inspection every four years or thereabouts, and that the UGC, itself under scrutiny, was forever demanding more information about staff and student numbers and the costs related to them. Less haphazard and better informed methods of managing resources were needed. Hitherto the processes of development had been much exposed to various forms of horse-trading and log-rolling. When the Council decided to release money for new developments, the deans of the faculties were asked to consult their colleagues 'informally' and to submit a series of proposals to the Senate Committee on University Development. As was explained in 1958, this body was a gathering of deans and representatives of faculties, all vehemently backing their own projects, with victory going to the man who bayed loudest and longest (one thinks of the defeat of Frank Kermode at the hands of Bernard Lovell, mentioned in an earlier chapter). It was sometimes described as a 'thieves' kitchen'. Wishing to see more orderly and equitable methods adopted, in July 1969 a joint working party of Senate and Council advocated the system of control by a Joint Committee for University Development (JCUD) which was to come into full operation under the new Vice-Chancellor, Arthur Armitage. 'To control our future', declared the working party, 'we shall need to be masters of the facts of our environment and its costs.' In prosperous times one could develop a university simply by adding new activities to existing ones. In leaner years it might well prove necessary to redeploy resources in order to keep the University alive. Should a post fall vacant in some obscure and redundant subject for which there was little demand, it might be necessary to transfer the resources which had supported it to some more dynamic activity.

The new system would be designed to bring the concerns of Senate and Council together, to co-ordinate academic and financial viewpoints. JCUD's tentacles would reach down into faculties. There would be a sub-committee responsible to it in each faculty or group of faculties. Arrangements would be founded on 'small Committees of disinterested members who would meet frequently and might be expected to take the larger view since they represent neither department nor Faculty'. They would not be elected by the faculties, but appointed by the JCUD after consultation with the appropriate dean (they became known at one point as 'the dean's friends'). They would be expected to act as an impartial jury, adjudicating claims laid before them to new or replacement posts. The deans, or some of them, would now be caused to assume a double role – both as representatives of their faculties to higher authority in the University, and as representatives to their faculties of the JCUD. A weak democratic principle and a strong hierarchical principle were therefore to meet in the person of the same senior academic. In times of the most acute stringency, which still lay some years ahead, there would be strong pressure to add elected members to the development sub-committees, and deans would have to struggle to retain both the confidence of their colleagues in the faculty and that of their bosses who controlled the University's resources.

The 1960s had been a decade of optimism and frustration, which had raised high hopes only to dash them, and the prospect of creating a more egalitarian society, a community of scholars on a generous scale, seemed increasingly remote. Universities were financed mainly by Treasury grants, their students drawn from a wider area and subsidised by their own education authorities. But local businessmen and

professional men still held the majority of seats on their chief executive bodies; they had, indeed, made a new appearance in the guise of
a bulwark against creeping government control and a guarantor of
that elusive concept, academic freedom, in which everyone was
bound to believe. Professorial control over promotion and patronage
appeared to be a threat to that freedom, even if the obligation to consult was being more formally acknowledged. If concessions to democracy were being cautiously made in the field of educational policy
making, hierarchical principles were being asserted in that of resource
management. It remained to be seen whether some lecturers, impatient of the caution and delay that attended University reform, would
lean towards their students rather than their professors. Perhaps they
would sympathise strongly, if not make common cause with, student
demands for greater participation in University affairs.

9

Anxiety and dissent

In the early 1960s experts conducted at least two extensive surveys of the social origins and opinions of Manchester students, of their attitudes to politics, society and themselves. From an office provided by the students' Union in the summer of 1962, the sociologist Ferdynand Zweig conducted over 100 lengthy interviews with a random sample of students, seventy-nine undergraduates and twenty-four postgraduates. His inquiry set out to compare the qualities and outlook of students attending an archetypal redbrick, departmental university, where science and engineering were a strong presence, with those of their counterparts in the ancient collegiate University of Oxford, where the arts and humanities reigned supreme. In March 1963, the Union itself distributed a questionnaire to a much larger random sample of students and succeeded in eliciting 736 returns. Conceived by a postgraduate student of accounting, Andrew Balcombe, the survey depended on thirty-nine questions drafted by Richard Rose, one of Professor Mackenzie's bright young men in the Government Department, co-author of a book entitled *Must Labour Lose?* The main purpose of this operation was to discover the voting intentions of British students, even if they were not yet legally entitled to vote: would they vote as their parents did, or would they strike out on a path of their own?

Both surveys depicted a student population mainly but not wholly of middle middle or lower middle-class origins, mostly educated in grammar schools, drawn heavily but not exclusively from the North West, or at least from the North of England. Students seemed fairly confident of their own prospects of success in society, either teaching in schools or else working in some capacity for large corporations and industrial concerns. Nevertheless they were inclined to be critical both of that society and of the politicians who aspired to rule it. According to the Union survey, almost 40 per cent of students thought that they belonged to no particular social class, as though the experience of going to university had cut them loose from family moorings.

Zweig saw middle-class values triumphing over those of the working class in the attitudes and behaviour of those he interviewed. He, in particular, believed that the critical attitudes fostered by a university education were breeding a deep distrust of extremist or dogmatic politics of any kind and exerting a strong pull towards the centre. The Union survey did not disagree, but indicated that political preferences varied markedly from one faculty or group of subjects to another: that budding engineers, for example, were 47 per cent Conservative and 24 per cent Labour, while students pursuing social studies inclined quite the other way – 60 per cent were Labour supporters, and only 19 per cent adhered to the Conservative Party.

Each survey found a degree of dissatisfaction with the University on the part of perhaps 20 per cent of the student population. Such discontent was more clearly expressed by Zweig's respondents, who were encouraged to comment freely. Not surprisingly, students in large, impersonal departments seemed to be the most disaffected. Fifty-three of his 103 students were enjoying University life; thirty-four were moderately critical, complaining especially of the remoteness of their teachers, of an obsession with acquiring good qualifications rather than a good education, of a lack of community spirit, of depressing surroundings, and – where they came from outside the region – of a drab provincialism. Sixteen were sharply critical, calling the place, for example, 'Little more than a technical night-school'.

The Union survey, which did not allow free comment, seemed to elicit stronger support for the University. Thirty-eight per cent of respondents agreed with the proposition that 'It is a very rewarding experience and I am glad to be here', 43 per cent with the judicious pronouncement that 'There are a few drawbacks, but on balance it's a good life'. However, 8 per cent were 'lukewarm' and 12 per cent murmured moderately that 'There are a number of things I would like changed'. Only one student in 200 was prepared to say 'It is just a waste of time'. More than 80 per cent of respondents, whatever they thought of university life in general, were essentially satisfied with their courses or even enthusiastic about their academic work. There seemed to be no cause for alarm.

Both in his Oxford and in his Manchester subjects, however, Zweig detected a certain joylessness, a kind of earnestness and puritanism which inspired him to plead on their behalf for brighter surroundings, a lightening of the atmosphere, a development of university medical services with special attention to mental health and the provision of counselling. Indeed, he warned that 'The university can over-reach itself by breeding a too serious-minded, too studious and industrious student, over-laden with care and worry, unstable and neurotic, who seeks refuge only in day-dreams ... There is not only a complete divorce between learning and pleasure, but one can often sense a close link between learning and displeasure, boredom, tension and fatigue.' Seven years after the appearance of his book, *The Student in the Age of Anxiety*, a large part of the student population – perhaps at least three thousand – found relief and pleasure in a strange 'happening', a fortnight of coming together in Manchester's first sit-in on a grand scale. The occupation of the Whitworth Hall and the administration buildings between 26th February and 12th March 1970, an unscheduled winter festival and a 'bit of a gig' for many participants, originated in widespread anxiety: in the 'grand peur' (as the historian E.P. Thompson put it) that universities in general were keeping political files on the activities of radical students and dissident members of their own staff. Centrist politics seemed to have been eclipsed by a fear that the centre could not hold, giving way to a polarisation of Left and Right, to socialist criticism of the shortcomings of a Labour government, to the highly politicised Union elections of 1969 which had resulted in the election as President of a Communist student of Politics and Modern History, the likeable David Wynn.

In the previous two years, 1968–70, a large part of the student population had been indifferent to the student troubles; the contrast between attitudes in Engineering and in Social Studies, noted in 1963, seemed as strong as ever. But in the late winter of 1969–70 dissent had spread, for the time being, far beyond the 'small but powerfully vocal group of students who had interested themselves in Union and public affairs' whom the Vice-Chancellor had described to Senate on 1st February 1968. Anxiety about the endless, repetitive grinding of the examination machinery had given rise to earnest debates concerning the fairness, efficiency and consistency of the assessment apparatus. It had long been represented as infallible; but was it really so? Paradoxically, even tragically, a Vice-Chancellor of working-class origins, high principled, a champion of the rule of law, an administrator endowed with a strong Nonconformist conscience, sincerely devoted according to his lights to the well-being of the students in his paternal care, found himself cast in the role of a reactionary villain. Sadly, Sir William Mansfield Cooper, who would certainly have claimed to be a defender of academic freedom, was charged with making a clumsy and unjustified attempt at interfering with free speech in the University by an ill-advised use of old-fashioned legal devices. He left his office an unhappy man, unable to understand that very able students, who were neither ne'er-do-wells nor professional agitators, were capable of seeing grave faults in the system under which they were educated.

Open disrespect for authority had not been unknown in the early 1960s, but it had been easier to contain. Early in 1961 a new student newspaper, *Manchester Independent*, had reason to declare that 'Last term was possibly the most confusing in the history of Manchester University.' *News Bulletin*, the fortnightly journal subsidised by the students' Union, had courted retribution by publishing two sensational stories containing allegations which it had failed to verify. The first of these was an attack on the commanding figure of the Bursar, Rainford, as if he were personally contributing to the so-called brain drain of distinguished scientists from the United Kingdom to the United States. Involved in the tale were the Langworthy Professor of Physics, Samuel Devons, and an expensive piece of scientific plant, a heavy ion linear accelerator installed at 259–61 Oxford Road, and eventually costing between £300,000 and £400,000. In the wake of the Jodrell Bank affair, as Lord Flowers remembers, the University was understandably concerned at any hint of unbridled extravagance in the Physics Department, and quick to censure Devons when they discovered flaws in his financial control of the accelerator. Having been for some months a visiting professor at Columbia University, Devons took umbrage and decided not to return to the machinery installed at his instigation. Seizing with glee on a prepared statement read by a member of the Physics Department to the effect that 'This is the greatest loss to British Physics since the war', *News Bulletin* chose to portray the Bursar, though not quite in so many words, as a pettifogging accountant who failed to appreciate great science. For this piece of innuendo the students' Union subsequently apologised, both by a personal visit of the officers to Rainford and by the issue of a special broadsheet disavowing the remarks of their newspaper.

A second essay in tabloid journalism threatened to bring students in general into disrepute when *News Bulletin* carried a front-page account of a lurid attack on the morals of his student tenants by a disgruntled landlord, Jan Danilewicz, said to be the owner of about sixty flats. Having been informed that between 3,600 and 3,800 copies of each issue were printed, and that complimentary copies were sent to the editors of all other University Union newspapers and to a number of news agencies, the Vice-Chancellor resolved upon stern action. Two student journalists were disciplined, and all Union publications were suppressed for the time being until a suitable system of censorship could be devised. Such incidents contributed to the fall from office of the Union's first woman President, Elva Corrie. Not only did she share the technical responsibility of Union officers for the publication, but she had also, it seemed, made certain unfortunate remarks at the conference of the National Union of Students at Margate. Publicly embarrassing the University was an offence not easily forgiven, on this occasion and on several others in the future.

These events revealed two of the preoccupations – fear of adverse publicity and misgivings about the misuse of public money – which were to explain several of the Vice-Chancellor's actions during the 1960s. The Union was proud of its autonomy, and it generated some income by selling goods and services to its members. But it could not survive financially without the capitation fee paid by local education authorities alongside the tuition fee of each student. Public money provided the Union subscription because the University compelled students to belong to the Union, which was not, as in Oxford or Cambridge, merely a debating club to be joined by those who chose to do so. However, the fee was not paid directly to the Union itself, but rather to the University, which felt justified in withholding the money should it believe that the Union was engaged in improper activities. With regard to the affair in 1960, the Vice-Chancellor told the University Council that he 'had always followed the policy of allowing the students as much freedom as possible in the management of their Union and of their publications, but submitted that the University was a trustee of public moneys handed over to the students and could not disclaim a certain liability for events'.

More than once in the future Mansfield Cooper was to use this argument to discourage or curb student enterprises of which he and his Council did not approve. Control over public funds could be used for disciplinary ends on occasions when the Union had failed to prevent distasteful conduct liable to bring the University into disrepute. Late in 1964 the Rag Committee attracted the wrong kind of publicity by engaging a stripper to entertain a social gathering at which pressmen were present. On that occasion the Vice-Chancellor obtained authority from Council to use his discretion 'to withhold payments of funds from public sources to the University Union' if and when it proved unable to run a tighter ship.

In the interests of diplomacy, however, the University established in 1960–61 a committee on relations between the student body and the University (a move which seemed to imply that they were separate entities), and instructed it 'in particular to consider and report upon the role of the Union in University affairs and how this role may be most satisfactorily fulfilled'. Under a skilful and sensitive chairman, Sir Raymond Streat, this committee, comprising the Vice-Chancellor, three members of Council, four academics and four students appointed by the Union, was reasonably successful for several years in promoting amiable relations through top brass talking to top brass. It did not talk about purely academic matters, but discussed the provision of amenities, the amount of the capitation fee, and other sensitive and potentially awkward affairs connected with student welfare.

Though it seemed a harsh repressive measure, the suspension of Union publications did not silence student journalism for long. The solution lay in separating the principal student paper from the Union, so that the Union could no longer be held responsible for the paper's vagaries, and establishing a paper which would own itself, a publishing company 'without outside interest' and therefore free of censorship, but obliged like all publications to take account of the law of libel. Hence the birth of *Manchester Independent*, which first appeared on 17th February 1961. It announced three main objectives: 'Firstly to provide an exhaustive news service covering the whole of Manchester University and the student world in general. Secondly to give a medium in which members of the University can express their views on any subject. And perhaps most importantly to become a voice in University affairs. A responsible, fair but strong-minded voice ... ' Two years later, the Union President proposed the formation of a Trust, modelled on one recently established at Oxford to manage a number of undergraduate publications. This Trust would buy the paper from its current owners, Independent University Publications. Among the trustees would be two members of the University staff, two members elected by the Union Council, and one elected by the Union of the Faculty of Technology. The trustees would then co-opt two additional members, 'one to be connected with journalism and the other to be a Bank Manager'. Eventually, in July 1964, two academics, John Jump, soon to become a Professor of English Literature, and Geoffrey North, Warden of St Anselm Hall and a Lecturer in Geography, were appointed to the Council of Management, as it was now called.

Geoffrey North, who eventually became Chairman of this Council, was not supposed to be a censor. But he remembers learning much about the laws of libel and having to exercise his powers of persuasion with some conviction, for he might himself be sued if the paper defamed somebody with the means to take legal proceedings – 'For

God's sake be careful how you say this and how you say that!' *Independent* kept out of serious trouble until early in 1970, when it was more than once forced to apologise for publishing defamatory statements about members of the University staff. During the 1960s it developed into a serious newspaper of high quality, which achieved most of its stated ambitions and won recognition outside Manchester. In *The Daily Mirror*'s annual competition for student newspapers in 1962 it earned high commendation for 'successful sobriety in presentation', for its good use of photographs and cartoons, and its attention to layout. David Murphy's columns, 'Against the Grain', were described by the assistant editor of *The Mirror* as 'the funniest I have ever read in student journalism'. In 1964 *Independent* was runner-up to Oxford's *Cherwell*, and in 1967 it succeeded in breaking the Oxford-Cambridge monopoly of the highest award. Among its essays in serious journalism that year was a series of 'liberal in-depth probes' into social and moral as well as educational issues, on such matters as 'Moss Side', 'Homosexuality' and 'Examination Systems'. Lyn Silver, the editor who received the award on behalf of the paper, had herself written on 'The National Disgrace of Britain's Prisons'. Whilst one strain in student opinion portrayed students themselves as an oppressed class, another in student journalism depicted them as incomparably better off than their close neighbours in the grimmer districts of Manchester. It was in this kind of vivid reporting, which described social conditions without patronising the people who had to endure them, that *Independent* excelled.

Independent was the only student publication to appear regularly throughout the decade. It was normally issued fortnightly during term, and sometimes came out weekly in times of high drama. To resolve the crisis of 1960–61, a majority of the Union Council had meekly agreed that they would themselves act as censors of all Union publications. In 1964 they again began issuing a bulletin of their own, *Mancunion*, which was intended to explain the doings of the Union officers and Council to their constituents, in case they did not receive satisfactory coverage in *Independent*. *Mancunion* was originally a free newspaper, distributed without charge and subsidised by advertisements, but at intervals it ran into financial trouble, and unlike *Independent* it appeared only as a result of periodic bursts of energy during interludes of solvency.

An article in *Independent* in 1964 suggested that the Union had good reason to be grateful to the University, for bar extensions, Rag concessions, and the Union building itself, of which the University was landlord. The writer gave warning that despite the clauses in the tenancy agreement which were intended to forestall University intervention in Union affairs and administration, the University had 'eventual control'. By this time the University was considering another act of grace – the possibility of allowing Union Presidents to interrupt their courses for a year and devote themselves entirely to Union affairs during their spell of office, so that neither the Union itself nor their prospects of taking a good degree need suffer. In the recent past the academic careers of some Presidents had been chequered, subject to interruptions, and unduly prolonged. One who had entered the University to study dentistry in 1956 had ended up with a degree in Commerce seven years later. It was perhaps unfortunate that when the principle of sabbatical leave for Union officers was put to the test in 1965, the Medical Faculty felt obliged to oppose an extension for the successful candidate, who had started his course in 1955 and interrupted it to work for the World Youth and Students' Festival and to tour Russia, the Communist satellite countries and the Middle East. He failed his examinations and had to abandon his presidency. By the end of the decade, the University was prepared to make similar concessions to the Welfare Vice-President of the Union, as though recognising the job as equally responsible and arduous.

At least one President, Anna Ford (1966–67), a former left-winger driven, as she now says, by a 'vicarage conscience', and described by an old tutor as 'a militant determined to be moderate', got on splendidly with the Vice-Chancellor. She thereby infuriated radical colleagues who thought that Vice-Chancellors were not to be trusted and could never be allies in their struggle. As she now recalls, 'I just found him so easy to talk to, because there was this man with this rather left-wing background, who was tremendously interested in listening ... I felt I could go, whenever I wanted, and say, "I think this is reasonable and that is unreasonable. What are you going to do about it?" So I didn't feel there was any of the oppression that there was in the European universities ... '

On at least two issues the Vice-Chancellor was firmly on the side of student opinion. He was, with other Vice-Chancellors and Principals, opposed to charging higher fees to overseas students, and he was against substituting loans for maintenance grants to home students. Internationalist sentiment was strong among students, arrivals from overseas were welcomed at railway stations and airports at the start of the academic year, and special attention was given (at least in the Economics Faculty) to providing them with accommodation. An

International Club, opened in Fallowfield in October 1966, later, under the name of the International Society, occupied the house in Plymouth Grove which had once belonged to the novelist Elizabeth Gaskell and her husband. According to *Independent* there were just over a thousand overseas students in Manchester, almost half of them from Commonwealth countries, and only the Universities of Oxford and London attracted larger numbers. The sensibilities of both students and Vice-Chancellors were deeply offended just before Christmas 1966 by one of the Labour government's economy measures. This proposal to introduce a higher fee for overseas students breached the principle that all students should be treated equally and it therefore incurred charges of racial discrimination. Educating overseas students at less than the actual cost had long been regarded as an important form of overseas aid. Worse still, it also seemed that there would be no compensation elsewhere, since cuts were falling on the Ministry of Overseas Development and on the BBC's overseas service. As Mansfield Cooper memorably declared, 'No one who is engaged in the pursuit of knowledge is a foreigner.'

Anthony Crosland, the Secretary of State for Education and Science, announced that tuition fees for university courses now averaged about £70 per student per annum. Although the government had no wish to impose a general increase of fees during the next quinquennium, it had calculated that more than 30,000 students from outside the country were receiving higher education in the United Kingdom, and that of these 7,000 hailed 'from countries with fully developed systems of higher education'. The next quinquennial settlement would assume that every overseas student who began a course in the next academic year would pay a fee of £250. To opponents it mattered little that the fee still fell far short of the cost of the courses, or that there would be safeguards for existing students. Crosland's measure was rendered doubly offensive by the absence of any consultation with university authorities, and by the all-too-plain demonstration that governments were in a position to manipulate university finances by assuming a certain level of fees.

Unusually, academics and students combined in planning a brief strike in protest against this discriminatory action, which seemed to foreshadow other unpalatable economies. Equally unusually, the Vice-Chancellor seemed to approve of the strike, or at least not to oppose it. He chose to issue only the mildest of cautions: 'If we did decide to strike we should make sure we did not harm ourselves by prolonging it unduly.' Two years later, a Parliamentary Select Committee on student relations was to depict the Vice-Chancellors, basking in gratifying student approval, as sorcerers' apprentices calling forth dark forces of student activism which they would prove unable to control. Somewhat unkindly, they quoted a remark of Mansfield Cooper's, that 'in the realm of spiritual and intellectual ideas you cannot strike a balance to suit the British Treasury', and suggested that students could very easily alter this to read 'in the realm of spiritual and intellectual ideas you cannot strike a balance to suit university authorities'.

However, despite the protests of the Vice-Chancellors, the National Union of Students and others, it proved impossible for the University to resist indefinitely the requirement that it should charge the higher, discriminatory fee. On 26th July 1967 the Vice-Chancellor advised his Council that should the University not fall in with the government's proposals it would incur a loss of about £70,000 per annum. The University's total income for 1967–68 was to be in the region of £7.6 million, including £5.9 million from Treasury recurrent grant and just over £600,000 from fees for tuition, registration, examination and graduation. Budgeting was tight; it seemed that even a reduction of 1 per cent in income could not be sustained. Hence Council accepted the recommendation that the higher fee be charged, though it did so on the understanding that a committee should be established to consider cases of hardship and examine applications for assistance on the part of students already at the University.

Much controversy surrounded the question of United Kingdom students' maintenance grants, as distinct from their fees. Gravely resented was the practice of applying a means test to the students' parents which determined the level of grant, while the practice of requiring parents to make up the shortfall and provide students with enough to live on was a possible cause of family tension. Many students hated asking their parents for money, and some parents were reluctant to give it. These arrangements seemed to deny students the independence and the adult status which many of them craved. Some students objected to the implication that they were living on charity rather than earning a living by study, which, after all, was believed (as the Robbins report had proclaimed) to benefit the country, and surely deserved not an allowance but a wage.

There was even stronger resistance to any proposal that grants should be replaced by loans and students be liable to repay them after graduation. Loan proposals were usually justified by the argument that students' earning power would be enhanced by the possession of a degree, and that in recognition of the benefits bestowed on them personally they ought to make some restitution to the country which had supported them. After rehearsing the arguments for and against loans, the Robbins Report had advised against introducing them for the time being, partly on the grounds that first-time buyers of higher education might well be daunted by the prospect of a large mortgage and, as they put it, a 'negative dowry' for young women who wanted to marry. But Robbins had allowed for 'some experiment in this direction' at a later date. In Manchester Professor Brook put the case for students repaying grants after graduation; Dan Brennan, President of the Union in 1965, countered that society should be 'conscious of its indebtedness to graduates', and Pamela Gascoigne of the English Department suggested that perhaps the University staff might be called upon to repay research grants when they had finished doing the work for which they were given (and, presumably, gained professional advancement by carrying it out and publishing the results).

At a general meeting in the Union in November 1965 rumours circulated to the effect that the Vice-Chancellor had supported a government plan to convert grants into loans. This suggestion he strongly repudiated. True, he believed that the present system of grants would prove too costly to the country to be continued, but he 'would like to see any repayment scheme based on a graduated income tax system. This would eliminate the burden of repayment which would otherwise be placed on the young graduate.' Speaking at the Union in December 1967 he told his audience 'with great emotion' (as *Independent* reported) 'how he had battled against loans to students all his life', and how 'he would have had to have sacked members of his staff if he refused to charge overseas students' fees, which he so strongly opposed'.

On other issues there was less meeting of minds, particularly those related to sexual morality and early student marriages. Caution or disapproval on the part of senior administrators and lay officers inevitably exposed them to accusations of being stuffy and unhelpful, and of failing to move with the times. Once again questions arose concerning the proper use of public money and the University's power to curb the independence of the students' Union. High authority could be accused of insensitivity to the needs of women students, on whom the burden of unwanted pregnancies and the demands of a young family would most heavily descend, and also to the needs of women lecturers with young children, who were expected to make their careers in exactly the same way as men.

By 1964–65 the proportion of women students at Owens had increased to 32 per cent, compared with 25.2 per cent in 1951–52. Some faculties were now almost evenly divided between men and women: 948 women students were registered to 951 men in Arts, 178 women to 159 men in Education, and there were now 17 women to 23 men taking full-time degrees in Theology, though they were heavily outnumbered by male colleagues in the part-time courses in that faculty. Women were still making relatively little impression on the Science Faculty. Here they accounted for no more than one-sixth of the total (357 women to 1,821 men). But among these women, as Joan Walsh remembers, were some very good mathematicians, driven to Manchester by the limits on the number of places available to women in Oxford and Cambridge, as well as being attracted by the high reputation of Max Newman's prestigious department.

Women were invading other male preserves and arguing strongly (as did a socialist Vice-President of the Union, Annie Reid, and her successor, Anna Ford) that they should be prepared to compete with men on equal terms and not rely on a quota of reserved places on the Union Council. In the mid-1960s a student journalist wrote of a convention whereby the President of the Union should generally be a man and the Vice-President an elegant woman with a strong dress sense who would act as First Lady and entertain visitors in style. But a male candidate for the presidency, David Clark (afterwards Chancellor of the Duchy of Lancaster in Tony Blair's administration) had defeated a female rival, Sue Baddeley, by only four votes in 1963. Any such convention was decisively broken in 1966 by the triumph of Anna Ford. *Independent* appointed its first woman sports editor, Helen Woolsey, in January 1964, and won the *Daily Mirror* award in 1967 under a woman editor, Lyn Silver. It was true that many left-wing student politicians in the 1960s were not aware of feminist issues or feminine sensibilities (some were surprised and piqued when reproved by Pip Cotterill for swearing by items of female anatomy). But women's voices were growing stronger and more assertive, especially in matters concerning the well-being of women students and the younger women academics.

For the University, as for Philip Larkin, it was broadly true that

Sexual intercourse began
In nineteen sixty-three
(Which was rather late for me) -
Between the end of the *Chatterley* ban
And the Beatles' first LP.

Greater frankness if not greater licence, more open discussion of sexual morality, gradually became customary. *Independent* ventured circumspectly into the subject of birth control in November 1964 in an article which risked offending the powerful Catholic lobby ('we hope that R.C.'s merely disregard this article rather than let it enrage them'). This piece pointed out that students could not afford to marry early and might well enter into five-year engagements, during which they could easily be overpowered, not by the temptations of promiscuity, but by an irresistible desire for sex in anticipation of marriage. 'The tragedy is that sometimes a child results' – a tragic event in the familiar sense that domestic responsibilities, arriving too early, brought with them poverty, loss of freedom, and the postponement if not the end of a promising career. Birth control clinics were for married women only and tended 'to have an anti-man bias'. Potentially a liberator, the contraceptive pill was usually reserved for married women. 'What is needed is courage. Courage on behalf of the Student Health Centre, on behalf of the Family Planning Association to help students in this matter, to provide safe, usable contraceptives.' A complication, however, was that the long-term effects of the pill were the subject of doubt and hesitation among doctors, and that the Health Centre might on those grounds be reluctant to sign the necessary forms to be taken to a clinic which would dispense the pill. Serious problems, too, could arise from sheer ignorance on the part of many students. So the Health Centre seemed to acknowledge when in October 1965 it instituted a Sex Education Week to show films on such subjects as 'Anatomy', 'Contraception' and 'Venereal Disease'. *Independent* began to carry discreet small advertisements for male contraceptives ('Send 10/- for 14 assorted'), which could be obtained through the post.

Not surprisingly, the Union Council wanted far more than this, and began to campaign for a University birth control and family planning clinic under the auspices of the Student Health Centre. Faced with this request in June 1966, the University Council discussed the matter seriously in the light of the Vice-Chancellor's caveat that if the proposal were accepted advice should not be offered to students under the age of twenty-one without their parents' prior consent. They concluded, however, that 'the provision of a service would not be an appropriate function of the University, though the Medical Officers of the Student Health Service should remain free to give whatever advice was justified on health grounds'. Doctors could hardly have been expected to do anything else. General meetings of the Union reaffirmed the Union's policy on the matter and proposed that if its pleas again fell on deaf ears the Union should itself open a clinic on two evenings a week with the help of local doctors. But Council again stood firm after hearing the Vice-Chancellor's opinion that the Union would not be entitled to use public funds for the purpose, though on this occasion he was advancing an administrative and financial rather than a moral argument. The UGC had agreed to an increase in the *per capita* grant to the Union, but only on condition that there be no new forms of expenditure, unless increased numbers or changed circumstances called for them; changes in the moral climate could not, presumably, be regarded as changes of circumstances within the meaning of the agreement.

A crude alternative to the clinic, mooted in November 1967, was a proposal to install contraceptive dispensers in the men's lavatories of the Union. Ostensibly designed to counter the notorious 'Saturday night syndrome' (casual or impulsive couplings after a Union hop and the pregnancies that followed for a few unlucky girls), the measure met opposition on the grounds that it would encourage rather than prevent irresponsible behaviour. Basil Hetherington, the Church of England chaplain, thought that the decision to have intercourse ought to be carefully considered. He also objected to a clinic which would give purely mechanical and not psychological advice. On this particular subject young men needed counselling more than young women did. The chaplain of St Anselm Hall questioned the reliability of contraceptives, especially when used by uninstructed parties. The case for the right kind of clinic seemed to be getting stronger, even as the case for machinery weakened. Sounding a familiar note, the Vice-Chancellor warned that the installation of such apparatus 'would change the character of the Union and result in its becoming a voluntary organisation and having to collect its own fees'. To his relief he was able to tell Senate that the proposal had been 'overturned' by the Union's own members.

Independent sought to solve the problem in its own way by making sure that its readers were properly informed. On 23rd January 1968 it published accounts of contraceptive devices, comparing their costs and their various degrees of reliability. The centre pages of this issue were devoted to the question of unwanted pregnancies, and made the claim that some forty unmarried pregnant students sought the assistance of the Health Centre every year.

Parallel to the campaign for the clinic was the struggle to establish a day nursery for the children of students and of academics, especially women lecturers. The University authorities generally took the view that students should 'wait': that even senior students and postgraduates should defer sex, marriage and domesticity, and that women students with children should interrupt their courses rather than attempt to be students and parents at the same time. About the beginning of 1965 Michael Costello, a member of the Union Council, told the Vice-Chancellor of twenty-seven babies born to students (only one to an unmarried couple) who needed a nursery if their mothers were to continue their courses. There were also several student fathers with working wives. He predicted confidently that there would be no lack of student volunteers to help with the nursery. Once again the Vice-Chancellor saw insuperable obstacles, both legal and financial, to pursuing the project. Such institutions, he said, would be subject to 'stringent statutory requirements and inspection', and an annual income of £4,500 would be required to run a day nursery for even twenty children. He therefore advised Council not to support the proposal.

During the year, however, the Union, spurred on by one of its Vice-Presidents, Judith Gray, decided to start the nursery with aid from its own funds. By October 1965 it had found premises in a church hall in Oxford Place with the approval of the vicar of St David's, who was prepared to sit on the management committee. Due to open the following spring, it was proudly claimed as another Manchester first. Unimpressed, the Vice-Chancellor told the Union 'that the name of the University must not be associated in any way with the project and that public funds must not be used in its support'. The proposed grant from the Union to the nursery must be a loan and nothing more, though the University eventually relented on this point when it became clear that the nursery would never be able to repay the £640 which it had been lent.

However unpromising the circumstances, the nursery continued to run and, in its modest way, to serve the needs and safeguard the careers of younger academic staff as well as of students. A crisis occurred in 1968 when the nursery was required either to leave the premises in Oxford Place or purchase them for £20,000. Again the University withheld support and justified its decision partly on the grounds that the nursery would benefit only a small minority, partly by invoking the rule against new projects that had been cited against the birth control clinic, partly by arguing that students should not start families while they were reading for degrees. Putting the case for the nursery in *Staff Comment*, Sylvia Dixon reminded readers that

'Some first degrees take five or six years, some second degrees much
longer. How long should your M.D. candidate wait for a family? And
what of the mature female student who already has small children?'
'Our whole society is undergoing fundamental change. Early marriages and working mothers are going (whether we like it or not – and
we *should*) to be the norm.'

UMIST came to the rescue by offering, for five years, the premises
of the Oxford Wine Bar at 63 Oxford Road, near All Saints. Here, by
the end of 1969, the nursery was breaking even financially and the
matron was providing seventy children with lunch and tea for five
days a week at a modest cost of £6 per head. Diana Kloss, a Law lecturer and treasurer of the nursery, regretted that the University's attitude still appeared grudging. The converted wine bar would
eventually be demolished, and the University would, it seemed, be
prepared to set aside part of the proposed new Health Centre for a
nursery. But in exchange for such a concession it seemed to be
demanding the impossible. The nursery itself would have to raise the
sum needed to construct that part of the building (about £18,000) and
secure at least the promise of the money by the end of the current academic year. Should it fail to do so it would be excluded from the
Precinct plans. 'Our only hope at the moment is to ask the City to
provide a nursery for children of both University and Polytechnic
students to be financed by the City alone.'

Articles written in the early 1970s testified that the nursery was still
struggling on, but apparently with much smaller numbers: it was
accommodating only about twenty children, with a waiting-list of fifty.
Of the forty parents of the twenty children attending at the beginning
of 1972, eighteen were undergraduates, seven were postgraduates, five
were engaged in teacher training, and ten were working. About half
were at the University and the remainder were at the Polytechnic or the
Colleges of Education. There were long waiting lists for Corporation
nurseries, and the students would never get places in them for their
children. As Fred Tye, a veteran member of Council, recalls, the University's argument against itself providing a nursery was that 'it's not
possible for the University to make it possible for a student to become
a student'. Rather, the University's task was to supervise the studies,
and students must be expected to make their own arrangements for
their children. The issue of the nursery was to be for some years to
come an item on the agenda of the University–Union Relations Committee, and to be the subject of several surveys and inquiries designed
to establish the extent of the need for child care.

There were no boycotts, sit-ins or other protests over the birth control clinic or the day nursery. Both were examples of almost inevitable, not particularly sinister, conflict between generations. The older generation of administrators and councillors continued to watch anxiously over the morals of students, urging them to be provident, defer gratification and cause no public scandal. Arguably they did too little to provide positive support and encouragement for these enterprising responses to a changing world, about which students felt strongly. No doubt the managers of the University's finances were conscious of higher priorities than the day nursery and rightly reluctant to infringe the UGC's rules. But the University's control over public funding was an unwelcome reminder of the limits imposed on the Union's autonomy, of the constraints on a student population which could not govern itself fully even in domestic and welfare matters, and still existed in a kind of transitional state between adolescence and adulthood. In some fields the University authorities had shared the students' idealism, especially over the treatment of comrades from overseas. But had they been tenacious enough, and had they been too ready to allow prosaic economic arguments to triumph in the end? Were they not themselves too much at the mercy of the government which provided annually some four-fifths of their funds, and could the existence of the UGC as buffer between government and the universities continue to conceal that fact?

10

Participation and protest

In his book *The Modern University*, published in 1965, Leslie Brook, Professor of English Language, sometime Pro-Vice-Chancellor and Presenter of Honorary Graduands, observed comfortably that 'There seems to be no very strong demand for students to have a larger share in the control and administration of the universities to which they belong.' He saw nothing amiss, however, with the prospect of a joint standing committee of staff and students which might tackle such momentous issues as 'whether Wednesday afternoons should be kept free from lectures for the sake of students who wished to play games, whether certain tables or rooms in the refectory should be set aside for the exclusive use of staff or students, or whether the university library should remain open in the evenings'.

Within three or four years, however, students would be seeking direct representation on Senate, Council, Court, Faculty Boards, the Charter Revision Committee and all the most powerful university bodies, and at one point demanding a third or even half of the seats. Nor would their interest be confined to domestic matters. Their voice would be heard in demands for control, or at least for strong influence, over the curriculum, methods of teaching, forms of assessment, the appointment of academic staff, the choice of a new Vice-Chancellor – in short, for the conversion of their place of work into a democracy, rather than a specialised institution for communicating knowledge and understanding from those who knew more to those who knew less. Radical students, an active minority, sought the destruction or root-and-branch reform of the authoritarian system which sought to rule their lives in the present and to shape their future existence by the qualifications it awarded, the conformity it demanded, the ambitions it instilled.

At its most far-reaching the movement for student power was an attack on universities as instruments of a capitalist society. Radical critics accused them of serving capitalism's needs by slotting the mass-

produced graduates of the Faculties of Science, Technology and Economics (if no others) into their pre-ordained places in the corporate
structures of big business. It was as if industry and commerce had
become a kind of Minotaur to which innocent graduates were annually sacrificed. The University of Manchester was open to attacks on
these grounds which superficially made sense. Like most civic universities Manchester submitted to financial control by a Council on
which businessmen and professional men held a majority of the seats,
and the promised new Charter would make no substantive difference
to this arrangement. By establishing the Business School, or so it
would be said, the University had lost its 'academic neutrality'
between the Confederation of British Industries and the Trade Union
Congress. University Councillors, it would be pointed out, were
directors of companies which engaged in unsavoury activities in
Southern Africa and implicated the University in giving tacit support
to exploitative, racist regimes. Some of the University's research activities were said to be assisting the aggressive war waged in Vietnam by
the United States. Industrial society in general was associated with
soulless, utilitarian and impersonal forms of mass instruction, with the
operation, indeed, of a 'knowledge factory' which produced information and not argument or analysis, and which discouraged both freedom of thought and criticism of authority. Students, it seemed, were
controlled through the University's power to assess them, particularly
by methods that imposed considerable strain and anxiety and, when
themselves examined, proved to be inefficient as well as inhuman.
Only through high levels of student participation in the making of
decisions could the institution be purged of corruption. Parliamentary
democracy was not enough; it amounted to nothing more, some
argued, than the right to make a choice every five years between one
elite and another. The place where democracy mattered was the place
of work. All too often democracy had no place within it, and this
arrangement was quite at odds with the academic ideal that students
should be taught to question all accepted authority and think for
themselves.

For the radical student, nothing more than token concessions
would ever be gained through orthodox approaches to university
authorities. It was no good using the channels which those authorities
had themselves devised and observing the procedures which they had
themselves laid down, because these were not impartial and were
designed to frustrate or delay change. Direct action, non-violent
protests by the use of tactics such as the sit-in, boycotts of lectures and

tutorials, disruption of administrative routines, the picketing of Senate – such measures would have to be employed to make the University take heed. Authority would not budge except under some form of duress. Wrangling around a committee table was likely to achieve little more than the mutation of student leaders into university bureaucrats; the recommendations of consultative committees would find favour only if it suited authority to accept them. At a Manchester Senate debate in March 1970 a pessimistic speaker thought the mass sit-in which was then in progress 'the culmination of a concerted attempt to disrupt the work of the University, to attack the essential values without which academic work was not possible and to replace them with a system the nature of which was never specified'.

Manchester was not a prime mover in the campaign for student power and participation. Several of its major incidents were ignited by events elsewhere, particularly at the London School of Economics and at the University of Warwick. In 1966 the issues which had arisen at Berkeley in California, originating in disputes over the right to sell political literature on campus and broadening into a struggle over the nature of the university itself, were discussed in an article in *Manchester Independent*. Anna Ford sent a telegram of sympathy to David Adelstein, President of the students' Union at LSE, who had been censured for writing to *The Times* without the current Director's permission concerning the controversial appointment of Dr Walter Adams as Director of the School. But she disapproved of the militant tactics that were tried out during her presidency. Opponents of the war in Vietnam objected to any kind of military presence on University premises, and threatened to seize guns or weapons from the Royal Observer Corps stall in the Union lounge; they planned to burst in upon a Union debate with placards proclaiming 'No Guns in our Union' and 'End the War in Vietnam'. But the President warned the minders of the stall and no such thing happened. When planning the mass protest against overseas students' fees, the Union Executive fell out with the Action Committee which it had itself appointed. This body, headed by an American chairman, Bob Lubetsky, appeared to be planning actions – such as a sit-in at the Manchester offices of the Department of Education and Science – which the Union as a whole would not support, and which risked alienating the University administration at a time when it seemed for once to be sympathetic to student protest.

In an article published in *Independent* in February 1967, Lubetsky argued fiercely against any notion that universities ought to be instruments of national purpose or stooges for big business. To prevent them from becoming such, students should be able to organise their own environment, through 'student-autonomous control over their own Halls of Residence and Union, and student–faculty committees to rule over the hiring and firing of professors, salary scales and course content. Administrators need to be reminded that their task is to administer and not make policy decisions; and professors need to be reminded that at the University their primary task is to aid in the educational process'. Early in 1967 the newly formed Radical Student Alliance (described by *The Sunday Times* as 'a popular front ginger group within the NUS') had held its first conference at LSE. It set out to challenge the costive policies of the studiously moderate executive of the National Union of Students. To radicals it seemed that this cautious body possessed, as one critic remarked, 'all the passion of an ashtray' and about as much power to promote the interests of students. At a conference of the North West branch of the Alliance, held in Manchester in the autumn term of 1967, the new organisation was described as a 'broad grouping of individuals who aim to make students more militant in the pursuit of their own interests while increasing their general level of political consciousness'. Much discussed at the conference was the possibility of making both student Unions and the Alliance itself into bodies much more like trade unions, which should ally with other workers' organisations in a common struggle. 'Students have gradually changed from regarding themselves as privileged members of the middle class to realising that they are a class which can play a meaningful part in changing society if sufficiently organised.' Strikes, boycotts, sit-ins and other forms of disruption were no longer to be eschewed. In the winter of 1967–68 there was some student support for workers in a prolonged industrial dispute at an engineering factory, Roberts-Arundel, in Stockport; two students were arrested for allegedly assaulting the police on the picket line, and the Amalgamated Engineering Union thanked students for their support. It seemed as though workers of the hand and brain might indeed come together in a common enterprise.

In Manchester, as in most universities, only a few students had the passion and energy for regular and sustained political action, only a few believed in the possibility of revolution, and unrest affected some parts of the University far more than others. Senior administrators associated upheavals particularly with the Radical Student Alliance; with the Socialist Society, generally known as Soc. Soc.; with students and lecturers in the Social Sciences and in some parts of the Faculty of

Arts. They were inclined to attribute student protest to poor academic motivation and to connect it with non-vocational subjects. An opportunity to analyse student militancy in public arose early in 1969 when, after the formation of a Commons Select Committee on Student Relations in the universities and colleges, a panel of MPs (Sub-committee B) arrived to take evidence in Manchester. In his evidence Vincent Knowles remarked 'that it is in the fields of political history, politics, modern history and sociology that the motivation may not be quite so easy to see as in medicine, town planning and architecture. This may well have something to do with the unrest of those young people who do not see where they are going and leads to instability in their behaviour, perhaps.' However, the Parliamentary Committee, in their final report, gave more weight to the opinion that social science students were 'being trained properly to ask basic questions about the nature of the institutions of which they are part, whereas this is not by and large true of people who study medicine and science and such like'. In Manchester's Social Sciences Faculty the dissection of social theories, including Marxism, formed part of academic courses; students were naturally attracted to journalism and politics; the School of Politics and Modern History supplied a number of prominent Union officers; and historians were inclined, by the nature of their discipline, to suspect authority of being up to no good.

As the Union survey had found in 1963, there was still a strong link between subjects studied and political attitudes and activity. Engineers, as the natural servants rather than critics of industrial society, seemed inclined to concentrate on making things work rather than on questioning what they were working for. Ed Straw, a student of civil engineering, brother of Jack Straw, then President of NUS, was elected President of the students' Union in February 1970, but he was not aligned with any particular left-wing group. Students in professional schools could expect to exert relatively little influence on a curriculum determined in large measure by professional bodies outside the University. Scientists, dentists and others often complained of being too busy to protest and seemed to despise and envy those who had the leisure to make a nuisance of themselves. 'Two disgruntled dental students' remarked in February 1969 that 'students that do protest just don't realise how bloody well-off they are'. Professor Morton, who was a Professor of Chemical Engineering at UMIST and a Pro-Vice-Chancellor of the University, told the visiting MP's that students of Medicine, Science and Technology seldom attended the lunch-time general meetings of the Union 'because they have lectures at 1.30 and they are keen on doing their work'. It would be wrong, though, to ascribe the passivity of scientists solely to enslavement by the demands of lectures and practical work in laboratories: in some departments, such as Physics, attempts had been made to overhaul teaching, to communicate information about examination results, to involve students in departmental affairs, to teach in small, intimate tutorials. Professor Willmott, Director of the Physical Laboratories, told the visiting parliamentarians that in his department students were already represented on committees dealing with course content, laboratories, workshops, and the departmental library.

Halls of residence and their rules were sometimes the targets of organised protest. But some of them acted as a counter-revolutionary or at least as a stabilising force. Relations between youngish tutors and students were often closer, and opportunities for discussing issues far into the night more plentiful, in the halls than in many academic departments. Gerard McKenna, who had recently joined the Registrar's Department and was then a tutor in Allen Hall, became conscious that 'meetings were being held in the Hall by student groups who were seeking to counter some of the wilder elements'. 'Scatter-gun radicalism', as a historian has called it, had opponents in many quarters. Early in 1969 a Union motion, voted on by postal ballot, that 'There should be a boycott of all lectures and tutorials on Thursday February 6th, and the day should be devoted to discussion in the Arts building on the exam system and the role of staff and students in academic decision making', suffered defeat by 2,490 votes to 1,644. The result was said to have been swayed by the hall vote, and there were rueful references to 'an inordinately high vote from Owens Park', as if this were somehow the product of an unfair tactic. The result may have echoed a long-standing rivalry between the central Union and the outlying halls, both of which made claims on students' loyalties and competed for their custom. Woolton Hall, in particular, remained resolutely philistine and a-political. Undertaken in the spirit of Rag rather than Revolution, its main contribution to the struggle was to try to kidnap the presidential candidates when they made their customary tour of the halls in search of votes. If Wooltonians could, for example, handcuff aspiring politicians and put them on the train to London the proceedings would be cleansed of undue solemnity and pomposity. On the eve of Manchester's largest and most prolonged sit-in in 1970, the Junior Common Room of Woolton objected that the 'supposedly democratic constitution' of the Union was suffering from 'the manipulation of the Emergency General

Meetings by pretentious political minorities, both to the Left and the Right'.

It was also broadly true that protest seldom permeated the whole academic year; it was seasonal rather than continuous, and the most vigorous forms of it usually erupted between late January and early March. They were so timed in 1968 (over Vietnam and over the visit of a Labour politician); in 1969 (over examination procedures and over events at LSE); in 1970 (over the contents of students' files and an alleged denial of free speech). Events in other months of the year, particularly the announcement of the new Vice-Chancellor's appointment in the autumn of 1969, could trigger angry reactions and prolonged protests. But trouble could be expected in the Lent term almost as a matter of routine, and was generally quietened down by the Easter vacation and the approach of the main examination season. Since the student body dispersed at the end of each academic year and reassembled in October, its composition greatly changed, time was needed to build up a fresh impetus and to acquaint newcomers with the issues at stake. February was the month of the Union elections, when causes were most vociferously pleaded. It was also a season (though not the only one) at which candidates for office would try to make a name for themselves by accusing the existing Union officers of impropriety, feebleness or gross incompetence in the conduct of Union business. Furthermore, some departments held their 'terminal' or 'course' examinations in January, and these served as an irritant, calling into question the utility of examinations. As mere 'mocks' or rehearsals they were easier to challenge than the summer examinations which actually contributed to a degree.

Protest, too, could be seen as not far removed from the old form of carnival, an extravaganza which lightened the gloom of the influenza season. Rag, too, after the occasional quiet year in the early 1960s, showed signs of getting out of hand. In February 1968 old-style and new-style forms of disturbance coincided. The Manchester and Salford Students' Rag (as it now was) extended its buffoonery across the country and was found increasingly irresponsible and unfunny. It daubed slogans on Stonehenge, damaged the runway of Speke Airport at Liverpool, and perpetrated (so Senate was informed) 'a hoax at Ramsgate which had wasted the time of the police and the armed forces'. Whereas Rag, which turned outwards, exasperated the public, student protest, which turned inwards on the University itself, inspired genuine fear and unhappiness on the part of senior administrators and academics, and also attracted public attention of an unwelcome kind.

Discussing student relations with the visiting MP's in 1969, Mansfield Cooper spoke of three 'broad bands' within the student population. More than 50 per cent of them were not interested in political or social issues or in the government of the University. They should not be condemned as 'apathetic'; rather, they had 'come up to University to do a job' and wanted only to be allowed to get on with it. There was also, the Vice-Chancellor conceded, a considerable body of students who were 'very deeply interested in the problems of society and the University', 'to whom the University would be wise to pay a lot of attention'. But there was another 'tiny layer' who would not be appeased, whatever the University did, because they belonged (as he had said earlier) to 'the world of student agitation and protest and exploitation of every kind of difficulty and grievance'.

The student officers of the Union had discussed a similar question with the Parliamentary Sub-committee, and two of the officers, R.V. Porter and J.L. Terry, had spoken of a hard core of anything between thirty and fifty militants, who commanded a following of about 200 (the Union then had 7,850 members). Joe Terry, the Events Vice-President, defending Manchester's activists against the charge of being 'academic thugs', said carefully, 'I would not say we have anyone here whose sole concern is merely to disrupt the life of the University. We certainly have some idealists, albeit wild ones. But in their own way they are fairly justified, in that they are people who believe in their point of view ... ' A problem which the officers frankly acknowledged was that General Meetings of the Union could easily be manipulated by a small but determined body of members. Under an antiquated rule, which had been in force for forty years and reflected a time when numbers were much smaller, an Emergency General Meeting could be summoned at the behest of only thirty people, and 100 people could form a quorum. The officers drew attention to the very high levels of attendance at meetings which discussed topics of universal interest such as examinations or representation. But they admitted that otherwise 'general meetings seem to be left very much to a group of union-conscious people fluctuating anywhere between 100 and 300, most of whom have political alignments one way or the other'.

Complaints about student apathy were almost as common as complaints about student militancy. Some said that the passivity of the majority allowed the minority to get away with far too much, and others berated the majority for failing to support the minority of lively and interested dissenters. Much would plainly depend on the political skills of University administrators and on their ability to retain the support of moderate student opinion. Many senior people, unfortunately, were unused to any kind of challenge, inclined to see student protest as intrinsically violent, nervously aware of the lack of force at their own disposal and conscious of the reluctance of the police to intervene in domestic disputes on University premises. One of their fears was that young lecturers might side with rebels at a time when it was important for academics to close ranks. But it was not entirely surprising that some junior academics, estranged from the hierarchy and closer to the students in age, should be drawn to their students rather than their seniors. Younger tutors might well feel that they understood students as their elders did not. Sometimes, at least, they strove, not to stir up student protest, but to calm students down and reconcile them with the University.

Examination issues were a subject on which most students felt strongly, and were not just the concern of an aggressive minority. They had been discussed throughout the 1960s. Was there no alternative to the traditional, three-hour, 'unseen' examination? In this rite of passage candidates were isolated from each other and thrown back on any resources which they carried in their heads, cut off from books, dictionaries, encyclopaedias and most other aids to study, and required to prove themselves by a short burst of energy. Critics said that this system put a premium on a retentive memory, called for the regurgitation of knowledge that had been mugged up only to be forgotten again, failed to test analytical and argumentative skills, and caused considerable anxiety on the part of a number of students. Providing much-needed facts, a member of the Health Service reported that in May and June 1968 222 students had attended the Medical Centres suffering from examination strain. This he defined as 'an environmental hazard imposed by the University producing stress which manifests itself by physical and mental symptoms – diarrhoea, vomiting, insomnia, feelings of panic, writer's cramp, lack of concentration, blackouts and abnormal behaviour – all familiar to some members of staff'. Nobody knew how many more students had suffered from these ills but not sought professional help. Faced with such complaints, however, higher authority was inclined to be bracing. Interviewed in May 1966, the Vice-Chancellor had said: 'Life is a perpetual examination; take marriage, for example – looking for a partner is one long succession of examinations and a person who is afraid of examinations is afraid of life.'

Any evidence that the examination system was foolish and fallible was seized upon eagerly and given embarrassing publicity. In January

1969 twenty-two out of thirty-four first-year students in the School of Politics and Modern History refused to take the course examination set for them. They were potential martyrs, and the University wisely decided to offer them another set of papers to sit. The dashing Professor M.R.D. Foot, official historian of the Special Operations Executive in the Second World War and editor of the Gladstone diaries, told them that if they refused this lifeline 'I'm afraid your university careers will be finished. The University is not spoiling for a fight, but we do intend to maintain the kind of University we want – a rational university, a community of scholars.' The students gave way, and it was duly suggested that they had been 'threatened, bullied and cajoled into surrender', a most unlikely role for the enlightened Foot to play.

The facts seem to have been rather different. By their action the students had intended to provoke discussion with their tutors and had booked a room for the purpose of meeting them. A colleague of Foot's, Brian Manning, later wrote that the University authorities had not consulted the tutors concerned and had advised them not to go to any such meeting, presumably for fear that by agreeing to talk they might appear to condone the students' rebellion. But some tutors had ignored the advice and it was they who had persuaded the students to accept the University's offer, thereby avoiding a good deal of embarrassment, since any attempt to discipline the rebels would certainly have brought many others out in sympathy. 'The lesson that should be drawn from this,' wrote Manning, 'is that the myth of the inhuman administration can be overcome if the university will place greater trust in tutors.'

Soon afterwards there was a dramatic breach of the confidentiality which normally protected examiners, when *Independent* published a leaked document. This consisted of a stern rebuke issued by a social anthropologist, Professor Emrys Peters, to his colleagues concerning the misconduct of an examiners' meeting, presumably one which had been held the previous summer. Assurance had been given that examining boards, when judging students in danger of failing, would take account of their academic record during the year. But Peters's letter conveyed the strong impression that some first-year students had suffered injustice because evidence about their performance was missing and the tutors themselves, having found more entertaining things to do elsewhere, had failed to attend the meeting. 'Instead of mouthing the need to help students', said the letter sternly, 'it would be more fitting if staff began by fulfilling their contractual obligations.' When the story broke, Peters hastened to explain that he had saved the situation by consulting faculty record cards and speaking to external examiners. The severity of the reprimand may have seemed reassuring; as Anna Ford testifies, Peters himself cared about students and dealt with them imaginatively. But in the face of such stories it became increasingly difficult to maintain that the examining system was always efficient and fair.

The most radical position was that all examinations, however conducted, were simply a means of asserting power and dividing the academic community. Dick Atkinson, a temporary lecturer in Sociology, argued that the rituals of examining and grading hampered the free exchange that ought to take place between the teacher and the pupil, the teacher being in truth nothing more than a student who happened to be a little further down the road. ' … assessment gives me power over you, and the system has power over me because it forces me to assess you'. However, politics being the art of the possible, few students dreamed of abolition. Most thought of more limited objectives – of an automatic right to resit failed examinations, of the right not to sit more than one examination on the same day, of the returning of marked scripts.

Some progress was made on the subject of forms of assessment designed to test qualities neglected by the three-hour examination, tests which would reward the long-distance runner as well as the sprinter. In October 1969 the Department of American Studies introduced a system of assessment which depended half upon essays submitted during the year and half upon the usual type of three-hour examination. Would this actually reduce strain, or was it essentially a means of making students work harder and more consistently, providing them with short-term objectives to make them organise themselves better? Would it create an examination atmosphere which permeated the whole year and immediately turned tutors into judges, the students being more at their mercy than ever before? Some of those educated in Oxford or Cambridge found the idea repulsive, because in their view essays ought to be simply teaching instruments, a focus for discussion, not final statements to be solemnly weighed and assessed and never subsequently improved. Dennis Welland, who was then Professor of American Literature, remembers that the students who had advocated such assessment in his department were disconcerted to find it being introduced before they had had time to leave. Whatever the rights and wrongs of it, however, the new belt-and-braces system seemed to promise reassurance to a great many anxious students and appeared likely to spread widely in the University. It seemed more practicable than other proposed reforms, such as the introduction of multiple-choice examination papers (which would indeed have put a premium on factual knowledge), or essays on a set subject which could be written over a day or two with any aids that a student cared to employ.

The old system had many defenders, and among the most articulate was Brian Cox, one of the Professors of English Literature, who gained national fame (or notoriety) as co-editor of the volume of *Black Papers on Education*, published in 1969 under the auspices of his journal *Critical Quarterly*. Cox was no simple reactionary. On arriving from Hull in 1966 he had, as he now recalls, found the University of Manchester 'an extremely conservative organisation, in many of the bad senses of that word'. He had chafed against the regime of Professor Brook, 'who really felt that God created the rules of Manchester and they should never be changed'. Cox had first-hand experience of Berkeley, the scene of student unrest as early as 1964, and had much admired the idealism and courage of the students concerned. But, in common with many other Manchester academics, he felt that the grievances of English students were trifling by comparison. For him the attack on examinations formed part of a campaign to undermine the rigorous standards that ought to govern education. Indeed, he argued that 'Without exams, which impose an authoritative concept of the subject, the individual teacher is left very much to his own devices ... Exams make people work hard. Much opposition to them is based on the belief that people work better without reward or incentive, a naïveté which is against all knowledge of human nature. All life depends upon passing exams ... To create an education system without examinations is to fail to prepare children and students for the realities of adult life.' In this matter at least Professor Cox was at one with the Vice-Chancellor, who had spoken of examinations as a metaphor for life itself.

As he recalls, Cox was much in favour of consulting students, as consumers of goods and services, on matters affecting the domestic side of University government. But he and others disliked the idea of students exerting control over the curriculum, 'because the whole point of a curriculum is that you can't really know what is right or wrong until you graduate ... I'm a great believer in flexibility in curricula, so that students have areas of choice where that's possible. But a decision on what is basic to a subject must come from professional teachers ... ' However, the Vice-Chancellors and Principals were ready to be a shade more accommodating and by October 1968 had arrived at an influential agreement with the National Union of Students. This was to be translated slowly into action in Manchester in the course of the next two years. It was never likely to satisfy radicals, savouring as it did of 'co-optation', i.e. of taking one's opponents into the government in order to soften them up, of putting them on committees to draw their fangs. In time the NUS was to make higher demands, but the Vice-Chancellors did not agree a new document.

Circulated generally throughout universities, the emollient October agreement recognised that 'men and women of student age are expected to bear the full responsibilities of adult life much earlier than would have been thought reasonable a year ago'. They were no doubt referring to the Family Law Reform and Representation of the People Acts of 1968, which had made young people of eighteen legally adults and given them voting rights. The agreement distinguished between three areas: first, student welfare; second, courses, curricula, planning and development; third, decisions on such matters as appointments and promotions of members of staff, the admission of individual students to the University, and their academic assessment. Students should be directly involved in the first two matters. In the third area, students would not be allowed to discuss individual cases and these would be treated as confidential 'reserved' business, kept from student eyes and ears, but students would none the less be entitled to discuss the general principles involved in such decisions and have their views taken into account. To this end, the joint statement was generally in favour of joint staff/student consultative committees at university, faculty and departmental levels, members of those committees being of equal status and serving as representatives free to exercise their own judgment and modify it if they chose in the light of discussion. They were not to be mandated delegates, obliged to stick to a predetermined position and obliged to refer back to their constituents before they could change it. Student members of such committees should be allowed to attend the boards which discussed their recommendations, for all items of 'unreserved' business.

In Manchester the implications of the agreement were gradually worked out, though in May 1969 a General Meeting of the students' Union delayed the process by rejecting the report of the working party set up by the Senate to consider the matter. Although the working party contained plenty of students, it was thought not to have obtained enough concessions. Union presidents, both from Owens and from UMIST, began to attend and speak at Senate meetings from the end of 1969 onwards. It remained to be seen how seriously anyone would take the recommendations of staff–student committees and whether consultation with students would prove to be genuine. Student officers told the visiting MP's that the Drama Department in particular had held a full and helpful discussion on examinations, but in other places the professors too often seemed interested only in explaining the present system and were indifferent to anyone else's point of view.

In July 1968, Sir William Mansfield Cooper announced his intention to retire in two years' time, thus enabling the search for his successor to begin. He was unfortunately destined to spend the last years of a distinguished career contending with a movement he could neither understand nor sympathise with. He had himself struggled to enter higher education and triumphed against heavy odds. How could those young men and women who now had it so much easier fail to regard higher education as a privilege, how could they presume to criticise their educators, and how could they misuse the grants bestowed upon them by using the precious time to challenge the principles on which a great institution was run? Trained as an academic lawyer before he became an administrator, he adopted a somewhat legalistic approach to most problems, and had a misplaced confidence in the power of the law to subdue people who had no respect for law. Faced with requests to suspend university teaching for a day or two in order to allow all staff and students to attend 'teach-ins' at which important educational issues would be discussed, he was inclined to invoke, somewhat drily, the law of contract. The University had undertaken to provide lectures and tutorials at the appointed times, and provide them it must. He was shocked by breaches of confidentiality and seemed readier to object to them than to correct the faults which they exposed. A cartoon in *Independent* depicted an invisible figure at a desk (presumably representing him) interviewing a senior colleague with a face like a skull: 'Never mind the efficiency of your department, professor. Who let the cat out of the bag?' His scrupulous care for the proper use of public money led him to hint at the possibility that grants might be withdrawn from student troublemakers, a procedure that could seem like blackmail, and could be construed as part of a plan to break the students' Union when it began to express unacceptable opinions.

There was much to try his patience. Early in 1968 the University first collided with the Radical Student Alliance. This body had 'brought to light' at a convention in London the news that Manchester scientists appeared to be doing research work for the United States

Defense Department. Opposition to the war in Vietnam had become a sacred cause. Pleas for peace and an end to the inhumanity of modern industrial warfare had figured in student politics for the past three years. Expose the complicity of one's own university in the brutal campaign of an advanced industrial nation against a people of peasant farmers, and there would be a chance of protesting effectively against the war, since universities were more vulnerable than governments and more open to persuasion. A prominent figure in the ensuing events was Andrew Hornung, a student in the German Department who had distinguished himself as a journalist. He had written a convoluted column in *Independent* and edited his own magazine, *Idiom*. In style more Cavalier than Roundhead, he had once been described as 'an elegant, effete, teutonic goatee standing up in a debate to protest against the ungallant treatment of a lady debater'. Hornung was now much in favour of an alliance between workers and students. Only through such a combination could radical change in the University come about. Through the Union he and a fellow left-winger, Dave Clark, launched their assault on the Chemistry Department. It had allegedly received a grant from the Dow Chemical Company, which among other things manufactured napalm. At the very least, they argued, the department was releasing American scientists to do war work by performing their other, less harmful duties for them. Three students were charged with illegal billposting, the posters in question showing dead civilians and under their image the legend 'Killed by Manchester University?' However, in this debate, a research chemist, Bob Ayerst, was able to win the day by arguing that the University had a policy of not accepting classified war work, and maintaining that the department was merely undertaking research into polystyrene, which had a great variety of uses. The left-wingers failed to carry their motion in the Union, but still attempted to send a deputation to Senate. Wisely, the Vice-Chancellor issued a press statement explaining that the University had indeed received $1,452,839 from American sources, but of these $1,420,039 were designed to support work in 'fundamental science'. This meant, in effect, research by astronomers (they had, for example, been photographing the moon from the observatory at the Pic du Midi in the Pyrenees, with the aid of project assistants paid for by the United States Air Force). 'The fact that some processes or materials on which scientists work could be applied in war, is entirely coincidental.'

Questions concerning unsavoury military researches continued to come up occasionally, as they did in December 1968, when a small demonstration at the Appointments Board objected to an advertisement for a research post at the Chemical Defence Experimental Establishment at Porton Down. The students concerned were told 'that the Board did not act as a moral censor on such matters and that it believed the attitude of students towards such posts was a matter for their individual consciences'. The demonstration ended peaceably. Fortunately for Manchester, the issues of Porton Down and free speech, arising separately, did not come together in the same way as they did at Essex – where the Vice-Chancellor sent down three students for preventing a scientist from Porton Down from giving a lecture, and thereby provoked a sit-in and a series of other events.

Lecture disruption occurred in Manchester on 1st March 1968. A group of students – perhaps 150, according to the report in *The Times* – prevented the delivery of a much-advertised lecture in the University by Patrick Gordon Walker, the Secretary of State for Education and Science. He was to have explored the subject of the new polytechnics, which were more directly concerned with vocational training and were under local authority control, and the relationship of polytechnics to universities. The lecture was due to be recorded for the BBC Third Programme. Interrupters were not taking a moral stand, but pursuing student self-interest. They demanded that the Minister should talk about first things first – by which they meant student grants (no one could attend a university or a polytechnic without adequate financial support). Andrew Hornung, who had initiated the disturbance, proclaimed as the chanting of his allies swelled about him, 'This is not a demonstration, it is an attempt to get a direct confrontation with the Minister.' Mr Gordon Walker left the hall, stepping over the bodies of students who were sitting in the doorway to block his exit. He later received apologies from the Presidents of the University Union and of Didsbury College of Education.

Since the event had not been a Union function but an authorised extra-mural lecture on University premises, there was a case for disciplinary action, not by the Union officers, but by the University authorities. The Vice-Chancellor summoned a council of deans of the faculties; a Professor of Law, Peter Bromley, having led the majority which urged the need for action, found himself appointed chairman of a disciplinary committee. After a lengthy hearing, the committee pronounced sentence on Hornung and a fellow activist, Glyn Carver. Both were suspended and officially excluded from University buildings for the remainder of the academic year, though with a proviso that they should be allowed to return and take their examinations (it was reported that both continued to attend lectures nonetheless). A large body of students approved of the University's disciplinary proceedings. Indeed, David Worsley, the past President of the students' Union, told the visiting MP's a year later that the group which had disrupted the lecture 'suddenly realised how isolated they were from the rest of the University. The petition which went round the University collected 4,000 signatures in the last week of term, and that petition supported the action taken against these people.'

However, there was still a possibility that things might go disastrously wrong. Bombarded with letters from the public disapproving of student behaviour, the University seemed on the verge of making martyrs. It received twenty-four 'confessions' from students who claimed to have been just as guilty in the matter as Hornung and Carver. Wisely disclaiming any wish to proceed further on its own account, the administration asked these students if they too wished to be disciplined. When replies were not received, the Vice-Chancellor wrote to the students' education authorities to make them aware of the situation before they issued grant cheques at the start of the summer term: 'We feel that your authority might have a justifiable grievance if a full grant were made available when possible proceedings were pending.' The snowball threatened to swell into an avalanche, with students making representations to MP's, but the trouble subsided when it was realised that the students had 'relied on not replying' to convey the message that they did not want to suffer punishment.

A new ritual was established. As part of the process of pacification, it was important to institute an inquiry into something – in this case, into 'the relationship between staff and students and the administration in the University'. In the hands of Peter Worsley, Professor of Sociology, this inquiry developed into an ambitious project financed by an external research grant and also involving the University of Edinburgh. Senior academics from one University would prepare 'an objective, scientifically based' and 'diagnostic' study of the other, by means of interviews and questionnaires. By 1969–70 the project was under way, enjoying a grant from the Social Science Research Council, and proceeding under the direction of Worsley of Manchester and Tom Burns of Edinburgh.

Early in the academic year 1968–69 the University Senate, realising that student troubles would be with them for some time yet, took the precaution of establishing a Student Affairs Committee. This consisted of seven professors, of Lord Bowden, and of two others (Geoffrey North and John Parker) with whom the Vice-Chancellor would be able to consult rapidly in matters concerning student unrest. It became known as the Fire Brigade. The name served not just as a joke but as a form of code, though its use could cause problems. Once, when the Vice-Chancellor's secretary rang the Geography Department and asked 'Will you tell Mr North it's the Fire Brigade?', the Geography secretary answered 'There's no fire here', put the telephone down, and failed to pass the message on.

In the spring of 1968 the Vice-Chancellor was still prepared to proclaim his confidence in the good sense of most of the student body and in the capacity of Union members to resolve issues responsibly. He was the first signatory of a letter to that effect to *Staff Comment*, also signed by Anna Ford (then in the Registrar's Department), the Anglican and Catholic chaplains, and several academics. Early in 1969, however, some of that confidence seemed to be evaporating; he was receiving 'demands' from the Union that he dissociate himself from Dr Adams, the Director of LSE, and give undertakings that he himself would never imitate Adams's actions by closing the University or summoning the police on to University premises. When he refused, there was a brief sit-in on 17th February. Students tried to enter his office. Finding the way blocked, they occupied the Registrar's office for about two hours. It was no more than a 'token solidarity demonstration', inspired by a visit from Nicholas Bateson, a lecturer facing disciplinary action at LSE, and was followed by a not-very-determined attempt to gain entry to Senate to hear it discuss the demands. The tone of Mansfield Cooper's report to Senate suggested that he was dealing with a small, rather ineffectual and not very stout-hearted body ('their discretion by far exceeding their valour'), who were not successful in persuading other students to join them. That being so, he might well have been confident of eventual victory. But he was clearly exasperated by 'the utter irresponsibility which had now gripped a section of the student body'. Now openly attacking the Vice-Chancellor, writers in the student press represented him as rattled if not terrified, and therefore inclined to resort to acts of intimidation. They made something of the text of a letter he had sent to graduates of the University, in which he again appeared to be hinting at the withdrawal of grants from troublemakers and arguing that since the 'dissidents' were not quarrelling with the University alone but with the 'society' that supported it, that society would have to lend its aid to enable 'reason' to prevail. Let taxpayers protest heartily at the misuse of their money.

In the spring of 1969 other protests focused on a long-standing irritant – the regulations in halls of residence, including the relatively liberal 'midnight rule' in Owens Park. Ashburne Hall was an obvious target. But administrators were learning not to overreact, and when sitters-in approached and settled down in the place for an hour or two Vincent Knowles advised the Warden, 'Don't call the police – that's what they want.' A paper in the name of the Owens Park Student Action Committee announced their intention to 'free Halls of Residence from the paternal attitudes of an unrepresentative minority of Wardens and Managers'. The demonstration at Ashburne originated from outside its walls, but was said to be supported from within by a number of Ashburne students who wished 'to remain anonymous for fear of reprisals'. As the protesters explained, their intention was 'To demonstrate the impotence of the authorities when faced with collective disobedience of *their* regulations.' Much exaggerated language took the air and emotive words were underlined as in a Victorian letter – 'the warden of Ashburne Hall has tried to *terrorize* the girls into thinking that this movement is one initiated by the Socialist Society and in this way she hopes to avoid the *crucial issue* which the movement is bringing to the attention of the residents: namely that they should start questioning the decisions made on their behalf, about their lives yet without their participation'. However, since nobody in Manchester was compelled to live in a hall of residence as Oxford and Cambridge students were compelled to live in a college or in licensed lodgings, it was comparatively easy to argue that students should study the regulations of a residence before they applied to it and make other arrangements if they found that they could not accept the rules.

During 1968–69 the University was seeking a successor to Mansfield Cooper. It set about the task in its usual discreet fashion by keeping the matter to a small circle of people and setting up a joint committee of Senate and Council (eight members from each) to 'consider and report on the office of Vice-Chancellor'. Eminent people were expected to be interested in the job and it seemed, as always, vital that their interest should not be broadcast. But the committee was responsible for discussing general principles concerning the nature of the Vice-Chancellor's office, and it might have been possible for them to share some of their views more widely, even, perhaps, to seek the opinions of students, as the agreement of October 1968 seemed to suggest. Speakers at a Union meeting in November 1969 claimed that students had been fully consulted over the appointment of a new Vice-Chancellor at Leeds, and that the nearby Polytechnic had permitted the governor elected by the students 'to take a full part in the election of their principal administrator'.

Much information was revealed about the process at Manchester, but only when it was effectively over. *Manchester Independent* made a scoop on 7th October 1969 by announcing that the new Vice-Chancellor appeared to be Arthur Armitage, the President of Queens' College Cambridge. This paper also, then and later, published the names of other distinguished gentlemen said to have been interested – those of Lord Boyle, who in fact went to Leeds as Vice-Chancellor, and Sir Brian Flowers, then on secondment from Manchester as Chairman of the Science Research Council (and later to become Rector of Imperial College). Technically the committee's proposal was not a decision, but a recommendation to Council, Senate and Court of a kind they could hardly refuse to accept. It reached Senate only on 30th October. Dick Atkinson, temporary lecturer in Sociology, pointed out that constitutionally the Court of Governors were not bound to accept the committee's proposals and argued that they should regard the appointment as an open question. A General Meeting of the Union objected all but unanimously to the method of appointing the Vice-Chancellor, and twenty-four members of the University teaching staff expressed concern about the procedures. The issue was not merely the choice of Armitage, but the process by which the University habitually made decisions.

A Pro-Vice-Chancellor, Frank Morton, eventually gave an account of the principles involved both to Senate and to a meeting of Staff Forum. About eighty names had been mentioned in connection with the post, and the committee had arrived at a short-list of thirteen, from which Armitage had emerged as first choice. They had identified a number of ideal types which might fit the job, including 'an outstanding academic who also had experience of University administration, in particular of the Government's approach to University administration', 'a well-known public figure who would be the University's "ambassador at large"' and 'an outstanding industrialist interested in University life'. Armitage, who had served his time as Vice-Chancellor of the University of Cambridge (a post rotated among the heads of colleges), approximated most closely to the first of these models. A lawyer and a magistrate, interested in torts and in the criminal law, he enjoyed in the eyes of students the reputation of a formidable defender of law and order, more to be feared than the mild if shockable Mansfield Cooper. He was the head of a college in which opinion was strikingly polarised between radicals and conservatives. An intelligent pragmatist, he had moved quickly to modify the college's regulations when its Senior Tutor came under fire after an unfortunate interview with a student journalist. But radical critics, suspecting that he had no intention of making concessions on more vital matters, had been unimpressed and he had fallen out with the most aggressive organs of radical opinion in Cambridge, particularly the left-wing *Shilling Newspaper*, which had attacked him with great relish.

Student protest in Manchester gathered momentum and led to an occupation of the Whitworth Hall on 9th and 10th December 1969 in which slogans of 'Armitage Out – Student Power' were painted on the roof. The Union subsequently received a bill of £450 for damage inflicted during this sit-in. Early in the New Year, when Armitage was making his first official appearances in Manchester and attending stormy meetings of Senate, the Union was campaigning to deny him recognition as the rightful Vice-Chancellor. Moreover, at least some of the student officers were, logically if churlishly, refusing to accept Sir William Mansfield Cooper's hospitality and meet the new Vice-Chancellor at dinner. Young Liberals, more carnivalesque in mood, proposed to install a donkey as Vice-Chancellor: 'As the new Donkey V.C. stands on the University lawns in Lime Grove next term, paying close attention to the grass roots, let this be a public example to the University administration to end the V.C. Comedy, to silence the braying of the undemocratic professorial factions, to recommence the electoral system – and above all to CONSULT, CONSIDER and RESPECT their GRASS ROOTS – US.' At least one of the Union officers, Liz Loughran, the Welfare Vice-President, was beginning by mid-February to regret the discourtesy shown to the new Vice-Chancellor, with whom the Union would have to work in future. The incumbent Vice-Chancellor was outraged: 'How much longer the University can go on compelling students to be members of the Union in the face of this kind of activity I do not know. The Union itself seems to be intent on committing suicide.' In March 1970 he confided to Council his fears about the conduct of Union business – the President, David Wynn, was ignoring the advice of his Executive and Council, seeking advice only from personal friends who might or might not be part of those bodies, and choosing to rule through General Meetings. Two responsible students in the Union had resigned over this issue, and their resignations were 'part of a crumbling system of confidence' within the Union itself.

Another issue supervened, obscured the Armitage question for the time being, and led to a more sustained protest marked by a general breakdown of confidence in the University authorities and one not confined to holders of extreme views. In December 1969 the Vice-Chancellor appeared to have told *The Sunday Telegraph* 'that he was compiling a dossier of student trouble-makers'. He was later to explain to Senate that this remark referred to student troubles in general and not to Manchester students in particular; but his papers did contain references to students who had been involved in disciplinary proceedings or to students who had written to him. He had 'no files, punitive or police-like in substance, nor would I keep such, but I have ... caused to be preserved all papers which could amount to the ordinary records of the University'. It was not the most unambiguous or reassuring of statements. When the parliamentarians visited Manchester in February 1969, the Vice-Chancellor had referred to a written 'analysis' of the distribution of activists among the different faculties of the University, and his remarks on that occasion had also suggested that records of political activities if not of political views were being kept.

Events at the University of Warwick in February 1970 embarrassed Mansfield Cooper personally by leading to the discovery of what became known as the 'Dear Jack' letter, addressed by him in confidence to Jack Butterworth, the Vice-Chancellor of Warwick. Students occupying the Administration Buildings at Warwick had first opened a file marked 'Student–University Relations' which had not been locked away, and then, perturbed by what they found in it, had decided to break into locked filing cabinets and explore the contents. Their discoveries suggested that the University of Warwick was engaged in surveillance, amounting in some cases to espionage, of the political activities of students and of academics, and that at least one headmaster had supplied information concerning the political activities of one of his pupils. Found in the Warwick files, the 'Dear Jack' letter arrived in Manchester on 17th–18th February and was subsequently published in a broadsheet, 'Ballot No. 3'. David Wynn, the President of the Union, read a paragraph from it at a Senate meeting on 5th March. Dated 6th December 1968, the letter implied that the Vice-Chancellor of Manchester had for some time been planning repressive action by resort to legal process, perhaps even waiting for an opportunity to use the weapons which the law afforded him. 'You can see that what I want to do is to invoke either the civil or the criminal law – preferably the former because the process is slower and we shall be the longer protected by the *sub judice* rules – which will keep dissident members of staff quiet also. I'm sure that it is only on these lines that some respite might be won.'

It was the Vice-Chancellor's resort to legal process at Manchester that now threatened to divide the University. A motion was put down at the Union in the names of Janette Anderson, the news editor of *Independent* and a former member of the Socialist Society, and Peter Cockcroft, the Socialist Society's candidate for the Union presidency. Proclaiming that 'An academic community is founded on mutual trust', it accused the University of violating that trust by collecting 'dossiers on the educational and political views and activities of members of the Union and of staff'. It proposed to remedy the abuse by immediate occupation of the Main Building until assurances were received that the offending material had been destroyed, that no more would be collected, and that the persons responsible for collecting it would be reprimanded. There was no proposal to commit an act of theft by breaking into filing cabinets as distinct from an act of trespass by occupying University property. A subsequent inquiry was to encounter hearsay evidence to the effect that the Vice-Chancellor had received a visit from a student who had advised him that an attack on filing cabinets had been planned. This mysterious figure was sometimes said to be a member of the Socialist Society – a mole, perhaps, or an agent sent to provoke the Vice-Chancellor into acting unwisely. Without consulting the majority of his Fire Brigade or informing the Registrar, the Vice-Chancellor approached the University solicitors and on their advice had injunctions served on five students. Two were the proposers of the offending motion and the other three, Peter Gibbon, Kenneth Green and Glyn Carver, were believed to be officers of the Socialist Society. This information was out of date because the officers of that body frequently changed. The injunctions were designed to restrain the persons concerned from inciting their fellows to commit an illegal act of trespass (it would have been difficult for one of the injunctees to do this, because he was away from Manchester and carrying out research in Belfast). But no political hydra could ever be killed by attempting to sever a mere five heads, and events soon showed that hundreds would swiftly grow in their places.

Although it was later said that the injunctions had been carefully worded so as not to preclude discussion of the issue of political files, they seemed an unwarranted interference with free speech and with the Union. Peter Bromley, the lawyer most experienced in matters related to student discipline, thought that the University had made the wrong application and had obtained injunctions seemingly intended to frustrate debate, rather than injunctions directed against the sit-in itself. They appeared to deny Union members the right to react to the Anderson–Cockcroft motion and perhaps to demonstrate their good sense and moderation by defeating it. David Wynn, the Union President, said that he would himself have voted against the motion and that the Union officers could have prevented it from even being put. Indeed, if put freely, it would probably have obtained little support. At least one senior academic believed that the injunctions served as an effective deterrent, in that they saved the University's confidential filing cabinets from violation. Almost certainly, however, they provoked a sit-in on an unprecedented scale which would not otherwise have happened and was supported even by moderate Conservative opinion. On 26th February 1970, after a General Meeting in the Union attended by about 1,500 students, there was an occupation of the Whitworth Hall and parts of the Main Building. However, as the subsequent inquiry reported, 'with only one minor exception, no administrative offices were entered and none of the University's files were broken into. In the rest of the University lectures and tutorials continued throughout.' At the Senate meeting on 5th March the President of the Union spoke of an occupation of University buildings, which had now lasted about a week, by between 3,000 and 5,000 students. Whatever the exact numbers involved, the event clearly differed in kind and in scale from the minority disturbances and token sit-ins which had gone before.

The Vice-Chancellor's distress was great. Of the injunctions he said to Senate, 'this represents the complete defeat of all my policies in relation to students. Rightly or wrongly I have sought all the time to be a peacemaker ... but this policy is in ruins and the University must defend itself ... ' The Senate remained overwhelmingly loyal to him, but there was a grave loss of confidence in their elders on the part of a fair number of 'junior' staff. Dr Martin Southwold, who had been a vigorous critic of the University in the pages of *Staff Comment*, approached the Vice-Chancellor on 3rd March with three colleagues and soon afterwards presented a petition carrying 187 signatures and asking for 'adequate representation of the non-professorial staff in any negotiations to resolve the present crisis in the University'. Southwold and his colleagues were 'in vigorous disagreement' with the Vice-Chancellor about 'the resort to the injunctions and the use of "archaic" legal procedures'. It was not right for the Senate to represent the non-professorial staff, because 'the professoriate and older generation were out of touch with students', and because 'the really junior staff, i.e. probationers, were not even eligible for election to Senate'. The crisis was again raising fundamental questions about the institutional structure of the University, which seemed to lack the resilience and adaptability to cope with a general protest. It appeared that too many decisions were being made by administrators and managers far from the chalk-face and the shop floor, by people whose primary duty was not to teach students and give them advice.

Anthony Arblaster, then a temporary lecturer in Philosophy and himself to become the subject of bitter controversy, remembers feeling: 'I really wish this wasn't happening.' Few could avoid taking sides. About forty staff members met regularly during the occupation and formed a new group called SPUR, an acronym for Staff Pressure for University Reform. At its first meeting the historian Brian Manning offered suggestions as to why the University was badly governed. These did not greatly differ from those put forward in more general terms twelve years earlier by Gerald Aylmer. Attributing a kind of Machiavellian ingenuity to the authorities, Manning suggested that the University's ruling oligarchy 'used a number of devices to bolster its rule, among which were the encouragement of parochialism, the creation of secrecy and complexity in its decision-making processes, and the assertion of prerogative in the areas of finance and appointments. These stratagems needed to be seen for what they really were by the majority of staff and had to be exposed and contested.'

Alarmingly serious on one level, the mass sit-in was exciting and entertaining for many of those who took part. Briefly at least, it developed into a kind of free university in which serious issues were eagerly debated. Some academics who visited the sit-in found the level of discussion higher than in the formal seminars they were accustomed to hold. It was important to keep the occupiers stimulated and entertained, and the sit-in went hand-in-hand with a teach-in. Teach-ins were popular in the 1960s; they were sometimes marathon events which devoted a day or more to exploring a theme of wide interest – the War in Vietnam, Class Structure, Trade Unions, Examinations, University Development in the 1970s – through talks, lectures, discussions and perhaps films. They had been held in Manchester at intervals since 1965. Visiting speakers came to the occupation, including Bernadette Devlin, the young MP for Mid-Ulster (Independent Unity), and Jack Straw, the future Home Secretary, then President of the NUS, bound to Manchester by family ties, since his brother Ed was President-elect of the Union. Bernadette Devlin, contemptuous of the file-keepers' explanation that the information collected was to be used

only for the good of the individual student, reminded her audience
learnedly how students had controlled the hiring and firing of professors in the medieval University of Bologna. Jack Straw accused the
Vice-Chancellor of attempting to break the power of the students'
Union and said that his injunctions 'represented a greater denial of
free speech than I have ever seen before'. Allegedly they were worse
than anything seen at LSE or Warwick, where the injunctions did at
least arise out of illegal acts that had already taken place, such as the
purloining of documents at Warwick. He too called for fundamental
changes in the structure of a University that could permit or even
cause such things to happen. Stan Cole, a trade unionist, President of
the Manchester Branch of the Amalgamated Engineering Federation,
addressed the teach-in and seemed to recognise parallels between the
Unions' and the students' struggle for democracy in the workplace. A
message of solidarity arrived from workers at the Shell building site at
Carrington. Such indications that public opinion was not wholly
against students and that manual workers did not despise them were
greatly prized.

Two temporary lecturers, Arblaster and Atkinson, spoke at the
teach-in. Atkinson, who had been involved with student politics both
at LSE and at Birmingham, had published several articles with *Independent*. In its issue of 3rd March 1970, the paper published a discussion between the two on the subject of academic freedom. Here
Arblaster spoke of the need for students and junior staff to make common cause – but 'the whole structure of the University is aimed at
keeping staff and students apart – outside of formal and semi-formal
occasions'. He disarmingly confessed to 'ill-concealed fink-like ten-
dencies' and to seeing 'some value in the old "elitist" tradition of the
liberal education for gentlemen', as distinct from the crudely utilitarian notions of education which were being forced on universities. Academics professing to defend the humanities failed to realise that
radical students were actually on the same side – that students
resented, just as much as they did, the proposition that education
should be made to serve a particular kind of society.

The sit-in set out to be organised and controlled. It seemed important to prove that students could discipline themselves. Among its literary products were the shilling souvenir paper, *Insitter*, which
carried photographs of the sit-in, the text of the Devlin speech, a well
written article by Lord Bowden on the necessity of keeping files, a
piece on student radical politics by Lawrence Freedman (later Professor of War Studies at King's College London), and a large photograph

of the Vice-Chancellor. This seemed calculated to represent him as a grey and unfriendly bureaucrat, besuited and bi-focalled, writing at his desk – a very different image from that presented in his official portrait, where the Vice-Chancellor seems a trifle overwhelmed by his robes of office. A sixpenny duplicated typescript entitled 'Dossier' purported to give details of the business interests of members of the University Council and seems in retrospect like a Manchester parallel to E.P. Thompson's Penguin Special, *Warwick University Ltd.* Cheerful essays in satire included a spoof letter to Arthur Longarse Junior from his disapproving father in the style of *Private Eye* ('Quite frankly, your lazy student friends should have their grants stopped, they are nothing but parasites on society', etc.). Parodying a headmaster's report found in the Warwick files, somebody compiled references for such noted subversives as John Stuart Mill and George Bernard Shaw, and embellished each of them, in the manner of the Vice-Chancellor of Warwick, with the instruction 'Reject this man'.

Live entertainment was laid on to keep up morale in austere conditions and maintain the festive atmosphere. As Pip Cotterill remembers, 'There was a group, most of whom went into the media and became relatively famous locally, called "Occupational Hazard", who put a play on, a sort of skit on, every night. And people learnt to play "Go" and "War Games", and, you know ... it was really good fun.' 'We did a lot of things by candlelight, so they'd probably turned the electricity off ... People kept coming back to report how negotiations were going, but I have to say that most of us weren't particularly interested ... ' 'I never had a sense of pushing against any authority that had any influence over me directly ... the University authorities were actually very little more real to me than Lyndon Johnson ... or Harold Wilson ... ' It was said that some hall wardens threatened to discipline students for staying out all night. Sister Marie Murphy, the wise and liberal nun who ruled St Gabriel's, merely suggested to Margaret Jacobs (as Margaret Brazier then was) that she should take plenty of blankets to insulate herself against the prevailing chill. There is a tradition – remembered by David Pailin, now Professor of the Philosophy of Religion – to the effect that the sit-in was prolonged by an extra day because the drama group were presenting a soap opera and had left it on a cliffhanger: 'so they had to go on for the next night's instalment, to draw everything to a conclusion!' On departing, the rump of the sit-in gave three rousing cheers for the Vice-Chancellor, whose unfortunate letter had provided the pretext for having such an enjoyable time.

Insitter carried a photograph of the dignified, formal portrait of a former Vice-Chancellor, Sir Walter Moberly, in the Whitworth Hall. Taped to the glass was a placard bearing the four points for negotiation in a simplified form:

1. An independent public enquiry.
2. Immediate withdrawal of injunctions.
3. No victimisation of students or staff.
4. Full student representation.

After much haggling, a compromise was reached, the injunctions were withdrawn, and the University agreed to set up an inquiry. This investigation was to be conducted by three members of the Bar. Senate nominated a prominent local Queen's Counsel, Iain Glidewell (who later became Lord Justice Glidewell); the students' Union, Ian Macdonald; the local branch of the AUT, Alan Prichard, a Reader in Law at the University of Nottingham. There was much dispute over the precise terms of reference and the procedures the inquiry was expected to adopt. In essence, however, it was clear to everyone that it should be charged with examining the circumstances which had led to the issuing of the injunctions (why had those five students been singled out?) and with investigating the contents of the official files kept by the University (did they contain improper references to the political activities and opinions of students or staff?). Arguments about procedure delayed the start of the inquiry's operations until January 1971, when memories of events had begun to fade, and it did not report until the summer of that year. No disciplinary action followed against students, although there was to be some dispute with the Union over the bill for damage allegedly inflicted during the sit-in. Grave suspicion was to arise that appointments committees had discriminated on non-academic grounds against the two temporary lecturers who had addressed the sit-in as part of the teach-in: against Arblaster, who failed to get a permanent appointment in Manchester, and against Atkinson, who was unsuccessful at Birmingham.

Soon after the event, Basil Hetherington, the Anglican chaplain, attempted an impartial assessment of the sit-in and included it in his report to the Friends of the Chaplaincy. For some time he had been pleading for better communication within the University, and now noted the fact that for seven days the University had issued no comment and had not made out a reasoned case for the issue of injunctions. There were inconsistencies, however, on the students' side. What did they mean by free speech when they were themselves capable of shouting unpopular speakers down or denying them a platform? A student leader had admitted to the chaplain that he himself would be willing to use an injunction to prevent Enoch Powell from speaking. This admission suggested that the use of injunctions could not be absolutely condemned. Students demanded that they should not be judged politically, and yet they judged members of Council only by political and economic criteria and never by their academic records, as the literature of the sit-in showed. Would the inquiry be entitled to enquire into the chairing of student meetings, to see if this had been unduly manipulative, and would the University authorities be able to ask for representation on the Union Council – 'Or is enquiry and representation a one-way street with a No Entry sign outside the Union and the Whitworth Hall?' After asking these awkward questions, however, he spoke well of the sit-in itself, which to many senior figures in the University was a gross violation of law and order. 'The sit-in offered action and involvement, and there was an immense liberation and camaraderie during that time. It was one vast experimental workshop; it was fun, and students frankly enjoyed it. Were the Chaplain to be in any seat of power, he would be racking his brains to think up the constructive alternative to a sit-in.'

Present-day recollections of the student movement in general and of this affair in particular are greatly at variance with each other. The protests of the late 1960s and those which were to follow in the 1970s merge in the memory and the issues which gave rise to them are often forgotten. There is little agreement about the gravity of the vandalism and violence involved (violence towards people, property or the senses). Approval of the broad aims of the student movements sometimes combines with distaste for its tactics. Memories often focus on the pain inflicted on the Vice-Chancellor, 'a gentleman' and himself a 'students' man', as he had once called his predecessor Stopford. Vincent Knowles, the Registrar, said in his retirement speech in 1979: 'I found it hard if not impossible to forgive the way in which students treated a man who had worked all his life for them and their benefit.' But he admitted that the use of injunctions was misguided: 'Maybe we all underestimated the reaction to an injunction, which to a lawyer is an everyday occurrence, but seemed to many members of the student body and staff to be a threat to the liberty of the individual.'

Workers in the offices in the Main Building were most directly exposed to the effects of an occupation. Vincent Knowles remembers that in the course of one of the sit-ins 'My secretary was abused beyond belief', both physically and by being cursed and called a 'lackey of the Establishment'. Accidents could occur at moments when students were attempting to rush offices with a view to occupying them and porters, secretaries and clerks had instructions not to let them in. Olwen Williams found sitters-in pleasant and good-humoured, at least in the early days of such protests; it was easy enough to step over the recumbent figures on the office floor. Some administrators dealt with them robustly; Rainford the Bursar, faced with an occupation of the corridor outside his office, decided that the ceiling was in urgent need of a lick of paint, and summoned workmen bearing scaffolding, before whom the occupiers fled. Harry Kent warned them of the ill-will they would incur if their occupation interfered with the payment of the wages of support staff. Walter McCulloch, of the Photography Section in the University Library, wisely declined the request to go and photograph sitters-in – 'I'll get lynched … and I don't like to say it, but I'm probably in agreement with them.'

Dennis Welland remarks that student troubles were 'largely an infection and Manchester got it at a fairly early stage'. He remembers his own and other people's inability to understand why some members of the academic staff should sympathise with the students and apparently encourage them in revolt – 'why educated people, who ought to have had the sense to be discussing things positively, were just joining in this general hooligan affront all over the place'. Universities, in his view, were trapped between the demands of the public and the media that they should control their 'violent' students, and their own extreme reluctance to do so by calling the police on to the campus. 'It was really the breakdown of the old concept of a society of scholars, students and staff, that was just demolished. I don't think it has ever been recovered.'

Others would argue that the notion of an all-embracing academic community had already been lost in the hierarchical, increasingly impersonal, mass university of the post-war and post-Robbins days. If anything, it was the professoriate and the administrators who had destroyed it. Some of the so-called subversives were actually trying to recreate the community by means of a flattening of the hierarchy, a removal of the cast-iron divisions between professorial and non-professorial ranks, a reduction of the distance between 'staff' and 'students'. Perhaps, as the chaplain implied, the lost sense of community was recreated briefly by the mass sit-in itself. Jeffrey Denton, who became an assistant lecturer in History in 1965, had felt 'deeply alienated by the Institution', depressed by its new buildings and their discouragement of any sense of community, by the formal manners which prevailed in the History department. He himself visited sit-ins.

'Well, they annoyed people, of course, greatly, but, you know, a few sit-ins over a few days, the disruption was extraordinarily minimal ... I must say, I was completely sympathetic ... It's amazing how a sit-in of a relatively small number of students that stopped a few people in administration coming into work, got people cross. I mean, if they could have taken it lightly and said, "Oh, fine, we'll have a holiday for a couple of days, why worry?" Then, of course, they wouldn't have bothered sitting in ... I found it astonishing then, and I still find it astonishing, that they didn't realise that they were dealing with people with genuine attitudes towards education, and that you just go and talk to them.'

David Richardson, who joined the Registrar's staff in 1967, gives a balanced account which goes some way to explaining the sharp reactions on both sides. ' ... if it's never happened before, it's a frightening experience. It is a truly frightening experience to be invaded. There I'm using an emotive word ... meaning, if you are in an office, and somebody comes and invades your space, or you fear your space is going to be invaded, it is an intrusion. And, of course, until you've had one or two sit-ins, you don't know what the form is. You don't know they're not going to burn the place down. You don't know they're not going to leave messes on your carpet ... ' But 'once you know the pattern to it, you know you're going to threaten, you know they're going to threaten, you know there's going to be discussion, you're going to get them out, etc., etc. ... We didn't do too badly by comparison with elsewhere. And there wasn't a legacy of bitterness really ... The militancy of students came as a tremendous shock, because my senior colleagues had come here in the days of quietly spoken girls from grammar schools, and returning ex-servicemen, who almost saluted you!'

University students of the late 1960s were not as a whole a generation of militants. But they were perhaps – as the Union survey of 1963 was already suggesting – a generation much less given to accepting its parents' values without question, more conscious of forming a social grouping of their own, with its own manners, customs, coiffeur and style of dress. Many, perhaps, were less inclined to believe that they were privileged to be students, and more aware of the value of graduates to the country. If students were of value to society and the economy they were surely entitled to claim certain rights within universities, to have a say in what they were taught and how. One of the great agents of conformity, the experience of National Service or the prospect of having to do it, had been removed; it was easier to object to all aspects of militarism if there was no immediate likelihood of being part of it oneself, easier to dislike the authority exercised by the University if one had no experience of the much harsher discipline of the armed forces.

The lively and sometimes bitter debates of the 1960s had been marked by the pursuit of at least two elusive concepts in which most people professed to believe. The idea of the academic community and the idea of academic freedom were defined differently by different parties and each accused its opponents of destroying them. It was undoubtedly possible to build a sense of community in certain enclaves or fiefdoms within the University, in some fortunate departments or halls of residence; it was far more difficult to do so in the expanding University as a whole. Some shades of radical opinion held that a community could never be created within the University because it contained deep-seated conflicts of interest – academics, for example, had an interest in giving as much time as possible to their research, which brought them professional advancement, and students had an interest in demanding that academics give time to teaching and pastoral care. Was academic freedom – the right to speak one's mind and enquire into whatever one chose – threatened more gravely by the supposed irrationality of the student movement, or by the prospect of disapproval on the part of superiors intolerant of dissent? Did the gravest threat of all come from outside the academic community altogether, from government control and the influence of big business, calling for graduates of a suitable type?

The University had made concessions and had begun to allow student representation on academic bodies, though not on anything like the scale that student activists would have wished. Some thought, and still think, that these concessions would have been made in any case, that one of the few tangible results of student agitation was the fact that the University began to lock and even fortify its main buildings (previously left open, even at weekends) against possible student occupations. It may be, however, that genuine negotiations tend to take place only under some form of threat. Perhaps the desire to win over moderate student opinion prompted many modest concessions that would not otherwise have been granted. It remained to be seen whether, under a more pragmatic Vice-Chancellor, with a new Charter coming into operation, the University would be able to recover stability and peace.

III

The early 1970s

11

Aftermath of a crisis, 1970–73

'The chances that a single man can perform the duties of the present Vice-Chancellor are nil', confided a 'dedicated servant' of the University of Manchester to the journalist Christopher Driver on the accession of Arthur Armitage in 1970. 'When you grow up in a job you have an expertise no one else can have.' Unlike his predecessors Stopford and Mansfield Cooper, unlike the Bursar and Registrar, Armitage was an outsider who had not served his time in the ranks. He had presided for twelve years over a Cambridge college of four or five hundred male undergraduates, its ancient architecture intricate, domestic, reminiscent of a medieval manor house, its wooden mathematical bridge spanning a river best adapted to punting, its grace after meals imploring 'God preserve our Queen and Church'. Would such a man adapt to the complexities, the secularism, the forbidding urban environment of the University of Manchester? But Armitage, the 'Big Arthur' of Queens', was the son of a master draper in Oldham, had been educated at the Hulme Grammar School in that town, and had married a yarn agent's daughter. He was very much at home in the north. Some Cambridge colleagues murmured that he was a mill-owner at heart who had at last found in Manchester a big enough enterprise to run, perhaps twenty times the size of his Cambridge concern, and would now bring to it every scrap of his energy and enthusiasm.

As the nickname suggested, Armitage was physically imposing, burly, square-headed, blessed with spectacular eyebrows and strong, handsome features, and also with a capacity for expressive grimacing and conveying disapproval by eloquent body language, reclining in his chair and gazing abstractedly at the ceiling while unpalatable arguments were expounded. By nature he was an expansive, optimistic, generous, even bonhomous man with a talent for instilling in members of his organisation a sense of being loved and wanted, or at least appreciated, for what they did. He would insert himself into any vacant space in the crowded staff bar at lunchtime and talk to anyone who happened to be in his vicinity. There was something pugilistic in him and he did not shrink from fights, but was careful to choose good ground and not to take issue over trifling or indefensible things. Free speech, he was fond of reminding radical critics, cuts both ways, and he reserved the right to retaliate with interest. He was emotional, easily hurt by seeming disloyalty, exasperated by bloody-mindedness and boat-rocking, impatient of whingeing. He was capable of pushing a ready-made letter of resignation across his desk to someone identified as a troublemaker and suggesting (not in fact very ruthlessly) that he or she might like to sign it on the spot, or of pointing out to a woebegone science professor that he need not regard himself as inextricably bound to Manchester. An eminent but tactless theologian, intervening once too often to amend a motion before Senate, provoked a cry of 'God give me strength!' delivered by the Vice-Chancellor with scant respect for his tormentor's episcopal ring. His summoning voice on the telephone – 'Will you come up? Will you come up?' – was, to Harry Kent, the Establishment and Superannuation Officer with whom he spent much time, close to the voice of God. He could seem inarticulate, but his hesitancy had its uses. One of many theories was that he was a naturally open man, eager to share secrets, but constantly having to hold his candour in check. 'Write me a woolly letter', he would say to his assistant. Some said that he practised the art of selective deafness in Senate with consummate skill.

Margaret Brazier, who as Margaret Jacobs made the transition from law student to law lecturer in the early Armitage years, remembers him as neither a great liberal nor an ardent conservative, but as a diplomat determined to make the University work – 'it was more important that it worked than how it worked'. Alert to possible embarrassments, he refused to name anything in the University after the great Rutherford, who had hatched the nuclear theory of the atom while serving as Langworthy Professor of Physics in the early years of the century, lest the Campaign for Nuclear Disarmament take umbrage at the move. He once told the porters to open the doors of a building that students were determined to occupy, lest anyone be accidentally injured in a futile attempt to bar their way.

Throughout his term of office Arthur Armitage was supported by Vincent Knowles as Registrar and by Fred Ratcliffe as Librarian. But the old order changed in part with the retirement of Alan Rainford in 1971. His successor, Geoffrey McComas, the Bursar of UMIST, was neither a graduate of Manchester nor a product, as was Rainford, of many years of service in the University's offices. McComas was an Oxford man who had joined the Sudan Political Service in 1939 and risen to be deputy governor of a province. Before coming to UMIST he had been bursar of a public school in the Midlands, Uppingham. Within his kingdom the University created a new fief, an Establishment Unit responsible for the 2,720 'support staff' of the University – for the 698 clerical workers and secretaries, the 658 technicians, the 1,364 manual workers, and for their recruitment, training, rates of pay and conditions of service, and for negotiations with the trade unions which they were entitled to join. By 1972 perhaps a dozen unions could claim members among the University's staff, including ASTMS (the Association of Scientific, Technical and Managerial Staffs), NALGO (the National and Local Government Officers' Association) and NUPE (the National Union of Public Employees). Harry Kent headed the Unit, and was assisted by two personnel officers, Graham Stephenson and Philip Jackson, and by a welfare officer, Olwen Williams, who had been secretary in the 1950s to the beleaguered Mr McLeod, the first officer to work in this field.

Vincent Knowles's staff, meanwhile, were taking on the air of professional administrators, developing their own technical expertise, and some were forced to move away from their academic pursuits. It was difficult for one educated, as was the Deputy Registrar, Ken Kitchen, in a very lively discipline such as politics, to keep up with the burgeoning literature of the subject and continue to be, not only a mandarin, but an honorary lecturer in his field. The need for professional training had become doubly urgent since the Secretary of State for Education and Science had exposed the books of universities to inspection by the Comptroller and Auditor General, to say nothing of the UGC's demands for statistics and forecasts and the strain imposed by the need to prepare, every few years, the quinquennial submission on which the University's finances would depend. Kitchen and his colleague Jim Walsh managed to interest Manchester academics in setting up a course for senior administrators which began to run in September 1971. It included such matters as organisational behaviour, statistical techniques and computing, financial management, and law, and drew an audience, not only from Manchester, but also from other universities in the north.

More use was now to be made of Pro-Vice-Chancellors, senior professors who would act as the Vice-Chancellor's deputies, advise him, take responsibility for particular spheres of activity, and provide a system which would continue to function in the event of the Vice-Chancellor's illness or death. There was to be one full-timer among them capable of taking over should such an emergency arise. Pro-Vice-Chancellors would foregather at a so-called prayer meeting every Monday morning at half-past nine, to ensure that the left hand had some knowledge of the right hand's doings. Administration at the highest level was invigorated by the sympathy and understanding which developed between Arthur Armitage and George Kenyon, who succeeded Alan Symons as Chairman of Council in 1972, Symons becoming Treasurer. As Sir George has written, theirs was 'probably the most successful alliance in the University's history to date between a Vice-Chancellor and a Chairman of Council. This was because it was a meeting of minds and an association of two men who each brought to the other the full authority of Senate and Council respectively on an equal footing with due regard for the constitution and for the precarious balance of power which is the essential element for the success of the University ... Unlike Henry II and Thomas à Becket, Arthur Armitage and I managed to remain on good terms and preserve our respective forces intact.'

Even in the spring and summer of 1970 student protest had lost impetus with the coming of the Easter vacation, the approach of the examination season, and the promise of solemn enquiry into the events which had precipitated the sit-in. But several unresolved issues, hanging over from the last session, threatened to rekindle conflict and to test to the full the new Vice-Chancellor's diplomatic skills. Fortunately the students' Union soon recognised that it was impracticable to keep up their quarrel by insisting that Armitage was not the rightfully elected Vice-Chancellor. They needed someone with whom to negotiate and wisely shifted their attention to campaigning for students to be consulted over the appointment of the next Vice-Chancellor, whenever that should be.

An immediate problem arose over damage said to have been caused during the mass sit-in of February and March. *The Times Educational Supplement* had depicted it as a messy event which contrasted dramatically with a more savoury occupation of the main building at the University of Kent; at the time of the troubles the Registrar had made a statement to Senate referring to 'The physical and increasingly noisome brunt of the sit-in'. By mid-May the damage directly inflicted by the sit-in had been assessed at approximately £2,000 (although the figure was disputable). Over the summer the University officers appeared to be collecting the debt by withholding some of the fee income from local education authorities, destined for the Union but paid to it through the University. *Manchester Independent* headlined the story BACKLASH STARTS HERE, alluding to the long-expected counter-offensive by the government, the University authorities and the general public against student militancy in all its forms. But in October the Vice-Chancellor called three Union officers over to the main building, expressed his own wish to start with a clean slate, and announced that the sum withheld would be paid to the Union. He proposed to make life easier for them in future. It had been customary to pay the capitation fee (then £6 per head) in instalments, keeping back the considerable sum of £7,000 until a very late point in the financial year. He was prepared to increase the size of the early instalments, so that the Union would not have to wait so long for the bulk of its money. *Manchester Independent* was determined not to be impressed by his diplomacy and observed that 'Where University actions cause a major disturbance to which National Press coverage adopts a critical attitude, the University authorities then seek a return to the status quo. Such a return is couched in the form of a gracious concession.' Be that as it might, there were the germs of a working relationship between the Vice-Chancellor and the officers of the students' Union, who appeared to understand each other reasonably well. Even the comments of *Independent* began to take the form of cheerful satire too broad to be hurtful, as witness the appearance of a regular column called Mrs Knowall's Diary, set in The Armitage, 'Mr Arthur's' flat, and imagining the plots and intrigues between Arthur, Vincent and 'Mr Snowbound' (presumably Rainford), who was 'bent double under the weight of the money bags tethered to all points of his anatomy'. 'Dear Vincent has been in such a state and swears that he just does not know where his next register is coming from … '

Given to celebrating the power of the press, *Independent* was soon able to claim another triumph. Another front-page story raised the highly charged issue of academic freedom by suggesting that young lecturers were being punished for their outspoken opinions on university reform. Published on 13th October 1970, quick to attract media attention, this item bore the headline AND THEN THERE WAS ONE, indicating that two temporary assistant lecturers, Anthony Arblaster and Dick Atkinson, who had been prominent supporters of the sit-in, were no longer at Manchester. The one dissident left, though not named in the piece, was presumably Martin Southwold, whose position as a lecturer was more secure.

Arblaster's case promised to become a *cause célèbre*. It turned on events surrounding his failure to be appointed to a permanent post in

the Philosophy Department early in June 1970. It concentrated attention on issues of principle and public concern which were passionately
discussed and gave rise to accusations of deviousness, hypocrisy and
incomplete reporting. Was the University, though professing to be a
liberal institution, not capable in practice of tolerating dissent and
public criticism? Statute II.2 of the new draft Statutes prescribed
impeccably that no 'religious, racial or political test shall be imposed
by the University on any person in order to entitle him or her to be
admitted as a member, professor, teacher or student of the University'. Would this provision be strictly observed in practice? Should
appointments committees confine themselves to considering the intellectual qualities of the candidates before them, their achievements or
potential in research and their prowess as teachers? Or were they entitled to take other considerations into account, such as acceptability to
colleagues and willingness to collaborate with them? Might that not
mean preferring a mediocre conformist to a stimulating rebel or critic
of the established order? How far was a professor obliged, morally if
not legally or constitutionally, to respect the advice of his juniors
concerning the terms of appointments? Personal animosities became
entangled with intellectual disputes as to what did, or did not, constitute a legitimate kind of philosophy, fit to be taught in a Philosophy Department, rather than consigned to some other area of the
University.

By all accounts Anthony Arblaster was a well-liked teacher who, by
the summer of 1970, had held two temporary appointments as an
assistant lecturer in the field of political theory. At thirty-three, he was
more confident and worldly-wise than most people who held insecure
junior posts and he had extensive connections in the world of journalism. He had been assistant editor of *Tribune* and university teaching was a second career. He applied for a permanent post which had
been advertised in the Department of Philosophy. Since colleagues
had urged at a staff meeting in the Department that student demand
was strongest in his field and that the political theorists carried the
heaviest teaching burdens, his chances seemed excellent, the more so
because he enjoyed the support of powerful referees. Behind him
were Christopher Hill, the Master of Balliol, a celebrated Marxist historian of the English Civil War and of the economic problems of the
Church of England; Steven Lukes, a Fellow of the same college; and
Richard Wollheim, a Professor in the University of London. But
Arblaster appeared to be in disfavour with his professor at Manchester, Czeslaw Lejewski, who had, it seemed, rebuked him for disloyalty

to the University, and had done so (but not unwillingly) at the insti-gation of senior administrators.

Arblaster's offence was that he had written to *The Guardian* in Feb-ruary 1969 to complain of the University's handling of the visit of Sub-committee B of the Commons Select Committee investigating student relations with universities and colleges. One of his criticisms related to the composition of the panel of teachers which met the vis-itors (the panel had been selected by the Standing Committee of Sen-ate in consultation with the local branch of the AUT, and failed in Arblaster's view to represent a large section of University opinion, including his own). His other complaint was that the University administration had neglected to make it generally known that the visit was about to take place. There was a public gallery, but according to Professor Worsley of Sociology it was very thinly occupied by acade-mics – indeed, only by Worsley himself, by Professor Jevons of Liberal Studies in Science, and one or two others to whom Worsley happened to have mentioned the matter. Arblaster's complaints of the Univer-sity authorities were matched by student complaints that their Union officers had also concealed the impending meeting with the visiting MP's and arranged that they themselves should speak for the student body – presumably from fear that rowdy activists would present themselves and disrupt the proceedings. As Arblaster now reflects, 'I suppose criticising your employer in the press is on the whole rather a risky enterprise! But I also thought to myself, "Well, you know, uni-versities are supposed to be a bit more tolerant of criticism and dis-cussion."'

There was a suspicion that Lejewski, choosing to ignore the well-reasoned case put forward by members of the Philosophy staff, had changed the emphasis in the job specifications in such a way as to make it less likely that Arblaster would be chosen. Allegedly, there had been a 'devious regression' from calling, as the Department wished, for a political theorist who could also teach some general philosophy, to calling for a general philosopher who could also teach some polit-ical theory. It was also alleged that the professor had tried to weaken the case for a properly appointed political theorist by arranging for research students in the Department of Government to give tutorials in the subject – a practice deplored by the AUT as a device for obtain-ing teaching on the cheap.

When the story broke in October 1970, the students saw in Arblaster a man who had lost his job (though not through actual dis-missal) for speaking courageously in their cause. Since his non-appointment could perhaps be described as an act of victimisation arising out of the sit-in which he had addressed, the Union asked that the terms of reference of the Glidewell inquiry should be extended, and that they should be made responsible for investigating the Arblaster affair. Though supported by Professor Worsley, the Union's proposal was not formally put to Senate at its meeting on 29th October. But Senate was then, most unusually, summoned to a special meeting (held on 18th November) at the instigation of some members who feared that the Union would be affronted and the University pitched back into the chaos of the previous February and March. After debating the matter for several hours the Senate rejected by a large majority (seventy-one votes to twenty-six) the proposal to extend the inquiry's terms of reference. It also affirmed its 'confidence in the procedures followed by the Committee of Appointment to the Lectureship in Philosophy' (by sixty-eight votes in favour, with five against and fourteen abstentions). Several speakers urged 'that the case of those demanding an enquiry was being greatly overstated. There was a serious danger that the University was being placed in a situation in which, when candidates of outspoken political views applied for posts, appointments committees would be faced with either offering them appointments or facing a series of public enquiries.'

Since it was unthinkable that the merits of the candidates should be openly discussed in so public a forum as the Senate, there was no way of showing whether the best one had or had not won. Hence the argument could only focus on the questionable change in the specifications for the job, on Lejewski's entitlement to make it, and on the issue of whether it had been challenged from within the committee. But was the change inspired by political considerations, by repugnance for Arblaster's supposed disloyalty, or by the professor's lack of sympathy for political theorists in general and indeed for areas of logic and philosophy which were not his own? The students themselves had sensed the difficulty, since the Union's motion of 26th October, though starting from the premise that there had been 'victimisation', nevertheless acknowledged that 'it is difficult to prove that it has been the result of a person's political activities and beliefs'. At the same time it proclaimed that 'staff and students will not tolerate any interference with academic freedom' and asked not only for an inquiry but also for the appointment of 'an independent ombudsman' 'to investigate any future academic freedom violations'.

Although the University itself launched no official inquiry, an investigation was rapidly set in train by the Council for Academic Freedom and Democracy. This was a new organisation, more radical and out-spoken than the Association of University Teachers. Because the AUT had obligations to its professorial members as well as to rank-and-file academics, and therefore found it hard to take sides between them, the Association often faced charges of temporising and of failing to defend academic freedom. Membership of CAFD was linked to membership of the National Council for Civil Liberties and it described itself as 'both a watchdog and a campaigning body', which would 'take up and publicise cases where academic freedom has been attacked or threatened' and 'seek to democratise the institutional structures'. A deputation from CAFD arrived in Manchester at the end of October 1970 and set up shop in the Antrim Hotel hard by the Union building on Oxford Road, where it talked to anyone who was prepared to discuss the Arblaster affair and had good reason to understand it. The panel consisted of John Griffith of LSE, Professor of Public Law in the University of London, who had been counsel for the defence of students hailed before the Board of Discipline of his own institution; of John Saville, Reader in Economic History in the University of Hull; and of Tony Smythe, the General Secretary of the National Council for Civil Liberties.

CAFD's report, detailed, factual, documented where possible and studiously judicious in tone, concentrated on the more dubious aspects of the affair and again called for a judicial inquiry authorised by the University itself: 'The issues have now become public issues, and it is the wider community that must be satisfied. What is now in question is the integrity of the University of Manchester.' Among much else, the report censured all moves to discourage Arblaster and other academics from writing to the press or to reprove them for doing so: the proper reaction would have been to reply to them in the newspaper concerned. 'The friendly or unfriendly warning, the word in or out of season, the gentle or ungentle advice about the wisdom or unwisdom of types of conduct, these are the insidious methods frequently used in universities as in other forms of organisations. Their use can be highly subversive of the kind of societies which educational institutions should strive to be.' Publication of the CAFD report in a free-standing pamphlet towards the end of November 1970 gave rise to a brief sit-in, although, in the terminology of student leaders, it was a 'token sit-in' rather than a 'disruptive sit-in'. Ed Straw, the Union President, quoting crucial passages of the report, explained 'that the present "sit-in" was not intended as a complete confrontation. It was designed to underline the strength of feeling among students in their

view of the need for action in this affair. There was no intention of
continuing the occupation until such time as the requests to Senate
had been met.'

Meanwhile, other Manchester academics were pursuing a campaign which identified the foe of academic freedom not as the determination of the hierarchy to secure stability and loyalty, but as that of
students to get their way by disruption and intimidation. Brian Cox of
the English Department had secured 154 signatures for a manifesto in
the form of a letter to *The Times* which was eventually published,
after some leaks, on 23rd November 1970. This document identified
and condemned several forms of unacceptable protest, including sit-
ins, which 'necessarily involve the use of physical force', and called
upon universities to draw up codes of discipline 'to maintain freedom
and order'. It voiced misgivings about the wisdom of involving students in executive and decision-making bodies in universities and
regretted the time which had to be spent in explaining technicalities,
especially those connected with finance, to these uninformed recruits.
The manifesto resonantly proclaimed that 'For many decades British
universities have maintained the highest reputation for academic freedom. People with extreme political views, both left and right wing,
have been given a fair hearing at public lectures, accepted without
question as undergraduates, and appointed when properly qualified
to administrative and teaching posts.'

Shortly afterwards John Saville, a participant in the CAFD inquiry,
addressed an open letter to Cox (whom he had known as a colleague
at Hull) and suggested that if there were to be a disciplinary code for
students there should also be a code of conduct for the teaching and
administrative staffs of British universities. The enemies of academic
freedom might lie outside the student body. What did he, Cox, intend
to do about the allegations in the CAFD report? Over the next few
months Cox continued to collect signatures for his manifesto, but was
partially frustrated by the postmen's strike which began in 1971.
Arblaster, who now held an appointment at the University of
Sheffield, helped to circulate a letter inviting colleagues to contribute
to the Union of Post Office Workers' hardship fund. He received a letter from a senior lecturer observing that 'The views expressed in the
letter above make it very clear how right they were at Manchester
University not to appoint you to a permanent post.' As Arblaster
wrote in the book on *Academic Freedom* which he published in 1974,
'One can only marvel at the type of mind which sees the circulation
of an appeal for the strike funds of a trade union as grounds for aca-

demic non-appointment.' In 1971, CAFD was to investigate other alleged violations of academic freedom, one of which involved irregular procedures at the University of Birmingham. These seemed openly designed to prevent the appointment to a permanent post in Sociology of Dick Atkinson, who had also been prominent in Manchester affairs in 1969–70.

At Manchester the Arblaster case went gradually off the boil, the tensions in the larger academic community relaxing, although they persisted in the Philosophy Department. Another investigation was set on foot, this time by the National Executive of the AUT. Somewhat unfortunately, given the dichotomous view of academic society which saw it as divided into powerful professors and their impotent juniors, the inquiry was entrusted to two professors, one from Heriot-Watt University in Edinburgh and the other from Leeds, together with the General Secretary of the Association. Their report concluded that 'there was no political or other impropriety in the non-appointment of Mr Anthony Arblaster'. Given that the procedures were what they were and the constitution was what it was, no wrong had been done. 'Several of the witnesses told us, with commendable frankness, that they believed that political considerations had played a part, even a decisive part, in the non-appointment of Mr Arblaster. These same witnesses, with equal frankness, acknowledged that there was no convincing evidence that this had been the case … ' Predictably, the report was dismissed by members of the local branch of CAFD as a 'transparent whitewash' and they continued to stress the need for a more outspoken body to defend academic freedom. More moderately, the local executive of the AUT complained that the report did not question the propriety of the appointment procedures and remarked that these 'revealed a deep disagreement within the University on the proper way to arrive at academic decisions within a department'.

Some official action was taken, although in the prevailing confusion it would hardly have been possible to censure anyone for improper conduct. One member of the appointments committee had questioned the change in the terms of the appointment but had not formally asked for his objection to be recorded. In accordance with the growing practice of spelling out things which everyone had been expected to know by intuition, the Senate laid down rules for objecting formally to the decisions of an appointments committee. If supported by reasons, formal objections could be made and could give rise to investigation by the Vice-Chancellor. Since it had been suggested that the real problem lay in the antagonisms within the Department of Philosophy, Senate agreed that the Vice-Chancellor should use his 'good offices' to resolve the difficulties. He undertook to interview all members of the Department before Christmas, and in the spring of 1971 it was announced that two political theorists would be transferred to the Department of Government. Senate witnessed the rare spectacle of a professor thanking the Vice-Chancellor and the Dean of Arts for reducing the size of his department. Appointments in the field of political theory were subsequently made in the Department of Government; where other departments of Philosophy grew, Manchester's appeared to stand still.

There was, perhaps, now more readiness to question the right of professors to treat junior colleagues cavalierly, not only when making initial appointments, but also when recommending tenure. One lecturer who had failed to obtain tenure after seven years' apparently satisfactory service was successfully defended by the AUT, with some support from students who spoke well of her teaching. Faces were saved by allowing her ordinary lectureship to expire by 'effluxion of time', so that the Standing Committee of Senate would not have to reverse its decision, but appointing her to a special lectureship instead and thereby preserving her livelihood.

Like the granting of tenure, promotion to the rank of senior lecturer was a particularly delicate issue, since it depended heavily on a professor's advocacy as well on the opinions of referees from outside the University who were usually acquainted at first hand only with the candidate's research and publications. The status of senior lecturer was not a career grade at which all academics could expect to arrive in time; in theory at least, success in promotion exercises depended on demonstrating that an applicant possessed exceptional qualities and had done things beyond the call of duty. But there were enough senior lectureships available for academics who did not get them to feel a degree of bitterness or a depressing sense of failure. From 1970 the University offered some formal protection against prejudice or neglect on the part of a professor or head of department, by requiring faculties to appoint small review committees to examine the cases of lecturers who had occupied the same post for ten years or more without achieving promotion, and also those of lecturers who were approaching the highest points on the salary scale. Individual departments began to urge their professors to set up consultative committees which would allow all senior lecturers in the department to give opinions as to their junior colleagues' claims to promotion. In some departments lecturers, anxious to reduce the power and patronage at the disposal of their professors and to maintain good relations among themselves, advocated the principle of Buggins's Turn: that there should be as little competition as possible for senior lectureships and that the next one should be awarded to the most senior person in the line, unless he or she was manifestly incompetent at the job. Should Buggins be thin on publications, his slender bibliography could often be explained away (sometimes convincingly) by his dedication to teaching or his sound administrative work. It remained very difficult, however, for academics to obtain the desired promotion to higher status if they suffered from a writing block (elegantly called 'agraphia' by one Arts professor) or from a total reluctance to release their life works into publishers' hands.

For the time being academics of both left-wing and right-wing persuasion continued to suspect colleagues in the opposite camp of interfering with academic freedom by trying to impose orthodoxies, not only upon each other, but also upon students. Was examining, in certain fields which involved making political judgments, quite as unbiased as it ought to be? The twenty-five or so members of the Economics Department included five members of the Communist Party. David Purdy, late of LSE, and a colleague were on the verge of trouble for using the phrase 'advanced capitalist societies' in a second-year examination paper. Both were suspected of political bias by the external examiner, who protested to Professor Coppock, but were able to point out in their defence that they had awarded the best mark to an able student who had attacked Marxist analysis in several of his replies.

In the early 1970s the issues which had aroused such passion began to lose heat and fury, their fires banked down by the measured deliberations of committees and the long-delayed reports of inquirers. The Glidewell inquiry prepared a statement for a Senate meeting at the least inflammatory time of the year, in early July 1971. They had examined the files kept by the University on certain staff and students who had asked them to do so (ten students and a smaller number of staff), and they had also made a random selection of other files, taking care before they opened them to obtain the permission of the individuals concerned. These procedures had led them to examine the papers of about 1 per cent of the student population of the University. The results seemed reassuring. Where they had found references to political activities, made either by headmasters recommending candidates for admission or by members of the Appointments Board recommending graduands for jobs, these remarks were clearly intended to be complimentary and to improve candidates' chances rather than wreck their prospects. The Registry undoubtedly held a cache of documents relating to the ill-starred visit of Patrick Gordon Walker, and the papers therein could scarcely avoid naming those implicated in the plot to shout him down. But 'as far as we could see the file contained no other reference to the political opinions, affiliations or activities of any of the students named in it'. There arose, however, a difference of opinion between Glidewell and Prichard on the one hand (the two barristers named by the Senate and the AUT) and the Union's nominee, Macdonald, on the other. Submitting a dissenting note relating to certain points concerned both with the injunctions and with the files, Macdonald felt unable to accept his colleagues' statement that 'We are satisfied that there is no specific "student activists"' file kept in the University.' This verdict was rendered unsafe by Mansfield Cooper's mysterious references to a dossier and to an analysis of the distribution of student activists between faculties, and also by his unwillingness to co-operate with the inquiry. Not surprisingly, there were rumours that the University, hastily cleaning up its act, had hired pantechnicons to cart away quantities of embarrassing material before the investigators happened upon it. But they were never substantiated.

Understandably, the Senate concentrated on setting up machinery to provide reassurance in future that no improper records were being kept, and on establishing a committee of its own for the purpose. This staff–student panel, under the chairmanship of Peter Bromley, deliberated at intervals for three years and eventually recommended setting up a body called a 'watchdog'. It would investigate any complaints that information was being improperly recorded in the University's files or improperly divulged to outsiders who could claim no legitimate interest in it. Refuting the idea that political files, so much a live issue in 1970, had become a dead one four years later, the committee's report declared that 'a great deal of concern undoubtedly exists among staff as well as students over the amount of information which is currently being recorded about people generally, and by the possibilities for misuse afforded by this volume of information'. It was important that the University itself should not appear to be the agent of a Big Brother state which knew too much both about its own subjects and about visitors to the country. Controversial political activity, relatively dormant between the end of 1970 and the beginning of 1973, had resumed and taken the form of vehement demonstrations calling upon the University to sell all its shares in companies which had interests in Southern Africa. It was true that, as Peter Bromley reflects, there would have been nothing to prevent academics or administrators from keeping another set of files at home into which anything at all could have been inserted with impunity – to say nothing, one might add, about the information which they might carry in their heads and divulge to enquirers over the telephone. But there had been a demonstration of institutional disapproval of such practices. It gave reassurance, or provoked cynicism, or possibly both, because (to quote Bromley again) 'so far as I recall we were never asked by any student to look at files'.

In the early 1970s the University had benefited from the presence of a new Vice-Chancellor who, although at first regarded with the suspicion reserved for newcomers, had not himself been involved in the controversial events at Manchester. It was true that the integrity of the University, or at least that of powerful individuals within it, had been called into question. The University was suffering from 'not proven' verdicts which left uneasiness in their wake as much as from the pronouncement of 'guilty' made by CAFD. Manchester's official inquiries were dismissed by Arblaster in *Academic Freedom* as part of a 'classic defusing tactic'. No drastic remedies were on offer, and it is difficult to assess the impact of the events of the early 1970s. But they did sound a note of warning. They indicated to persons in authority that they might have to defend their conduct and find good reasons for doing what they did. The best way of covering their backs was generally to consult with colleagues and pay some respect to their opinions. It might well be unreasonable to expect all university teachers in the social sciences or humanities to approach their subjects, in the name of academic objectivity, in a totally bland manner which suppressed any political convictions that they might have. What mattered was that the institution as a whole should be impartial and tolerant, in being prepared to accommodate a range of opinions and approaches. And it should be magnanimous and confident enough not to fall into the trap of regarding criticism of its own ways, even if delivered to the press, as a disloyal and reprehensible act.

12

Stability and moral conflict, 1970–73

Most historians find it harder to account for spells of stability than for outbreaks of unrest. But some attempt can be made here to explain the comparative calm of the early 1970s. Universities and colleges had been relieved by the reduction in the age of majority from the need to behave as though they stood in the place of a parent to the younger students. Almost all students were, or soon would be, over the age of eighteen, and therefore legally adults. Hence the University had less obligation to do many of the things against which students had chafed – to concern itself with their morals, to discourage them from keeping late hours, to prevent them from entertaining visitors at unsuitable times, to reprove the Union for using public moneys for improper purposes. Partly for economic reasons, and partly out of respect for students' wishes for independence and self-government, the University built new residences in the form of self-catering flats which allowed students greater freedom. There were improvements in communication and public relations were better handled, partly through the widespread introduction of staff–student consultative committees and partly through better publicity and more accomplished dealings with the media.

At this time organised student political activity tended to fork in three rather different directions, certain students managing to follow all three paths. To some extent they struggled to promote their own economic interests, to improve their pay and conditions of service. They protested at the decline in the purchasing power of the standard maintenance grant in a period of steep inflation. They strove to defend the autonomy of students' Unions against government proposals designed, or so it was believed, to undermine the Unions in the hope of curtailing student militancy. But some of their concerns were more altruistic. They took up the cause of people less fortunate than themselves, recognising that students enrolled in polytechnics and local authority colleges were much worse off, and enjoyed much poorer facilities. But they were not just concerned with fellow students. The Union devoted some of its funds to organising and supporting politically conscious voluntary work among poor and deprived people in the city, as if it were acting upon the investigative journalism of *Manchester Independent*. The third concern, again representing the politics of conscience rather than those of self-interest, was with moral issues in international affairs, and above all with the evils of apartheid in the Republic of South Africa and of racism in other Southern African states. Moral gestures and demonstrations designed to show disapproval of apartheid and perhaps inflict some damage on the economy by boycotting South African goods had been part of student politics for several years. But they were to concentrate heavily on the University itself from the beginning of 1973 and to take the form of demands that the University should immediately agree in principle to sell all its holdings in companies which had subsidiaries or associates in South Africa, no matter what the financial consequences for the institution might prove to be.

It was possible for the University authorities and for the CVCP to sympathise strongly with student claims to better maintenance grants, not only out of humanity, but also because if students did not enjoy adequate financial support it would become impossible to exact economic rents for university residences. University authorities in general had no great desire to see alterations imposed on the existing arrangements for financing students' Unions or to find themselves obliged to supervise Union expenditure. They were therefore inclined to side with their Union officers against the government and join them in defending the autonomy of the students' Unions. It would have been hard not to sympathise with the students' social conscience and difficult to disapprove of the Community Action programme. But on the 'Sell the Shares' issue the University Council was to put up strong resistance to the more strident student demands for disengagement from South Africa. Demonstrations and other forms of action in Manchester were chiefly directed against members of the University Council. They, however, regarded the sale of the investments in question as an empty moral gesture incompatible with their duties of trusteeship and their obligation to maintain a balanced share portfolio.

During the winter of 1970–71 one analysis of the political situation by Ed Straw, the President of the Union, used the evocative phrase 'repressive tolerance' and suggested that students were now being faced with a new breed of Vice-Chancellor or at least with a new and subtle method of control. Vice-Chancellors no longer committed 'atrocities' and were more likely to wait for occupying forces to dis-integrate of their own accord than to feed protest movements by try-ing to identify and discipline their leaders. The force behind protests was being siphoned off into the endless deliberations of committees. '... the authorities act "sensibly", agree to discussions and participa-tory committees, – WHO CAN SIT-IN WHEN NEGOTIATIONS ARE GOING ON? It would appear also that V.C.'s are selected more on their political ability to hold an institution together than on any administrative or academic qualifications.' It would be said, before long, that Armitage was a 'master of repressive tolerance'.

Staff–student consultative committees began to spread through the deliberative system at all levels, from Senate and Council to faculties and departments, the places where most of the crucial decisions con-cerning the curriculum were made. Such committees had the power to make recommendations to the legislative and executive bodies which actually made decisions, and the student members were usually invited to attend the board meetings at which their proposals were discussed. There they were generally allowed to speak but not to vote. At the highest level there was a Staff–Student Consultative Commit-tee of Senate. Ten students representing the ten faculties were entitled to take part in this committee and to attend Senate, together with the Presidents of the University and UMIST Unions and their two Vice-Presidents for Academic Affairs. Up to four students were invited to attend meetings of the University Council – the President of the Union, the President-elect, when known, and two others chosen by the Staff–Student Consultative Committee of Senate (since UMIST had its own Council, UMIST students were not included in this arrangement). Introduced in 1970, these innovations were to be tried out for an initial period of three years, and because they were exper-iments they were not written into the revised charter. It was deter-mined in 1973 that they should continue indefinitely.

As might have been expected there were complaints in the early years that the entire system of student representation and participa-tion was nothing but a time-wasting charade, or else that students had so much information to absorb (particularly in general University committees) that they had no chance to contribute. There were tales of a professor in Town and Country Planning bringing unpopular pro-posals for compulsory field courses directly to his faculty without con-sulting the students whose plans for vacation employment would be directly affected. There were reports of recommendations being ignored because a staff–student committee in Sociology had refused to be manipulated and had delivered (by a narrow majority) an unacceptable solution to the problem of syllabus reform. Cynics and sceptics might regard the arrangements as no more than a device to deprive extremists of support and produce stability at all costs. But liberals and optimists clearly valued the students' contribution and reformists recognised, in the network of consultative committees, something promising which could be extended and improved.

Union moderates had an interest in extending the number of committees on which students were represented. Jim Hancock, President of the Union in 1972–73, pursued the matter doggedly, noting, for example, that 'We have no students in the powerful and influential Estimates and Stipends Committee' of Council, and campaigning for the abandonment of the concept of reserved business which must be hidden from student eyes. Since reserved business related to individual students and members of staff, their admission, appointments, progress and promotion, the removal of the concept would open the way to student membership of appointments committees. In these they could, because they were directly affected by the candidates' teaching abilities, claim a legitimate interest. Opposition came, however, from academics within the University as well as from the Privy Council, which was the body responsible for approving the statutes and charters of universities. The University Council had been told in October 1970 'that members of the staff would be most unlikely happily to concur in any arrangement under which information relating to their professional interests was made available to students, either for information or, still less, for discussion'. As Jim Hancock now reflects, 'the problem with student representation is that it's easy for the University to take sensitive matters into another committee structure altogether, so that there's always a danger that you get student representation on what I always describe as a shadow decision-making body, and that the real decisions are taken elsewhere'. Some suspected that the notion of reserved business might be stretched to include almost any matter about which the University did not want students to know.

There was some difficulty in persuading students to attend the committees on which seats had been won, for these bodies forfeited much of their charm when students began to listen to their deliberations. Fourteen students were entitled to attend Senate; at most meetings at the height of the autumn and spring terms in the first three years about half to two-thirds of them actually did so. As David Richardson of the Registrar's Department remembers, it was vital to keep the process going once it had been launched, since any move to close the committees down, even on the score of lack of interest, would at once create an issue. He himself devoted time to advising student officers on the etiquette of committee behaviour – arrive early, do not sit opposite the chairman in an attitude of confrontation, do not raise important issues without prior notice under 'Any Other Business', provide discussion papers in advance of the meeting and do not just spread them on the table as it proceeds, thereby flooding the committee with literature which it will never read. It was a course of instruction which many academics could profitably have attended.

Union politics, which had veered strongly to the left in 1969–70, once more became a struggle for the middle ground, in which few of the candidates, and none of those likely to succeed, were vowed to sharply defined ideological positions. A Labour government which was failing to behave like a socialist government had sown more trouble within universities than did a Conservative government which was cutting public spending. Government measures tended to provoke opposition both from students and from Vice-Chancellors. In the autumn of 1971 government proposals on the financing of students' unions appeared to threaten their independence. For some years the greater part of the Manchester Union's income had depended on the capitation fee paid by local education authorities, on the assumption that membership of the Union was not an option and that all registered students would be compelled to belong to it – although it was also true that a proportion of the Union's revenue (28.5 per cent in 1970–71) derived from its trading profits. There were now suggestions that students be permitted to choose not to be members of Unions, or that a proportion of the capitation fee might be paid to them directly, so that they could decide which political and cultural clubs they wanted to belong to, rather than being automatically entitled to membership of them all. Any system permitting students to opt out would clearly weaken the Union's authority, by diminishing its ability to speak on behalf of the entire student body.

At least one Conservative Member of Parliament had protested against the improper use of public money by Unions which had vowed support to various left-wing causes or had paid the fines of students convicted of public order offences. For a time there was a call for the appointment of a Registrar of Students' Unions who would be empowered to investigate their finances and their organisation. In the country at large this proposal won support from the Federation of Conservative Students, although the Manchester branch of that organisation did not agree. An alternative suggestion was that the universities themselves should supervise the expenditure of Unions. It was true that during the 1960s Sir William Mansfield Cooper had clearly felt responsible for curbing the improper use of Union funds and had warned of the consequences of abuses. But in these less paternalistic days the University authorities were much less eager to scrutinise Union expenditure. Another disquieting proposal was that public moneys destined for the support of the Union might be incorporated into the University's block grant from the UGC, and hence enter into competition with the funding for academic departments and be subjected to audit by the Comptroller and Auditor General. This seemed to be an ingenious, indeed almost infallible, recipe for conflict within universities. Neither the Manchester authorities nor the Vice-Chancellors' guild were anxious to rattle the cages afresh. There was much resentment of government hints that universities had been negligent in allowing the capitation fee to be fixed at too high a level.

In December 1971 the Committee on Relations between the University and the Union at Manchester issued an ample statement which affirmed the desire to respect the autonomy of the Union as an 'unincorporated body, separate from the University', 'empowered to employ its own staff, to conduct its own activities and to regulate its own constitutional arrangements, with few and clearly defined exceptions'. True, representatives of the University Council received the Union's annual budget and audited accounts and discussed them in detail with representatives of the Union, and they did examine together the case that might be made for any increase in the capitation grant. But further than this they saw no reason to go. Resistance to the government's proposals did at least win a respite, since the government agreed to postpone introducing any new system of financing the Unions until the parliamentary session of 1973–74.

Steep inflation in the early 1970s and government constraints on public spending resulted in a marked decline in the purchasing power of the standard student maintenance grant since the more prosperous early 1960s. That period was often used as the baseline for calculations and comparisons. An article in *Independent* in February 1971 complained of a rise in prices, bus fares and hall fees so steep that grants were in real terms worth at least 20 per cent less than they had been in 1962. In November 1972 the University Treasurer's report accepted that over the past ten years the monetary value of student grants had increased by only 35 per cent, whereas the cost of living was up by 69 per cent and hall fees had risen by 46 per cent over the same period. If the University were to restrain rises in hall fees, it would have to do so mainly by cutting services, by making life in the residences less comfortable and convenient, and by ensuring that residents got less for the same money, a series of expedients which delighted nobody.

There was some hope, admittedly, of balancing the books by putting the halls to profitable use during the vacations, at which time they would otherwise have represented a piece of costly unused plant. The tastes of many conference-goers were still spartan enough to enable them to tolerate the austerities of Owens Park and other halls, and conference income became an important item in the budget of University accommodation. As was explained in the autumn of 1972, the annual running costs of Owens Park were about £330,000. Student fees brought in some £250,000, other sources of income about £8,000, and vacation earnings, mainly from conferences, amounted to £70,000 and almost eliminated the deficit.

But there were other difficulties. Newly built University flats had to be financed to a large extent by means of loans raised on the open market, and the cost of servicing these loans had to be included in the rents which students paid. Should it charge fees for board and lodging which clearly exceeded the amount notionally allowed for them in the standard grant, the University would probably face a new form of protest advocated by the NUS. This was the rent strike, which involved withholding hall fees from halls but paying them instead into a special Union fund, a Rent Strike Account, from which they would be released only when the dispute was settled. By February 1973, rent strikes, total or partial, had been promised in several halls. But it seemed to be generally known and accepted that the Vice-Chancellor and the University Treasurer sympathised with the students' cause, and most of the odium was directed against the government, rather than the University itself.

At other levels, sympathy for the student cause was not whole-hearted. In the Awards Office some of the office workers objected to the contemptuous manner in which some students collected their cheques – 'Oh God, is that all, it'll just cover my cigarettes.' It was not the most compelling way of promoting their case. Jim Hancock remembers leading a student march down Oxford Road in favour of higher grants, only to be advised by derisive workers to get haircuts and return to work.

Much student energy and goodwill, however, turned outwards towards the social problems of a big city, rather than inwards upon the

University and the economic problems of student life, genuine though these were. Pip Cotterill, who had taken a first degree in American Studies, was appointed on a modest salary to be the first full-time organiser of Community Action. This was a comprehensive scheme for putting the knowledge, skills and spare time of Manchester students at the disposal of the people of Manchester, including immigrants, old folk, the homeless and the travellers. As she remembers, 'we began to recruit students to actually give benefits advice, to help tenants organise, you know, really mobilise them, and provide our resources. We were always very clear that we weren't leaders, we were there to resource ... where the Medical School is now, there was a site, and it was going to be empty for nine months or something, so we persuaded the University to move fifty travellers on to it (they were called gypsies in those days) ... The first Soup Run in Manchester was started by the students' Union for homeless people ... we'd encourage students to bring them into the Union, and say, "Don't give them money. Bring them in, buy them a drink, buy them a cup of tea, buy them a sandwich, talk to them ... " It had come to the period when, having pulled down everything that was completely falling down, the clearance machine was now moving into areas where people thought, "Well, I don't want to be cleared", and we were very involved, in the early 1970s, in helping groups of residents combat clearance, and we were successful.' Community Action also undertook investigations into social conditions, some of these at the request of the Housing Aid Department in the Town Hall, on whose behalf they carried out a survey in north Manchester identifying both reasonable landlords and those who were best avoided because they engaged in various forms of discrimination. At times workers for Community Action encountered resentment against the University's supposed habit of studying social conditions but doing nothing much to improve them ('If anybody else comes round here with a clipboard again, they're over that balcony!'). But, as the Union's External Affairs Vice-President proclaimed in February 1973, 'These projects bring credit on students generally, students of the University of Manchester in particular, and through them on the University. Indeed it is activities like Community Action that prevent a university being merely an ivory tower and help to show that it is directly involved in the social and environmental problems around it ... ' It was as if the University of the 1970s had devised its own equivalent to the Settlement of the 1890s.

At the height of the student troubles in March 1970, the Vice-Chancellor had confided to the University Council that 'He had felt desperately, in all that had happened, the need for a newspaper or other organ of communication.' Misunderstandings and breakdowns of trust were rightly blamed to some extent on lack of information and on the University's inability to present its own case. Philip Radcliffe's appointment as Communications Officer was described by *Manchester Independent* as one of the few tangible results of the great sit-in – 'all those sitting on the fence jumped for communications as the answer'. Some academics had been calling for a University newspaper which would be read by everybody and create a stronger sense of being a single community, rather than a series of separate constituencies each addressed by a journal of its own. *Staff Comment* and *Manchester Independent* could well, as one correspondent, the zoologist D.W. Yalden, suggested, be combined, for *Staff Comment* had difficulty in recruiting editors and *Independent* was in chronic financial difficulties. In his view, despite its perpetual 'lurch to port', *Independent* was capable of excellent journalism. Some academics had chosen to publish with *Independent,* and it fell to it to print an article on the Arblaster affair by Peter Worsley, Professor of Sociology, which had been declined by *Staff Comment*. Surely *Staff Comment*, since most of its contents were wholly innocuous, could drop the prissy notice on its cover, 'for private circulation among members of the Manchester University staff'. The journal continued, however, to carry these coy words. In the event, the principal existing publications retained their independence, and Philip Radcliffe added two others to the canon: a weekly news sheet entitled *This Week* and a not-quite-glossy magazine presenting the wholesome side of University life which appeared twice a term under the name of *Communication*. *Independent* was jealous of its own reputation for uncovering embarrassing facts, which no official paper was ever likely to emulate; it feared that the new magazine would compete with it for advertising revenue, though *Communication* did not in fact carry advertising material.

Philip Radcliffe's task, like that of the many other communications officers who were being appointed in British universities at this time, was to present the achievements of the University, and to convey a healthy impression of the place to the newspapers, radio and television. Other publications could be relied upon to expose the University's shortcomings. From the beginning he was given the status of a professor and installed next to the Vice-Chancellor, to whom he was directly responsible, in an office which was fortunately soon divested of its frosted-glass barricade. Some members of the community, as he recalls, might have preferred him to demonstrate his impartiality by pitching a tent in the middle of the campus. Radcliffe was invited to attend meetings of Senate and Council and began to carry out a policy of 'overt espionage' which included attendance at Union debates. At first this move aroused suspicion on the part of the Union officers, but he was able to disarm their misgivings in time. The Communications Officer was intended to be the University's first point of contact with the media, a channel through which all newsworthy items ought to pass on their way to the world outside, and he invited contributions from all parts of the University. By the autumn of 1971 he had established good relations with BBC Radio Manchester and set up a weekly half-hour programme on student affairs. This would present short news items concerning the University and UMIST, and there were prospects of developing another half-hour programme, which Radcliffe would himself produce, entirely devoted to goings-on in those institutions.

Communication, though not the weekly or fortnightly tabloid which some members of the University had hoped to see, was an informative if bland magazine which attempted to address all aspects of the University in a suitably demotic fashion. It dealt with the policies of the University and the students' Union and presented to the world the interesting people whom the University contained, from long-serving porters, cleaners and technicians through enterprising students embarking on expeditions to the imposing figures in the upper echelons of the administration or the University Council. The new journal consciously aimed to describe and communicate with and about all members of a working community of some 14,000 people (not including UMIST). At the beginning of 1972 some 3,500 copies were being printed. Miraculously resuscitated in the pages of *Staff Comment*, Gulliver greeted the new publications with hyperbole – 'For there through a meadow of margin ran a rivulet of print so pellucid, of prose so chaste, cartoons of the greatest craftsmanship, and likenesses taken by a master-hand. And as for news! – how this don was gone overseas and that one returned, and one had written a book and printed it too, and t'other won much money for his discipline and published the good news in the public prints, how some spoke well of a college newly built and others said it was the ugliest edifice ever seen. What richness, thought I, all human life is here, the tattlers and the prattlers are silenced for all time, now that all is open and known.'

Some less creditable information was made 'open and known', or at least asserted confidently and indignantly, by the student press. With the threatened rent strikes of spring 1973, protest had turned in a new direction. But there was still a determination to censure the University for any involvement it might have in dubious enterprises abroad, to ferret out and expose its moral weaknesses, and to demand – by direct action if need be – that it purify itself immediately of all contamination. It could always be argued that the businessmen who had undertaken to govern the material aspects of the University would inevitably seduce the institution into investing in areas in which they had extensive personal interests, and with which they saw nothing wrong.

Disapproval of apartheid had been a feature of student politics since 1964, when students had tried to prevail on shopkeepers and managers of chain store branches in Withington not to stock South African goods. After much controversy about the propriety of tying itself collectively to any political cause, the Union of that day had decided to affiliate to the Anti-Apartheid Movement. The winter of 1969 had seen demonstrations against the tour of the Springboks, the South African rugby team, and to the chagrin of Sir William Mansfield Cooper the Union had paid the fines of several Manchester students convicted of public order offences on those occasions. Enemies within were looked for and sometimes identified quite mistakenly. Sir William spoke with horror to Council in February 1970 of a defamatory Union motion which accused a member of staff of supporting apartheid, 'although it was known to all his senior colleagues that he had left South Africa because of his increasing distaste for its policies'. Threats of legal action forced the withdrawal of the motion at a noisy meeting and exacted an apology. In the early 1970s, political action began to focus on British firms which had, or were alleged to have, extensive interests in Southern Africa. Such firms, it was said, had an interest in at least tacitly supporting repulsive regimes and in swelling their own profits by exploiting black labour and paying starvation wages.

In October 1970 Barclays Bank became the prime target of student disapproval during Freshers' Week and the new arrivals were dissuaded from opening accounts at its new branch opposite the University. Students picketed this branch and refused the bank permission to keep a stall at one of the fairs. A leading article in *Manchester Independent* disapproved of the practice of selecting a single target in this way and wanted the assault launched across a much broader front. Although in October 1971 the paper carried a centre-page spread which called in general terms for the liquidation of both University and Union investments in South Africa, a more detailed case, based on estimates of the extent of the University's financial involvement, was put forward only in November 1972. An article headlined 'University Supports Apartheid' appeared in the name of Barry Munslow, who had graduated in Economics and had led a trans-Saharan expedition borne by Land Rovers to southern Africa. This piece declared succinctly that 'Manchester University supports the racialist regime in South Africa. It does not directly provide guns for the police, nor bricks and barbed wire for the concentration camps, but it does support the economic structure upon which apartheid is based. Approximately £7 million of this University's investments are in companies with subsidiaries or associates in South Africa.'

The next few months, indeed the next few years, were to witness a head-on collision between the idealism of the Anti-Apartheid and South African Liberation Movements and their supporters, on the one hand, and the more sober and cautious approach of the University officers, on the other. Anxiety that the University should adopt an ethical investment policy and thereby strengthen its moral authority was not confined to students but was shared by many senior members of the University. Disengagement from South Africa would bestow a right to condemn apartheid without hypocrisy – a right which could scarcely be claimed by anyone who was weeping all the way to the bank where his profits were stowed. Such a move would show solidarity with African resistance movements and give them heart. It might even provoke an economic crisis – something more than a temporary recession – which would bring down a profoundly evil and exploitative regime.

To the lay officers of the University these views and hopes appeared simplistic and naïve, mere essays in empty gesture politics, and the course of action recommended could hardly be reconciled with their legal duty to act as trustees of the University's funds. The law obliged them to maintain a balanced portfolio of investments, and should they have nothing to do with any firm that had even the most modest associations with South Africa it would become impossible to perform this task. In particular, they had a responsibility towards the support staff of the University, whose pensions depended directly upon the University's investments as those of the academic staff did not, for academics relied instead upon an outside body, the Federated Superannuation Scheme for Universities. The University officers had, they declared, no intention of supporting apartheid or of disavowing the responsibility of investors for the policies of those companies in which they held shares. But they believed that, rather than attempt anything so grandiose and futile as the overthrow of the regime by the application of sanctions, they could do more good by exerting influence on firms to induce them to pay reasonable wages and pursue liberal policies.

Opponents and critics, however, rejected any move that savoured of mere palliation and might actually have the effect of prolonging the regime's life by making it seem more tolerable. They suspected that by 'reasonable wages' the officers meant only wages at or slightly above subsistence level, the so-called 'poverty datum line'. Alan Symons, the University Treasurer, appeared to have advanced one suspect argument, since he had apparently invoked the new Statute II.2 in favour of not discriminating against South Africa (read in context, the statute was intended to forbid discrimination on religious, political or racial grounds against those seeking to be admitted to the University or appointed to posts within it, and it was hard to believe that it was also intended to govern the University's investment policy or its relationship with foreign regimes). The measured approach of the University authorities was swiftly attributed to self-interest on the part of the lay officers. Any evidence, however slender, that they were personally profiting from any racist regime in Southern Africa was seized upon and eagerly exploited. But aggressive tactics, raucous demonstrations, attempts to deafen or disrupt Council meetings, imprison councillors or stampede them into making hasty decisions tended only to stiffen resistance on their part, in which they enjoyed the Vice-Chancellor's firm support. 'What were we defending?' writes Sir George Kenyon. 'Certainly not the South African government nor apartheid. We were resisting an attack on authority by subversive means, roundabout means. We were resisting having our judgments and decisions overturned by unconstitutional and devious means, including force. Thrice the Vice-Chancellor and I with some members of Council were forcibly imprisoned. There were also illegal sit-ins and occupations causing disruption and damage over several weeks. I in particular was vilified in the student Press and oceans of erroneous statements and statistics were published.'

Positions were taken and the drama began to unfold early in 1973. Since the small, compact University Council was clearly responsible for the University's investments, concentrated pressure could be applied to it. Students began by using the constitutional channels which were open to them and the Council was willing to enter into dialogue. The Committee on Relations between the University and the Union received a request that 'the University should dispose of its investments in all companies which had subsidiaries or associates in

Southern Africa'. The Vice-Chancellor received a petition in support of the Union's request, signed by 130 members of the academic staff, and another petition, identically worded, which bore more than 1,800 signatures from student members of the Union. Eleven telegrams arrived from other institutions, such as universities, polytechnics and colleges, and one from the National Union of Students. Barry Munslow and Maria Brown (a Politics and Modern History student, who was the Welfare Vice-President of the Union) put the case for the Union first to Council and then to the Investment of Funds Committee of Council. Council decided on a cautious, diplomatic approach, declaring its own opposition to apartheid and undertaking to apply strong pressure to the firms in which it held shares. Should its representations have no effect, 'Council will consider divesting itself of investments in those firms'. Maria Brown made a formal request at the February meeting of Council that it should 'make a decision in principle not later than its next meeting'.

Council's reluctance to plump immediately for an unequivocal solution to the problem, its tendency to listen to its stockbrokers and to see complications and talk of legal responsibilities where others saw only the simplest moral issue, resulted in the first of many demonstrations designed to persuade it to change its mind. On 14th March 1973 students invaded the Council Chamber, blocked the doors, took over every available chair, and prevented members of Council from leaving. Led by the Vice-Chancellor, however, they managed to push their way out. Peter Cockcroft, an old campaigner of the 1960s who was now a research student, took the chair and presided over a meeting which lasted for four hours and rejected the latest statement made by Council. This the meeting called 'totally unacceptable. Our priority is not to bring the African population up to the poverty datum line, set by apartheid regimes as subsistence and no more, but to see the regime, as such, brought down. Part of that policy is the removal of all British support.'

The students were not alone in their concern. On 24th May 1973 the first meeting was held of the Assembly established by the new charter. About 200 members (10 per cent of those eligible) attended a debate on a motion proposed by Pat Devine of Economics and Clyde Mitchell of Sociology to the effect that the University should forthwith sell its shares in companies with subsidiaries or associates in Southern Africa. Deadlock was broken by means of an amendment proposed by Professor Collard, 'That Manchester University should sell its shares in companies with subsidiaries and associates in Southern Africa, unless they take steps to liquidate their interests there within one calendar year of this meeting. Further, that the University as a shareholder should propose a motion to that effect at the next shareholders' meeting of the companies in which we have interests.' This amendment was carried by 155 votes to 67. Since the Assembly had no executive powers, and could only opine and advise, its resolution was forwarded to Council, which duly 'took note' of it.

In the early 1970s relations between the student body, the University authorities and the University teachers had become more stable. Cynics might ascribe this state of affairs to the willingness of University administrators to learn from their initial mistakes, to cultivate the art of 'repressive tolerance', the skill of not over-reacting to provocation, the patience to conduct negotiations without intending to concede any really important point. Liberals might applaud the opportunities given to students to contribute to discussions of academic policy, there being no serious risk that they would impose their views on their teachers. There was a risk that students, having been co-opted into the system, might become bored with the 'procrascommitteeation' in which they had become ensnared; that they might lose heart at their failure to get quick results and simply stop bothering, or else try to simplify issues and tactics by resorting to direct action and chanting slogans rather than engaging in debate. Their sense of time, influenced by their brief life-span as students, could be very different from that of more permanent residents in the University, to whom hasty decisions were anathema. In some areas, such as the questions of Union autonomy and the level of student grants, there could be a genuine sympathy or at least a tactical alliance between University authorities and student leaders, even if the University became the immediate target of forms of action such as the withholding of rents. But 'repressive tolerance', studied moderation in dealing with students, could not avoid all forms of trouble. As the dispute over South African shares demonstrated, the University officers' cautious approach to what they saw as complex financial dilemmas began to clash dramatically with the demands of the moralists – of those people (not just students) who believed that in the interests of defending the University's honour there should be neither compromise nor delay.

13

Epilogue

In 1973 the University celebrated another centenary. One hundred years had now passed since the enlarged and extended Owens College had moved out of Quay Street and occupied the Waterhouse buildings on the Oxford Road site acquired at his own risk by Murray Gladstone, cousin to the Prime Minister and chairman of the Site Committee. The centenary happened to coincide with a project styled 'Focus on Manchester' intended to 'publish the City in all its aspects' and staged by the City Council, the Chamber of Commerce and Industry, and the Chamber of Trade. Aware of the need to proclaim itself, to win friends in the surrounding community and to arouse the curiosity of potential students, the University organised an Open Day on Saturday 19th May and welcomed, according to official estimates, between 25,000 and 29,000 visitors. As Philip Radcliffe, the Communications Officer, now says, 'you're conscious of people driving past on the bus on Oxford Road and seeing this great cathedral, and once you're inside it and working inside, I think you forget how daunting and how forbidding it looks'. Some of the mysteries of the great secular cathedral and its more commonplace subordinate buildings were now to be revealed.

The panelled offices, committee rooms, and remote attics of the Waterhouse buildings, the high-ceilinged corridors with their polished brass fittings and their memorial tablets to Francis Thomson the poet and George Gissing the novelist, the precipitous stairways of the upper floors, seemed to embody the heroic survival of the Victorian University into the third quarter of the twentieth century. They had been treated, recently, with a little more disrespect. But they commemorated the old civic pride in a regional University once financed by local philanthropy and designed for local people. Deserted by scientists and scholars, who had moved to more spacious premises elsewhere, the main buildings were mainly devoted to administration, to meetings of Senate and Council, to committee deliberations, to degree ceremonies, banquets and assemblies in the Whitworth Hall, and to the Manchester Museum. To some students they represented the stony, bureaucratic face of the University, the side of it which alienated and intimidated them. 'This place is worse than a bloody town hall', muttered one fresher, repelled by the frosted-glass partitions in the Bursar's and Registrar's Departments. On another student, Helen Pearson, who saw them some years later, the Gothic buildings were to make an entirely different impression, conveying a profound sense of permanence in an unstable world:

> Palatial architecture, wide-open squares,
> Splendid Owens in all its glory,
> Glossy flagstones, Victorian Quadrangle,
> A hint of Venice beneath the drizzle.

> Spiralling steps, Christie's corner,
> Learned threesome enshrined in glass.
> Panelled wood, mortars and gowns,
> Graduates leaving the Whitworth Hall.

> First editions, tomorrow's Journals,
> Rylands Library stocked to the ceiling.
> Red brick academia, Gothic skyline,
> Revered for centuries and centuries more.

Standing for the new order, for the national and international University responding to the needs of state and society, perhaps at the cost of some of its local roots, was the opening on 19th September 1973 of the new Medical School. This lay a few hundred yards to the south on the other side of Oxford Road, a gigantic deep-plan building and a shelter for high technology, whose box-like exterior concealed an inner quadrangle. 'Aesthetic relief', explained the University Planning Office hopefully, 'is gained by landscaping of the inner courts and surrounding areas.' It was Manchester's most ambitious modern undertaking, superseding even the Simon Engineering Laboratories and dwarfing the Computer Building. The Medical School, it was said, was one of the largest university buildings in the country and the biggest medical school in Europe. It was opened by Lord Todd, the Master of Christ's College Cambridge, a Nobel prizewinner who had been a Professor of Chemistry in Manchester during the war and had presided over the Royal Commission on Medical Education in 1965–68.

In the early 1970s the University was still in expansive mode and being spurred into further growth. But there was more parsimonious talk, more tendency to stress (in UGC parlance) the 'economy factor' rather than the 'improvement factor', more determination to reduce the cost per student and to practise economies of scale. The UGC was frowning on very small departments and suggesting that the average science department ought now to be accommodating at least 150 students and the average arts department 100 or more. It would still prove possible to maintain the principle of the five-year plan over the next quinquennium, 1972–77. But in a time of steep inflation there had to be some hope if not a guarantee that the block recurrent grants and equipment grants announced several years in advance would be 'supplemented', when it came to the point of actually receiving and spending them, in order to compensate for rising prices, wages and salaries. Without such supplements the grants would lose much of their purchasing power.

At first the UGC encouraged the University to plan for a total of 11,830 students at Owens in the last year of the quinquennium, of whom 5,500 would be engaged in what were broadly termed 'arts-based' subjects, and 6,330 in science. They admitted that, because A-level science had become less popular in sixth forms, it might well become difficult to maintain this desirable ratio of fifty-five science to every forty-five arts students. Unusually, the Grants Committee began peering still further ahead and straining to see as far into the future as 1981. In response to its enquiries the University estimated the capacity of its own area within the Manchester Education Precinct at 15,000 students, meaning that it could teach that number during the day rather than accommodate them overnight. By February 1973 the target for 1976–77 had been whittled down, the number of under-graduates increasing somewhat but the number of postgraduates dropping steeply. It was now set at 11,521. By the end of 1973 it was being estimated that in 1981–82 there might well be 13,700 students at Owens, including a small arts-based majority: the total would be composed of 7,000 students pursuing the arts and 6,700 the sciences.

From the start the University's planners envisaged that student numbers would grow faster than the recurrent grant from the Trea-sury and that the average academic would have to teach more pupils. When the quinquennial settlement was agreed it appeared that there would now be a reduction of 2 per cent in expenditure per student (this had risen by 5 per cent in the previous quinquennium). Staff–student ratios, so jealously defended in the 1960s, were expected to rise from 1:7.5 in 1971 to 1:9.5 by 1976–77 and even to 1:10 by

1980. Prognostications of coming economies had been common enough in the late 1960s, but now for the first time in recent memory the University found itself facing a deficit, of the order of £600,000, in the financial year 1972–73. The initial allocation of funds for the first year of the quinquennium, some £9.6 million, was announced by itself some months in advance and said by the Vice-Chancellor to be on 'barest minimum terms': he had 'a sad and sombre story' to tell, but at least the University would be getting the worst over at the beginning of the period, and there was some hope that the years would not be uniformly lean. Hence, in February 1973, he announced 'an immediate freeze on the filling of all vacant posts, whether academic, administrative, technical or secretarial'. The object of this manoeuvre was to save up to £300,000 in the current financial year and the same sum in the next one, with further savings of at least the same amount 'on the costs of the central services and the expenditure authorised by Council directly'. By employing such stringent measures it should prove possible to get the accounts into balance by July 1974. In subsequent years replacements and additional posts would have to be authorised in order to cope with the rising tide of undergraduate admissions to the University, but wherever possible the Joint Committee for University Development and its sub-committees in the faculties would be doing the work for which they had been established. They would be redistributing posts and allotting them to the growth areas which were pulling in students, at the expense of those which were not.

Fortunately the dark horizon began to lighten in March 1973 when the UGC responded to representations about the heavy running costs of the Computer Building and the Medical School, which had been constructed to serve those areas which the Grants Committee were most eager to favour. The Stopford Building, housing the Medical School, depended heavily on air conditioning and was a voracious consumer of artificial light. None of the windows of the Computer Building could be opened, lest polluted air waft in from the street and damage the computers; a mechanical plant for the purpose of ventilating the place, said to resemble 'the machine room of a gigantic ocean liner', was situated on the roof. True, there was an ingenious scheme in the Computer Building for recovering heat from the lights, from the bodies of users, and from the computers themselves; this energy was used to heat the perimeter of the building in winter. But the costs of both buildings remained high, and relief came only when the UGC agreed to supplement the grant by £1 million in order to cover them. The recurrent grant for 1972–73 eventually rose from the original £9.6 million to a total of £11.3 million and it was guaranteed that it would rise by some 21 per cent over the next four years to £13.65 million in 1976–77. Reassuringly, it was recognised that compensation would be made for expected increases in costs, and expected that it would be possible for the Joint Committee for University Development to finance about 150 new posts in 1974–77, over and above those authorised for 1973–74.

There were periods when undergraduate recruitment to the University appeared to be flagging, with ominous effects upon its future prospects. The University was well advised to appoint a Schools Liaison Officer, Leslie Shave, the former headmaster of Stockport School, who was charged with ensuring that schools were kept informed of the latest developments in University curricula, that a pleasing image of the University was presented to them, and that the University understood the needs of schools. Sensing, not for the first time, the danger of excessive dependence on government funding, the University also appointed a Research Consultancy Officer, Ken Tittle, whose task it was to explore the possible usefulness to industrial firms of research being carried out in the University, and to review the needs of those firms to see where the University might be able to help. At the end of 1973 Mr Tittle pointed out that in recent years about 80 per cent of external support for the University's research had derived from government sources. These were highly susceptible to changes in government policy over which the University would have no control, and it would be good to find alternatives. A further 14 per cent came from charitable trusts and funds, and only 5 or 6 per cent from industry. It should, in Tittle's view, prove possible to improve considerably on this modest figure.

As always, the University's capacity for expansion depended closely on its ability to provide more residential accommodation. In times of stringency there was inevitably more talk of students living at home, as a large proportion had been accustomed to do in the 1950s. But nobody liked the idea of the student who merely came into lectures and tutorials, enjoyed no social life within the University, and returned home in the evening to work in isolation, perhaps in conditions that were far from ideal. Hence, in 1972 the CVCP, in correspondence with the Secretary of State, pleaded that students residing at home should be given adequate travel allowances and furnished with 'additional communal and private study facilities on campus'. If these vital things were to be provided, how great would the economies prove to be in the end? In fact the University undertook to provide approximately 500 additional residential places in every year of the quinquennium, with a view to increasing the 3,000 places available in 1972 to over 5,000 in 1977. 'No other university has set itself such a formidable target', reported the Planning Officer in March 1973.

Official statistics for the late 1960s and early 1970s, which appeared to cover both Owens and UMIST, suggested that about one-third of students now lived in University residences; that about half of them lived in flats and lodgings (probably two-thirds of these students were in flats, for lodgings were becoming less popular); that the remainder, anything from 13 to 16 per cent of students, lived at home. In the late 1960s there was an alarming tendency for the University residences to lose ground and to absorb a smaller proportion of the student population. By October 1973 there were signs of recovery, though not of startling gains. Luckily the need for speed and economy in the construction and upkeep of student dwellings was easy to reconcile with students' desire for independence and self-government. Some students would have preferred to see older houses renovated and adapted to student use, but the University came down heavily in favour of blocks of new flats, specially built for student occupation. There was no prospect of building new halls: it was accepted that there was nothing so expensive to run as a traditional hall of residence with its supervised meals, its portering charges and its heavy bills for cleaning, decoration and maintenance. This proposition was especially true at a time of inflation, when wages and salaries were rising and there was an urgent need to bring women's wages more into line with men's. The Warden of Dalton Hall, E.W. Fox, drew attention to some of the most dramatic changes in hall budgets by comparing the period 1926–31 with the period 1970–72 and showing how the share of salaries and wages in total expenditure had risen between the two periods from 25 to 52 per cent.

New-style residences would have to be financed neither by appeals to private donors (as in the 1950s), nor by full grants from the UGC, as in the 1960s. Grosvenor Place, a UMIST residence at the northern end of the Precinct, was the last to be funded entirely by the Grants Committee, and was completed in 1972. Enterprises conceived in and after 1969 had to rely on a new scheme whereby the government, through the UGC, would buy the site, meet 25 per cent of the capital costs of building the residence, and also pay the rates. For its part, the University would be obliged to raise the remaining three-quarters of the cost of building and furnishing by borrowing on the open market from banks, insurance companies or building societies at the going rate of interest (the Vice-Chancellors' guild complained of the government's failure to arrange a central public source for loans which might have given them better terms). It was expected that residences would be supported by the rents paid by their occupants, and that they would not be subsidised out of central University funds – to draw on these would be to reduce the resources available to the majority of University students, about two-thirds of the whole, who did not live in University residences. Hence the cost of servicing the loans must needs be included in the students' rents, at a time when the student grant was losing its purchasing power.

Only low-cost housing schemes and somewhat austere dwellings could be contemplated. Students tended to lose space but gain central heating. John Crosby, the University Planning Officer, explained in 1973 that a study bedroom in the new style would probably have an area of about 90 square feet, which compared unfavourably with the 110–20 square feet of ten years earlier. Walls were less likely to be plastered, and 'fairface brickwork' confronted the first occupants of Cornbrook House, the new development in the Precinct Centre. In July 1972 the University Council conceded a small reduction in rent to inhabitants of Cornbrook House 'whose rooms it is necessary to enter in order to gain access to other rooms'. Meanwhile the Vice-Chancellors expressed misgivings about the lack of sound insulation in buildings of insufficient mass – a study bedroom reverberating with other people's noise and echoing to the merriment of their parties was one in which little reading and writing would be done. But when Fox of Dalton observed in *Staff Comment* that 'To those who see the traditional Halls as a vital service to University life, the creation of other types of residence based largely on loan finance seems more of a regrettable necessity than a desirable development', he provoked the advisers of Cornbrook House into defending the new order. They urged 'that the need to organise one's budget, shop for and cook all or most of one's meals, look after a flat, for which one has signed a contract, in fact be considered as an adult householder, as well as sharing a flat with four or five fellow-students who were possibly strangers before – all of these factors contribute considerably to a person's maturity, to his or her education for life in the broadest sense, in a much more practical way perhaps than, for example, contributing to a Hall play (which is, of course, a very worthwhile activity).'

The new developments depended on grouping the students together into cellular units of (it was hoped) mutually tolerant people, flats containing anything from five to eight bedrooms, with kitchens, bathrooms and sanitation shared, and all catering in the hands of the students themselves. Cornbrook House, named picturesquely after a stream which had now disappeared from view, offered 240 places in the Precinct Centre. In November 1970 the University Council determined to abandon the third and last phase in the planned development of Owens Park in Fallowfield and to fill the space with the Oak House Flats, which would shelter 480 students. A third development would take place in the so-called Southern Area of the Precinct to the west of Oxford Road between Dilworth Street and Whitworth Park, the blocks of flats being shaped as though to imitate Toblerone bars lying on a sweetshop counter. This, it was expected, would eventually provide more than 800 places, distributed between five separate blocks, the smallest containing 96 students and the largest 218; construction was scheduled to begin in March 1973.

Styles of building and spatial organisation varied somewhat. Cornbrook House contained no communal rooms for the whole residence, expecting, perhaps, to attract students seeking the bliss of solitude and the right to be unsociable. There would, in any case, soon be a pub in the Precinct Centre, and Cornbrook's situation as an outpost on the University's northern frontier invited its residents to head for the city in search of fun. Cornbrook's flats opened off long corridors, in the style of University departments of the 1960s, whereas those in Oak House were grouped around staircases, somewhat in the fashion of undergraduate sets in Oxford and Cambridge colleges. Oak House enjoyed a central amenity block which offered games rooms, storage space and a laundry; a relatively gracious house, No. 316 Oxford Road, was due to be converted to provide similar facilities for the Tobleroners, as soon as the Student Health Service and the University Press moved out.

In general the arrangements seemed to suit students well and to meet their desire for self-government. For the day-to-day tasks of running the residences were entrusted to a residents' association, and this assembly was in its turn responsible to a management committee, the chain of command continuing upwards until it eventually reached the University Council. Many of the flats were close to the University and did something to save the campus from becoming moribund at night. They relieved many students of the need to deal with private landlords and live in dilapidated, poorly heated premises, though some might argue that students only grew up through living in the city, learning their rights, and summoning unscrupulous landlords before rent tribunals: the University, as landlord, was too reasonable to reflect real life, and was still providing too much protection. The new residential schemes began to work out a compromise between surveillance and indifference: the resident tutors of the traditional halls and of Owens Park were replaced by paid advisers, members of the University who lived elsewhere but came regularly to the residence to be appealed to and to make suggestions designed to further the common weal. By the end of 1973 about one-seventh of all places in University and UMIST residences (710 out of a total of 4,800) had been financed by resorting to loans, and were provided economically within the framework of the self-catering flat.

With the accent now falling on economy, the older buildings in the vicinity of the University began to stand a slightly better chance of escaping demolition orders, unless they happened to lie directly in the path of the Southern Area development or impinged on the Union. The money might run out before the bulldozers reached them, even if the arguments of the conservationists did not prevail. The Union at last had prospects of acquiring its long-awaited extension, and the Antrim Hotel came down to make way for it, while the former Essex Hotel (renamed Grove House) ceded its place to a new Grove House, which was a Toblerone block of flats. On the corner of Brunswick Street and Oxford Road, the College Arms closed its doors at last. It was to be remembered with affection for providing an alcoholic oasis for guests attending the University's teetotal functions in the Whitworth Hall and nipping out for a snifter to raise their morale. The name lived on briefly in a cheerful modernised production of *The Canterbury Tales* by Contact Theatre, in which the hostess was the landlady of the College Arms. But one friendly local pub, the Ducie Arms, at the back of the University on Lloyd Street, survived the threat to level it together with the rest of the area destined to provide space for a new General Purposes Building and yet another car park.

There was some controversy over the merits of the old Dental Hospital, which was then housing the Department of Metallurgy, was attached to the Museum, and was threatened by the proposed Museum extension. One of its defenders, Ralph Ruddock of the Faculty of Education, who admired its imitation Queen Anne façade, declared that 'The building in question is on a human scale. It was built by hand for the use and pleasure of human-sized people', and asked: 'If it goes, does any reason remain why we should not replace our Waterhouse main building with a larger version of the Maths Tower?' The architects of the proposed Museum extension, who belonged to the Building Design Partnership, wrote off the façade as 'pseudo-Baroque' and thought it a poor neighbour to the magnificent Waterhouse building. But, for whatever reason, the old Dental Hospital survived and stands there to this day. So did the old cinema which housed the Music Faculty and the German church which provided a studio for the Department of Drama; both were dismissed as old-fashioned and inconvenient, but both added variety to the landscape. True, the musicians developed a sense of being under siege and were moved to utter, through the pages of *Communication*, some politically incorrect remarks about gypsies, whom they found to be trying neighbours, especially when destructive children were at large with hammers and axes and dogs were allowed to run loose. But the cinema still stood and was not overwhelmed by the Toblerone blocks which eventually came to join it at the Precinct's southern end.

The University of the early 1970s was still well placed to perform one last great act of preservation – another beneficent takeover of a great Manchester institution, once handsomely endowed by Victorian philanthropy but now fallen on hard times. For some years the John Rylands Library, sumptuously housed on Deansgate in a building constructed of the finest materials by the architect Basil Champneys, had been struggling (as had the Whitworth Art Gallery) to make ends meet. Its income had failed to keep pace with inflation and mounting costs. Mrs Rylands, the widow of a Manchester millionaire, had seized the opportunity to purchase whole libraries and collections which came on the market in the late nineteenth century, including the famous library of Althorp in Northamptonshire. This library's richly bound volumes had been sold by the financially embarrassed Lord Spencer and transported to Manchester in six hundred packing cases in the late summer of 1892, somewhat to the distress of their owner, who was inclined to depart for his hunting lodge rather than see them go. Another great acquisition had been the Crawford manuscripts, which spanned a vast period from the third millennium BC to modern times. They represented more than fifty different languages and cultures and were preserved, as Fred Ratcliffe wrote, 'on virtually every kind of material man has used for his records'. Reports on the library in the University Calendar and elsewhere dilated breathlessly on the wonders of 'the most complete collection ever formed of Aldine Press printings at Venice, a remarkable series of manuscript and printed Bibles, outstanding collections of Dante literature, French Revolution material, and pamphlets dealing with the Civil War, Popish Plot, Revolution of 1688' and so forth. Moreover, the three charter rooms contained 'over one quarter of a million legal and manorial documents, estate papers and family records dating from the twelfth century'.

Since the death of Mrs Rylands, who had personally presided over the governing body of the Library in Deansgate, successive Vice-Chancellors had taken the chair and had helped to form a strong bond, both intellectual and administrative, between the two institutions. Discussions concerning a merger began about 1967 under Sir William Mansfield Cooper, with a view to renaming the two libraries as the John Rylands University Library of Manchester and rationalising the arrangement of their contents. All rare books and manuscripts would be transferred to Deansgate, and periodicals which might be of great interest to academics would be concentrated on the main University site. There were many advantages for the underpaid staff of the Rylands Library, who were now, with the necessary approval of the University Grants Committee, taken on to the University's payroll and henceforth paid on academic scales, enjoying the prospect of suitable pensions. The merger gave them access to the bindery and other resources of the University.

An official press statement, issued towards the end of 1970, declared that 'The University will maintain the existing Trusts, excepting such as could be affected by any Court Order, and will undertake to preserve intact the Rylands Collections and that its resources will remain available as laid down by the foundress to "scholars, authors, students and serious readers generally" ... ' Legal formalities were completed on 19th July 1972, which became the official birthday of the new, amalgamated institution. Its rare book collection was now, it could be argued, superior even to that of the University of Cambridge. The Library had now grown to such dimensions and contained such remarkable treasures that the time seemed ripe, as Fred Ratcliffe proclaimed, to press for the establishment of a copyright library in the north of England. This would flourish in the midst of a great conurbation and a culture quite distinct from that of London, in a place distant from the existing copyright libraries in England, Scotland and Wales.

There were many proofs of the Library's, and the Librarian's, ability to attract valuable collections of archives, books and manuscripts. The archives of *The Manchester Evening News* and *The Manchester Guardian* were given in 1972, and there were plans to construct a replica of the famous corridor in the *Guardian* offices in Cross Street within the new Library extension building which was now on the cards. Soon afterwards there followed the extensive personal papers of Thomas Frederick Tout, the medievalist who founded the Manchester history school. Although a general supporter of Ratcliffe's entrepreneurial and acquisitive spirit, the Vice-Chancellor jibbed at last when faced with tentative proposals for taking over, as an adjunct to the Library, the great Catholic Church of the Holy Name on Oxford Road, which had lost many of its parishioners as a result of University expansion. 'You're not satisfied with one bloody cathedral on Deansgate, are you? You want another on Oxford Road!' It was clear that the acquisition of materials on such a heroic scale was outstripping the librarians' capacity for cataloguing their accessions, but Ratcliffe was unrepentant – 'I know libraries where they've had books waiting for two hundred years to be catalogued!' 'We must get them because they'll never come again.'

In these years, however, the librarians were forced to recognise the risk of losing the Library's treasures and even its more ordinary books through theft and mutilation, with users cutting out the pages of research monographs rather than go to the minimal trouble and expense of having them photocopied. Indeed, a Shakespeare First Folio was stolen from the Library in 1972, and it became generally necessary to tighten security, to search the papers and baggage of departing readers, and occasionally to challenge people at the bookstacks and ask to see their library cards. Sadly, there was much to dispel the atmosphere of trust which had prevailed in the Tyson years, when the most valuable and ancient works were on open shelves.

Although the Library's record of acquisition was hugely impressive, services to undergraduates were said to be less so, and the Library was urged to assemble a collection of less extraordinary works for short-term student borrowing. *Manchester Independent* complained that too small a proportion of University income was being spent on the Library and that Manchester was less generous than the average University in this respect. But extra grants to the Library, some of them earmarked for undergraduate use, began to be made in the early 1970s, and the Library's needs for extended premises rose to the top of the list of building priorities submitted annually to the UGC. Information technology, in the shape of a computerised ordering and accessions system, was beginning to come to the Library's aid. Christopher Hunt, the Sub-Librarian for Social Sciences, was on the point of launching a computerised circulation system when he departed for Australia in 1974.

On 12th February 1973, the new Charter and Statutes of the University, approved by the Privy Council, came into force. Since the summer of 1968, when a full draft of them and a draft petition to the Queen in Council had been prepared, work had continued on the Ordinances and General Regulations, laws of a less fundamental character which elaborated on the Charter and Statutes and established some detailed rules for their operation. In their desire to participate the students had been too late to influence significantly the revision of the Charter and Statutes, but they were invited to help with the lesser legislation. Argument continued about certain points in the Statutes, which were disputed by the AUT, anxious for representation and fearful of job losses. It seemed, in May 1970, that they and certain of the elected members of Senate were unhappy about the provisions for removal from office, the proportion of elected members of Senate (said to be 'less than in other charters recently granted by the Privy Council') and 'the general principles on which the composition of Senate is based'. One stumbling block was Clause 6(b) of the draft Statute XVII, which dealt with the grounds for dismissal and laid down the limitations of tenure. This clause appeared to give the Council, on receiving a report from a joint Committee of Council and Senate, power to terminate appointments, not only on grounds of misconduct or inefficiency, but also 'on any other ground stated in the report'. Such grounds could perhaps have included financial difficulties on the part of the University. A formula was eventually found in the summer of 1971, when the clause disappeared from the Statute, although there remained an Ordinance (XII.7) which empowered Council to dismiss on giving adequate notice, and did not expressly state that they could do so only on the grounds set forth in the Statute. In general, however, the Charter appeared to have strengthened tenure by alluding specifically to matters which had hitherto rested only on custom. Tenure, although its very existence was sometimes disputed, would prove to be a genuine obstacle to government plans for the pruning and rationalisation of universities during the 1980s.

Two meetings of the University Court, in July and September 1971, duly passed the new Charter and Statutes together with their appendages, and forwarded the Charter and Statutes to the Privy Council, which was invited to approve them. Even after that date it was still necessary to introduce emendations, for example to enable the University to borrow money on the security of mortgages and to give guarantees to building societies or other lending institutions – a necessary provision in view of the need to raise loans to build student flats. The documents passed the Privy Council's scrutiny largely unscathed, although the Deputy Registrar, Ken Kitchen, reported some raising of eyebrows at the reduction in the size of the lay majority on Council. Presumably this change could have given academics a decisive vote if lay persons' attendance had been slack, if academics had been more diligent than they, and if academics had voted as a block. It had been necessary to convince the Privy Council 'that the Council in this University was, unlike some others, a working body with all the lay members attending with great regularity and playing a substantial part in the University's affairs'.

For some years members of the University had been warned not to entertain great expectations of the new Charter, which would do little to alter the balance of power within the University or to flatten its hierarchies. The most striking innovation lay in the institution of departmental boards, and they were in principle given advisory powers only, executive authority resting only in the hands of the professors and the bodies to which they were responsible, the faculties and the Senate. A historian, Michael Bush, complained that 'the revised Charter repudiates democracy but not despotism. True, the despot is now bound to receive advice from below, but not to act upon it. In contrast, the departmental democracy is now given no recognition and the restrictions upon the activity of the despot are nothing compared with the restrictions which can now be imposed on the working of departmental democracy.' A professor of Gulliver's acquaintance said of the new 'cabals', empowered to do nothing but talk, 'for my part let them talk; in my discipline I command as absolutely as I have ever done, all beneath me must look to me to praise or blacken them before the world, and well they know what side their bread is buttered on'. The professor's responsibility for pleading the case for promotions would always, it was pleaded, act as a bar to the free expression of dissent.

On the other hand, the power of a departmental board to embarrass a recalcitrant professor by appealing over his head was greater than was generally believed, for boards had a constitutional right to communicate their opinions to higher authority in the shape of faculties and the Senate. It was not long before, to the chagrin of some diehards, departmental boards did acquire some quasi-executive powers, in the form of the right to give or withhold the certificates of satisfactory work and attendance on which undergraduates depended for the right to sit examinations and for the payment of their grants. Sam Moore, who was to become Acting Vice-Chancellor in the early 1990s, sees the Charter and Statutes as documents which favoured, not despotism, but indecision by placing too much authority in the hands of collectivities and not of individuals – a fault which had to be rectified in the interests of managerial efficiency during the 1980s and 1990s. In his view the Charter was 'a child of the 1960s, there is no doubt about that, and it has all the virtues and vices of that … Un-amended, it gave too much power to veto groups, groups who could stop things happening without having any responsibility to put in place a constructive alternative.' In Manchester, as in any university, there was no lack of clever, negative people of a sceptical, rather than a creative, turn of mind. There was a certain danger that, should a professor assume the role of an absentee landlord, and a department be riven by personal animosities and uncontrolled childish jealousies, its members might talk themselves to a standstill and no way out of the morass be found. Much would clearly depend, not on constitu-tional devices, but on good personal relations which might succeed in oiling the complicated machinery of balances and checks. A late word, if not the last one, should perhaps be allowed to Gulliver, the satirist of *Staff Comment*: '"Sir", said I … , "statutes and institutions may be square-rigged or foul-rigged, but without men of good intent to man them they are doomed to shipwreck."'

Nautical metaphors have often come to the minds of those who contemplate the University of Manchester. The lounge of Staff House has sometimes been compared, with gallows humour, to the public rooms of *The Titanic* on course for the fatal iceberg. But, as Bill Beswick, once the Executive Dean of the Medical School and later the Bursar, expresses it, 'the University will go on sailing irrespective of a lot of things. Winds have come along and buffeted it, but it's a great big tanker and it'll go on … as long as the guy at the top doesn't aim too closely at the rocks, and sometimes he has to go fairly close.' By the early 1970s the University had weathered the storm of student unrest and much of the force of that unrest had been directed into the constitutional channels through which it was now trickling away. Some discontent was directed against the government rather than the University, but liberal consciences had now, in the South African ques-tion, found a new issue, involving the University's honour rather than its constitution, on which to concentrate their fire. Protracted argu-ment about the distribution of power and authority in the University had resulted in the intricate compromises of the new Charter, which had created neither a democracy nor a self-governing community of scholars. But it had imposed certain restraints on autocratic behav-iour, avoided wholesale surrender to industrial and commercial control, spelt out things previously taken for granted, and provided clearer definitions of tenure.

Would the provisions of the Charter and Statutes prove compatible with the demands for efficiency and economy certain to arise in the face of increasing financial stringency? Many feared with good reason that public enthusiasm for the support of universities was beginning to wane; that despite changes in the legal definition of adulthood they were still seen as weak, indulgent parents who could not keep their spoilt, unruly children in order; that successive governments, ceasing to regard universities as very useful, would be able without provoking a public outcry to starve higher education of adequate support. They might do so by failing to protect universities' finances against inflation, or by openly cutting their income and forcing them to find other sources of funding, to make themselves more obviously useful to the economy. The University might well face the task of maintaining, like some decayed aristocrat on a reduced income, the costly buildings and the numerous academic and support staff that had come into being in response to the demands of a more expansive and optimistic age.

Sources and bibliography

Primary sources

This book draws on the following written records and other sources for information and opinions. For oral sources, see the list of people interviewed by Michele Abendstern in the next section.

Official records

Minutes of the University Council
Reports of Council to the Court of Governors
Minutes of the University Senate
Vice-Chancellor's Annual Statements
Calendars of the University

Reports and surveys

Students in Society: a Manchester Survey (Manchester: University of Manchester Union, 1963)
British Business Schools. A Report by Lord Franks, Worcester College, Oxford, 20 November 1963
British Business Schools. The Cost. Report by a Working Party under the Rt. Hon. Lord Normanbrook, P.C., G.C.B.
Interim Report of the Committee on the Revision of the Charter and Statutes, October 1965
'Tabulated Raw Data' of a Survey of Teaching and Staff Attitudes to Teaching in the University [Session 1964–65], conducted by the University Education Research Project. John Rylands University Library of Manchester 378.1.f.M1
Manchester Education Precinct. The Final Report of the Planning Consultants [Hugh Wilson and Lewis Womersley], 1967
Committee on the Revision of the Charter and Statutes: Draft Charter and Statutes, together with a Draft Petition, July 1968
The Arblaster Case. The Findings of a Commission of Inquiry Established by the Council for Academic Freedom and Democracy, 1970
The Atkinson Affair. The Findings of a Commission Established by the Council for Academic Freedom and Democracy, 1971

Report of the Injunctions and Files Enquiry conducted by Iain Glidewell, Ian A. Macdonald and Alan Prichard, considered at Senate, 5 July 1971

Report of the Committee on Student Files and Confidential Records chaired by Professor P.M. Bromley, approved by Senate, 8 July 1974

Newspapers, journals and occasional publications

News Bulletin
Manchester Independent
Staff Comment
Communication
Occasional issues of *Solem, The Serpent, Rag Rag, Mancunion*
Insitter

Student leaflets

Student leaflets, broadsheets and other material collected in the University Archives, UAS/70/451 – UAS/72/72–163

Parliamentary papers

House of Lords Debates, 5th series, vol. 223, Session 1959–60, coll. 615–732 (report of the debate on University and Other Higher Education, initiated by Lord Simon of Wythenshawe)

Higher Education. Report of the Committee appointed by the Prime Minister under the Chairmanship of Lord Robbins, 1961–63 (London. HMSO Cmnd 2154). Presented to Parliament, October 1963.

Parliamentary Papers, Session 1968-69, vols. VII and VIII: Minutes of Evidence taken by the Select Committee on Education and Science dealing with Student Relations, from the Committee of Vice-Chancellors and Principals, 21 January 1969, and by Sub-committee B of that Committee on its visit to Manchester, 13 February 1969

Report of the Select Committee on Education and Science, Session 1968–69: Student Relations (ordered by the House of Commons to be printed, 25 July 1969)

Private papers

Papers of Professor J.H. Denton relating to discussions held by the University Teachers' Group of the Christian Frontier Council and Student Christian Movement

Papers of Sir George Kenyon relating to his involvement with the University, 1955–88

Papers of Professor Joan Walsh relating to University affairs

Bibliography

This list includes a number of items which deal with earlier periods of the University's history and with subjects and institutions which are not discussed at length in this book. Readers may find them helpful to pursuing their own enquiries.

Arblaster, Anthony. *Academic Freedom* (Harmondsworth, 1974)

Ashburne Hall. The First Fifty Years, 1899–1949

Atkinson, Norman. *Sir Joseph Whitworth. 'The World's Best Mechanician'* (Stroud, 1996)

Aylmer, G.E. 'University government – but by whom?', *Universities Quarterly*, 13 (1958–59), 45–54

Bosworth, Stuart (ed.). *Beyond the Limelight. Essays on the Occasion of the Silver Jubilee of the Conference of University Administrators* (Reading, 1986)

Bowden, B.V. 'Too few academic eggs', *Universities Quarterly*, 14 (1959–60), 7–23

Brett, Lionel. 'Universities. 2. Today', *Architectural Review*, 122 (1957), 240–51

Broadbent, T.E. *Electrical Engineering at Manchester University. 125 Years of Achievement* (Manchester, 1998)

Brook, G.L. *The Modern University* (London, 1965)

Brooke, G.J. 'Manchester and the Dead Sea Scrolls' (unpublished Inaugural Lecture as Rylands Professor of Biblical Criticism and Exegesis, 1999)

Carswell, John. *Government and the Universities in Britain: Programme and Performance, 1960–1980* (Cambridge, 1985)

Chaloner, W.H. *The Movement for the Extension of Owens College, Manchester, 1863–1873* (Manchester, 1973)

Charlton, H.B. *Portrait of a University 1851–1951. To Commemorate the Centenary of Manchester University* (second edition, Manchester, 1952)

Charlton, W.A., and Cutter, E.G. *135 Years of Botany at Manchester* (Manchester, no date)

Clark, Wilfrid Le Gros, and Mansfield Cooper, William. 'John Sebastian Bach Stopford', *Biographical Memoirs of Fellows of the Royal Society*, 7 (1961), pp. 271–9

Cockburn, Alexander, and Blackburn, Robin (eds). *Student Power. Problems, Diagnosis, Action* (Harmondsworth, 1969)

Cox, Brian. *The Great Betrayal. Memoirs of a Life in Education* (London, 1992)

Cox, C.B., and Dyson, A.E. (eds). *Fight for Education. A Black Paper* (Critical Quarterly Society, 1969)

Dahrendorf, Ralf. *LSE. A History of the London School of Economics and Political Science, 1895–1995* (Oxford, 1995)

Divall, Colin. 'Fundamental science versus design: employers and engineering studies in British universities, 1935–1976', *Minerva*, 29 (1991), 167–94

Divall, Colin. 'Education for design and production: professional organization, employers, and the study of chemical engineering in British universities, 1922–1976', *Technology and Culture*, 35 (1994), 258–88

Driver, Christopher. *The Exploding University* (London, 1971)

Fiddes, Edward. *Chapters in the History of Owens College and Manchester University, 1851–1914* (Manchester, 1937)

Gregory, I.G. (ed.). *In Memory of Burlington Street. An Appreciation of the Manchester University Unions, 1861–1957* (Manchester, 1958)

Hodges, Andrew. *Alan Turing. The Enigma of Intelligence* (London, 1985)

Kelly, Thomas. *Outside the Walls. Sixty Years of University Extension at Manchester, 1886–1946* (Manchester, 1950)

Kenyon, George. 'Arthur Llewellyn Armitage', *Dictionary of National Biography, 1981–1985*

Kermode, Frank. *Not Entitled: a Memoir* (London, 1996)

Kilburn, Tom, and Piggott, L.S. 'Frederic Calland Williams', *Biographical Memoirs of Fellows of the Royal Society*, 24 (1978), pp. 583–604

Knowles, Vincent. 'The University of the Future', in *Manchester and its Region* (Manchester, 1962), pp. 244–53

Lawrenson, T.E. *Hall of Residence. Saint Anselm Hall in the University of Manchester, 1907–1957* (Manchester, 1957)

Lees, Colin, and Robertson, Alex. 'Owens College: A.J. Scott and the struggle against "prodigious antagonistic forces"', *Bulletin of the John Rylands University Library of Manchester*, 78 (1996), 155–72

Lees, Colin, and Robertson, Alex. 'Early students and the "University of the Busy": the Quay Street years of Owens College, 1851–1870', *Bulletin of the John Rylands University Library of Manchester*, 79 (1997), 161–94

Lovell, Bernard. 'Patrick Maynard Stuart Blackett', *Biographical Memoirs of Fellows of the Royal Society*, 21 (1975), pp. 1–115

Lovell, Bernard. *Astronomer by Chance* (Oxford, 1992)

Mansfield Cooper, William, and Platt, Harry. 'John Sebastian Bach Stopford', *Dictionary of National Biography, 1961–1970*

Marwick, Arthur. *The Sixties* (Oxford, 1998)

Pailin, David (ed.). *Seventy-Fifth Anniversary Papers of the University of Manchester Faculty of Theology, 1979* (Manchester, 1980)

Phillips, C.B. 'Thomas Stuart Willan, 1910–1994', *Proceedings of the British Academy, 101: 1998 Lectures and Memoirs*, pp. 557–63

Robbins, Lionel. *The University in the Modern World* (London, 1966)

Robertson, Alex. *A Century of Change. The Study of Education in the University of Manchester* (Manchester, 1990)

Robertson, Alex. '"Between the Devil and the deep sea": ambiguities in the development of professorships of education, 1899 to 1932', *British Journal of Educational Studies*, 38 (1990), 144–59

Robertson, Alex. 'College, community and teachers: the evolution of education as a subject of study in the University of Manchester, 1851–99', *Bulletin of the John Rylands University Library of Manchester*, 73 (1991), 135–58

Robertson, Alex. 'Manchester, Owens College and the higher education of women: "a large hole for the cat and a small one for the kitten"', *Bulletin of the John Rylands University Library of Manchester,* 77 (1995), 201–20

Rose, M.E. *Everything Went On at the Round House. A Hundred Years of the Manchester University Settlement* (Manchester, 1995)

Rose, Richard. 'William James Millar Mackenzie, 1909–1996', *Proceedings of the British Academy*, 101: *1998 Lectures and Memoirs*, pp. 465–85

Sadler, M.E. *The Department of Education in the University of Manchester, 1890–1911* (Manchester, 1911)

Saward, Dudley. *Bernard Lovell: a Biography* (London, 1984)

Searle, John. *The Campus War. A Sympathetic Look at the University in Agony* (Harmondsworth, 1972)

Simon, Ernest (First Baron Simon of Wythenshawe). 'A Royal Commission on the Universities?', *Universities Quarterly*, 13 (1958), 9–22

Stewart, W.A.C. *Higher Education in Postwar Britain* (Basingstoke, 1989)

Stocks, Mary. *Fifty Years in Every Street. The Story of the Manchester University Settlement* (second edition, Manchester, 1956)

Stocks, Mary. *Ernest Simon of Manchester* (Manchester, 1963)

Stocks, Mary. 'Ernest Emil Darwin Simon, first Baron Simon of Wythenshawe', *Dictionary of National Biography, 1961–1970*

Streat, Raymond. *Lancashire and Whitehall. The Diary of Sir Raymond Streat*, vol. II: *1939–57*, ed. Marguerite Dupree (Manchester, 1987)

Sutherland, G.A. *Dalton Hall. A Quaker Venture* (London, 1963)

Thompson, E.P. (ed.). *Warwick University Ltd. Industry, Management and the Universities* (Harmondsworth, 1970)

Thompson, Joseph. *The Owens College, its Foundation and Growth* (Manchester, 1886)

Tylecote, Mabel. *The Education of Women at Manchester University, 1883–1933* (Manchester, 1941)

University of Manchester Athletic Union, 1885–1985 (Manchester, 1985)

Woolton, Frederick James Marquis, first Earl of. *The Memoirs of the Rt Hon. The Earl of Woolton* (London, 1959)

Zweig, Ferdynand. *The Student in the Age of Anxiety. A Survey of Oxford and Manchester Students* (London, 1963)

People interviewed

This is a list of those people interviewed by Michele Abendstern whose testimony relates wholly or in part to the years 1951–73. The brief biographical notes given here are not intended to be complete. They are designed to focus mainly on people's connections with the University during that time, and sometimes on their activities immediately after leaving the University or in the interval between two periods at the University.

Arblaster, Anthony. Political theorist and journalist. Temporary Assistant Lecturer, Department of Philosophy, 1968–70. Subsequently joined the Department of Politics, University of Sheffield.

Beswick, F.B. (Bill). Doctor and administrator; retired as Bursar. Student, Medical School, 1943–48; taught in Department of Physiology, 1951–65; Secretary and Tutor to the Faculty of Medicine, 1962–66; Associate Dean, then Executive Dean, 1969–79.

Boucher, Joyce. Schoolteacher and lifelong resident of Fallowfield, active in the Civic Society. Undergraduate, Department of English, 1946–49.

Brazier, Margaret (born Margaret Jacobs). Authority on torts and medical law; now Professor of Law. Undergraduate, Faculty of Law, 1968–71. Resident of St Gabriel's Hall. Vice-President of the students' Union. Taught in the Faculty of Law from 1971.

Bromley, Peter. Authority on family law. Taught in the Faculty of Law, 1947–86. Professor of Law and three times Dean of the Faculty, 1965–86. Principal of Dalton Hall, 1958–65.

Buckley, Michael. Administrator; retired as Deputy Registrar. Joined Registrar's Department, 1966; particularly responsible at first for the Business School and later for the Academic Staffing Office. Honorary Lecturer in the Department of Overseas Studies.

Burchell, Robert. Historian of the United States, also famous for generous hospitality; retired as Professor of American Studies. Taught in the Department of American Studies, 1965–96. Tutor, later Senior Tutor, St Anselm Hall, 1967–71.

Cameron, Harry. Electrician and engineer. Joined Electrical Services Department, 1951: apprentice, subsequently electrician, planned maintenance engineer, Assistant Electrical Engineer (1978), Electrical Engineer (1981) and Assistant Chief Engineer (1985).

Carling, Ellen B. Secretary, from 1964 Personal Assistant, to the Professors of Astronomy (Professors Kopal, Kahn and Dyson), 1954–95.

Case, Patricia (born Patricia O'Gara). Teacher and politician (sometime Chairman and Conservative Leader of Lancashire County Council). Student, General Arts, 1950–53; resident of St Gabriel's Hall. Postgraduate Certificate in Education, 1953–54. President of the Women's Union, 1953–54. Later part-time student, B.A. (Econ.), early 1970s.

Cotterill, Pip. Local Government Officer, Manchester City Council. Undergraduate, Department of American Studies, 1966–69; subsequently postgraduate. First paid organiser of Community Action, 1971–73.

Cox, C. Brian. Poet, critic and writer on education. Professor of English Literature, 1966–76 (subsequently John Edward Taylor Professor). Co-editor of *Critical Quarterly* from 1959; of *Black Papers on Education*, 1969–77.

Cummings, Patricia. Librarian, particularly concerned with the Manchester Medical Collection. Joined the staff of the Medical Library as Library Assistant, 1950; later Assistant Librarian; Associate of the Library Association, 1971.

Davies, Rita. Secretary in the Dean's office, Faculty of Medicine, 1932–65 (became Dean's Secretary and later Personal Assistant); subsequently Public Relations Officer to the Blackpool and Fylde Hospital Management Committee.

Davies, Rodney. Radio astronomer; retired as Professor of Radio Astronomy and Director of the Nuffield Radio Astronomy Laboratories. Worked in the Radio Astronomy Group at the Jodrell Bank outstation from 1953.

Denton, Jeffrey. Historian of the medieval Church, now Research Professor of Medieval History. Taught in Department of History, 1965–97.

Flowers, Sir Brian (afterwards Lord Flowers). Physicist and academic statesman, now Chancellor of the University. Professor of Theoretical Physics, 1958–61; Langworthy Professor of Physics, 1961–72; Chairman of the Science Research Council, 1967–73. FRS, 1961; knighted, 1969; Hon. D.Sc. Manc. 1973. Subsequently Rector of Imperial College of Science and Technology.

Flowers, Mary (Lady Flowers). Born Mary Behrens, daughter of Sir Leonard Behrens, of the family which gave Behrens House to Ashburne Hall and Holly Royde (the residential college of the Extra-Mural Department) to the University. Married Brian Flowers, 1951. Hostess to the Department of Physics, 1958–67.

Ford, Anna. Television and radio presenter. Undergraduate, Department of Sociology and Social Anthropology, 1963–66; Vice-President of the students' Union, 1965; President, 1966–67; member of the Registrar's Department, particularly concerned with the International Society, 1967–69; Diploma in Adult Education, 1970.

Griffiths, Sheila (born Sheila Chapman). History teacher, active member of the Ashburne Association and of the Committee of Ashburne Hall with Sheavyn House. Undergraduate, Department of History, 1954–57. Resident of Ashburne Hall. Subsequently postgraduate student in Industrial Management, Manchester College of Science and Technology.

Haddy, Pamela. Clerical Supervisor. Joined the staff of the Registrar's Office as Clerical Assistant, 1949; Supervisor of the Awards Office, 1963–93.

Hancock, Jim. Television journalist, now member of the University Council. Student, General Arts, 1967–70. Resident and Senior Student of Dalton Hall. Qualification year for M.A., 1970–71; student activities, 1971–72; President of the students' Union, 1972–73.

Hunt, Christopher. University Librarian, John Rylands University Library of Manchester. Sub-Librarian, Social Sciences, 1968–74; left to become University Librarian, James Cook University, Queensland, Australia, 1974.

Imber, Kee Kok (born Kee Kok Lee, writes as Kee Kok Lee). Philosopher, with particular interest in environmental philosophy. Retired as Reader. Taught in Department of Philosophy, 1966–99.

Jones, Peter. Expert in micro-electronics; retired as Senior Lecturer. Undergraduate, Department of Electrical Engineering, 1955–58; M.Sc., 1959; Ph.D., 1962; Research Assistant, Atlas Computing Laboratory, 1961–63. Taught in Department of Electrical Engineering, and later in the School of Engineering, 1963–97.

Kent, Harry. Administrator. Joined Bursar's Department, 1947; Establishment and Superannuation Officer from 1971, retitled Deputy Bursar in Charge of Personnel; retired 1982.

Kenyon, George (afterwards Sir George). Engineer, industrialist and banker. Undergraduate, Department of Engineering, 1929–32 (Trevithick Scholar, 1930). Member of Court and lay administrator of the University, 1955–88; member of Council and Chairman of the Committee for Radiological Protection from 1960; Chairman of the Buildings Committee, 1962–70; Treasurer, 1970–72; Chairman of Council, 1972–80.

Kenyon, Honorah. English teacher. Undergraduate, Department of English, 1952–5. Postgraduate Certificate in Education, 1955–56.

Kitchen, Kenneth. Administrator (retired as Registrar). Joined Registrar's Department, 1965; Honorary Lecturer in Government. Secretary to the Charter Revision Committee. Deputy Registrar, 1971–79. Co-organiser, with James Walsh, of the Northern Universities Administrative Training Programme (first run in 1971).

Knowles, Vincent. Administrator. Undergraduate, Departments of Greek and Latin, 1931–35; Teachers Diploma, 1936; M.A. in Greek, 1938; Resident Tutor in Classics, Lancashire Independent College, 1938–51, and Part-time Lecturer in the University; Assistant Secretary, then Deputy Registrar and Joint Registrar (with William Mansfield Cooper), 1945–51; Registrar, 1951–79; Special Lecturer in Greek and Latin, 1948–79.

Leece, Norman. Engineer. Student, Department of Electrical Engineering,

1952–55. Resident of St Anselm Hall. Joined Ferranti's and worked for them in seven different jobs, 1955–89.

Lowe, Peter. Historian of diplomacy in the Far East; now Reader in History. Taught in Department of History from 1965. Elected member of Senate and of Standing Committee of Senate. Officeholder (on many occasions) in Manchester Branch of AUT. Involved in validating courses and assessing examinations for the B.Ed. degree in the Colleges of Education, 1969–75.

McCulloch, Walter. Chief Technician. Member of the University staff, 1935–81. 'Two-year laboratory boy', 1935–37; porter in the University Library; war service in the RAF; later joined the Photographic Section of the University Library. Sometime Chairman of William Kay House.

McKenna, Gerard. Administrator, retired as Assistant Registrar. Student, Departments of Greek and Latin, 1956–60; M.A., 1962. Foundation member of Woolton Hall, 1959–61, and of Allen Hall, 1961–62. Civil Servant, 1962–67. Joined Registrar's Department, 1967; Secretary to the Faculty of Medicine, 1970–80. Tutor and later Vice-Warden of Allen Hall, 1967–78.

Mays, Wolfe. Philosopher. Taught in Department of Philosophy, 1946–79; retired as Reader. Officeholder (on many occasions) in local branch of AUT.

Moore, Stuart Alfred (Sam). Econometrician and academic administrator (retired as Deputy Vice-Chancellor and Professor of Quantitative Studies). Computer assistant and part-time student, Faculty of Economic and Social Studies, 1960–64; M.A. (Econ.), 1967. Taught in Department of Econometrics, 1964–92.

Mulholland, Maureen (born Maureen O'Brien). Legal historian, also concerned with law and medicine. Undergraduate, Faculty of Law, 1957–60; postgraduate, LL.M.; has taught full-time and part-time in the Faculty of Law at various times since 1964. Sometime Tutor, Langdale Hall.

North, Geoffrey. Geographer; retired as Senior Lecturer. Taught in Department of Geography, 1954–93. Warden of St Anselm Hall, 1963–71. Adviser in the Central Academic Advisory Services from 1972. Chairman and member of numerous University committees (at one time between thirty and forty).

Pailin, David. Philosopher and theologian, now Professor of the Philosophy of Religion. M.A. in Theology through Hartley Victoria College, 1959–61; Methodist minister; joined Faculty of Theology and taught philosophy of religion from 1966; Ph.D.

Parry, Geraint. Political theorist and writer on politics; retired as Professor of Government. Taught in Department of Philosophy, 1960–71, and in Department of Government, 1971–74; left to become Edward Caird Professor of Politics, University of Glasgow, 1974–76 (returned to Manchester as W.J.M. Mackenzie Professor of Government, 1977)

Prothero, Iorwerth (Iori). Historian, especially of radical movements in the early nineteenth century; now Senior Lecturer. Undergraduate, Department of History, 1958–61; postgraduate, University of Cambridge, 1961–64, Ph.D.; taught in Department of History, Manchester, from 1964. Elected member of Senate and of Standing Committee of Senate. Officeholder in local branch of AUT.

Purdy, David. Economist, especially interested in the labour market and the social security interface; now Senior Lecturer. Taught in the Department of Economics, 1968–94 (then transferred to the Department of Social Policy and Social Work).

Radcliffe, Philip. Journalist and television producer. Head of Production, University/UMIST Television Service, 1969–70. Communications Officer (retitled Director of Communications 1978), 1970–95; Honorary Lecturer in Adult Education, 1974–95.

Ratcliffe, Frederick. Librarian; retired as University Librarian, Cambridge, and Fellow of Corpus Christi College, Cambridge. Undergraduate, Department of German, 1948–51; postgraduate, 1951–54; Ph.D.; Assistant Cataloguer, University of Manchester Library, 1954–62; Sub-Librarian, University of Glasgow Library, 1962–63; Deputy Librarian, University of Newcastle Library, 1963–65; Librarian, University of Manchester, 1965–80 (Director of the John Rylands University Library of Manchester, 1972–80).

Rhodes, Gay. Secretary (retired as Personal Assistant to the Dean of Medicine). Secretary in the Dean's Office, School of Medicine, 1968–79.

Richardson, David. Administrator (retired as Academic Secretary). Joined Registrar's Department, 1967; Arts Faculty Office, 1969–71; Assistant to the Vice-Chancellor (Arthur Armitage), 1970–74.

Rose, Michael. Social historian of the nineteenth and twentieth centuries (retired as Professor of Modern Social History). Taught in Department of History, 1962–99.

Smith, Ian. Civil engineer (now Professor of Geotechnics). Taught in Department of Civil Engineering (later in the School of Engineering) since 1967.

Tallentire, Alan. Pharmacist and sports enthusiast (retired as Professor of Pharmacy). Diploma student, Department of Pharmacy, 1948–50 (passed Pharmaceutical Chemist Qualifying Examination); M.Sc., 1953; Ph.D., 1958. Taught in Department of Pharmacy, 1953–96. Worked at Argonne National Laboratory, Illinois, 1961–62; Deputy Director of the Laboratory of Radiation Biology, University of Texas, 1967–68.

Taylor, Jean. Magistrate and voluntary worker for the Health Service and in the courts; sometime City Councillor and member of Manchester Health Authority; sometime Health Education Officer for Salford. Undergraduate, Department of Social Administration, 1952–55. Resident in the University Settlement, Ancoats.

Taylor, Peter. Dental surgeon, of Old Trafford. Dental student, 1953–58. Resident in the University Settlement, Ancoats.

Torr, Barbara. Dental surgeon and doctor, of Chorlton-cum-Hardy. Dental student, 1941–46; Assistant Lecturer in Periodontology, 1946–48; medical student, 1948–51; orthopaedic house surgeon, 1952; Assistant Lecturer in Operative Dentistry, 1952–55.

Torr, James Bernard Doughty. Dental surgeon and doctor, of Chorlton-cum-Hardy. Medical student, 1942–48; Medical Officer, RAF, 1950–51; Demonstrator in Anatomy, 1953; Assistant Lecturer in Anatomy, 1959; dental student, 1966–69; Part-time Lecturer in Oral Surgery, 1970.

Torrington, Derek. Authority on personnel management, retired as Professor of Human Resource Management, Manchester School of Management, UMIST. Undergraduate, Faculty of Economic and Social Studies, 1950–53. Held various posts in industry (ultimately Manager of Personnel and Training, Oldham International Ltd); re-entered academic life, 1970, as Lecturer in Industrial Relations, Manchester Polytechnic; M.Phil.; moved to UMIST, 1975.

Turnberg, Leslie (afterwards Sir Leslie). Physician and specialist in gastroenterology. Medical student, 1952–57; M.D., 1966; taught in the Medical School from 1968; Professor of Medicine, 1973–97, particularly concerned with the development of the academic community at Hope Hospital, Salford.

Tye, Frederick. Headmaster and trainer of headmasters (Director of the North West Educational Management Centre, 1972–81). Undergraduate, General Science, 1940–43; Teacher's Diploma, 1946–47. Senior Research Fellow in Social Administration, 1969–70. Member of Court, 1962–98, and of Council, 1967–92. Chairman of Convocation, early 1960s.

Walsh, Joan. Mathematician, with special interests in computing; retired as Professor of Applied Mathematics. Taught in Department of Mathematics, 1963–97.

Welland, Dennis. Literary scholar and academic administrator. Taught in Department of American Studies, 1962–83; Professor of American Literature, 1965–83. Chairman of Tutors of Owens Park, 1967–71.

Williams, Olwen. Administrator. Secretary to Staff Officer (Harry McLeod, later Max Westland) from 1955; Diploma in Personnel Management and Training and Member of the Institute of Personnel Management; Welfare Officer in the Establishment Unit, Bursar's Department, 1971–89.

Willmott, John. Physicist. Professor of Nuclear Structure, 1964–89; Director of the Physical Laboratories, 1967–89.

Young, Margaret L.M. French scholar, specialist in Renaissance literature; retired as Senior Lecturer. Taught in Department of French Studies, 1948–84. Adviser to Women Students, 1955–72, and in the Central Academic Advisory Service, 1972–8.

Zussman, Jack. Geologist. Taught in Department of Geology, 1952–62; Professor of Geology, 1967–89. Resident of Donner House; Tutor, Needham Hall, 1959–60. Reader in Mineralogy, University of Oxford, 1962–67.

Statistical appendix

by Michele Abendstern and Steve Chick

The following graphs are derived from contemporary data collected by the sections of the university concerned and supplied to the Council for their Annual Reports to the Court of Governors. They seek to give an impression of the trends and developments taking place between the early 1950s and the early 1970s in certain branches of University life: e.g. the rise in student numbers and the changing proportion of male and female students, the steady growth of some faculties and the decline followed by acceleration of others. Unfortunately records were sometimes incomplete for areas we would otherwise have wished to consider and we have largely steered clear of these rather than misrepresent them. Data about the numbers of students living in halls, lodgings and other forms of residence were amongst this category for this period.

What we are able to show is the enormous rise over the period in the amount of Treasury grants received by the University, though as a percentage of total income it remained roughly four-fifths of the total. The graphs show at a glance how the Medical Faculty grew from the mid-1960s, raising its total student intake by a third in a matter of eight years and also how the intake of women into the Faculty of Arts began to overtake men by the beginning of the 1970s, the only faculty to do so in this period.

As we hope the graphs speak for themselves no further extrapolations will be made here. It remains only to note that the figures for student numbers refer to the total student intakes for those years which include full and part-time undergraduates and all postgraduates.

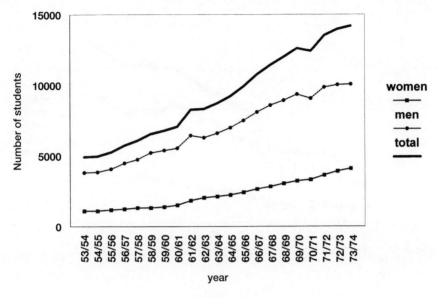

1 Total students

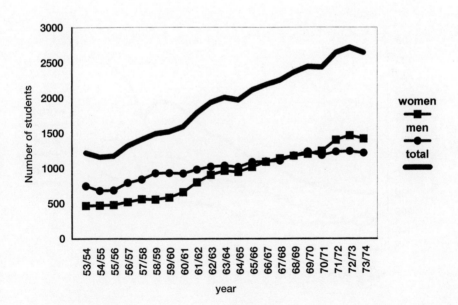

2 Arts

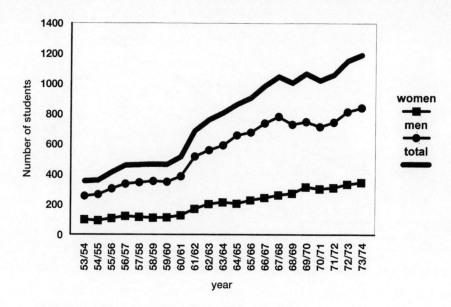

3 Economic and Social Studies

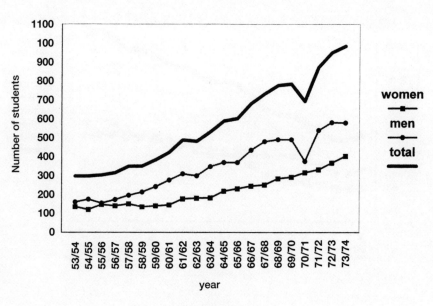

4 Education

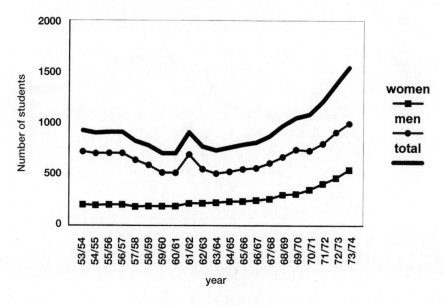

5 Faculty of Medicine

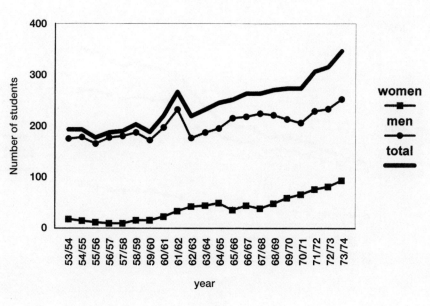

6 Law

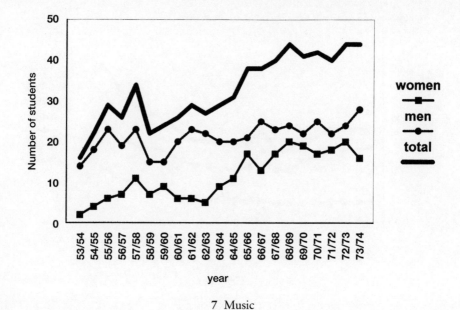

7 Music

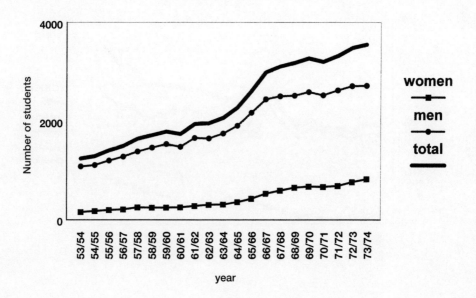

8 Science

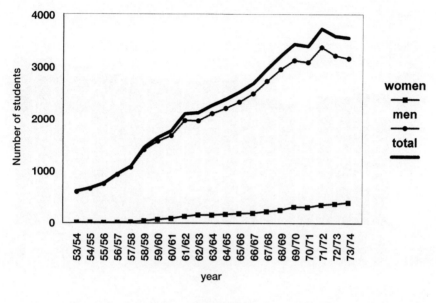

9 Technology

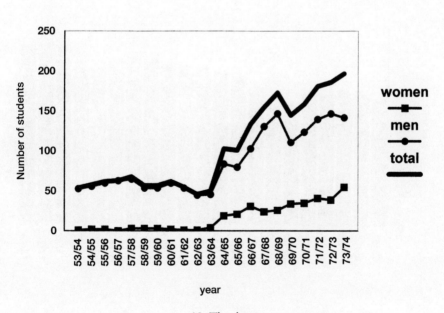

10 Theology

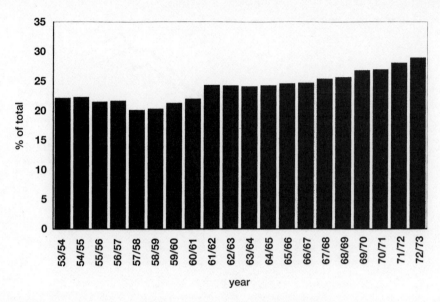

11 Percentage of women students (total)

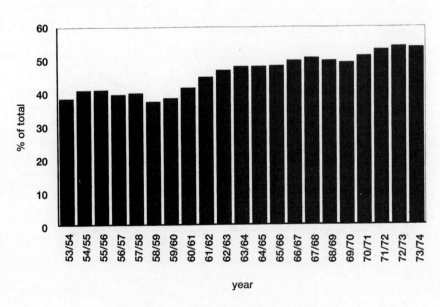

12 Percentage of women students (Arts)

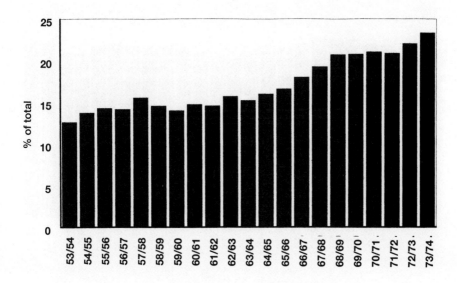

13 Percentage of women students (Science)

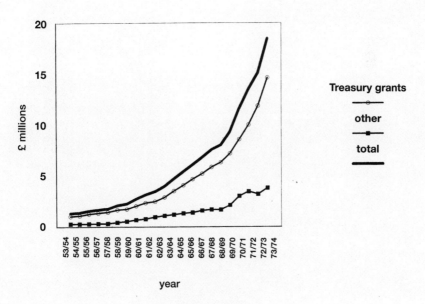

14 Income

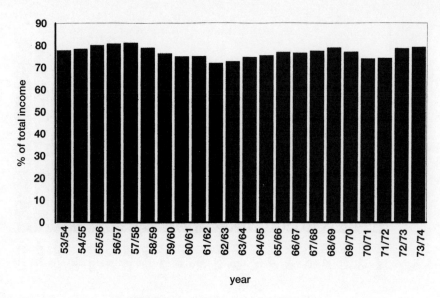

15 Treasury grants as a % of total income

Index